THE LIFE & TIMES

OF LOUIS LOMAX

The Life & Times of Louis Lomax

THE ART OF DELIBERATE DISUNITY

Thomas Aiello

DUKE UNIVERSITY PRESS   *Durham & London*   2021

Yes, my dear brethren, when I think of you which very often I do,

and the poor despised miserable state you are in, when I think

of your ignorance and stupidity and great wickedness of the

most of you, I am pained to the heart.

....

JUPITER HAMMON, 1786

Contents

Acknowledgments

As with any book, so many people have helped in its construction that I cannot name them all here. But I would particularly like to single out the staff of the Special Collections and University Archives at the University of Nevada, Reno. Jacquelyn Sundstrand went above and beyond to help me navigate a collection that was unprocessed when I began this project. It is, in some sense, a mystery as to why Lomax's widow chose UNR to house his papers. Lomax had no specific connection with the city or the university. But they are there, and they are now organized and available thanks to the hard work of Jacquelyn and her colleagues. She worked to process the collection even as I was sitting in the reading room reviewing the documents themselves. This book uses a variety of archival collections, of course, but it understandably relies most heavily on those from Lomax's personal papers. The book thus would not exist without Jacquelyn and the archivists at UNR. I hope that this book serves as a testament to their hard work and diligence.

Introduction

Louis Emanuel Lomax was an ex-con who served time in Illinois's Joliet Correctional Center for a confidence scheme of selling rented automobiles to used car dealers. He had uncontested domestic abuse claims on his record, two arrests for driving under the influence, and four divorces. He lied publicly about his collegiate education on a regular basis. Constantly in search of fame and media attention, he ingratiated himself to popular leaders on the fringes of both sides of the political spectrum and changed his position on key social issues when it suited his interest or audience. He criticized every major civil rights leader, engaged in hopeless assassination conspiracy theories, and took advantage of violent conflicts, both domestic and international, to draw attention to himself. In 1963, while giving the John B. Russworm Lecture at the California Negro Leadership Conference at Stanford, he told his audience that they needed to develop "the art of deliberate disunity," criticizing "the state of Negro euphoria, that seizure of silly happiness and emotional release that comes in the wake of a partial civil rights victory."[1]

No, wait.

Louis Emanuel Lomax rose from a childhood in the deepest of the Deep South, Valdosta, Georgia, to become one of the most successful Black journalists of the twentieth century. He introduced Malcolm X to the nation and remained a close ally of both Malcolm and Martin Luther King Jr. for the duration of their lives. He helped organize the 1968 Olympic boycott and was with Harry Edwards at the event's initial press conference. He was in the nation's capital for the success of the March on Washington and the confusion of Resurrection City. He was the opening act for Malcolm X's "The Ballot or the Bullet" speech and was on the telephone with Betty Shabazz the night he was killed. As the first Black man to host a syndicated television talk show and as the author of several best-selling and influential books, he was both a driver and a popularizer of virtually every element of the civil rights movement from the late 1950s to the late 1960s. In 1963, while giving the John B. Russworm Lecture at the California Negro Leadership Conference at Stanford, he told his audience that they needed to develop "the art of deliberate disunity," emphasizing that "only through diversity of opinion can we establish the basic prerequisite for the democratic process."[2]

Lomax told his Stanford audience that he wanted civil rights leaders to begin emphasizing economic and educational concerns, the building of infrastructure within the community that would allow the Black population to take advantage of any future political gains. He worried aloud about infighting in the movement, wherein competing groups jockeyed for power in an effort to become the public face of civil rights. It was a call for unity even as it defended functionally radical positions within the movement, a seemingly contradictory argument made all the more palatable because it contained something that appealed to everyone. It was sound and fury, signifying both nothing and everything, and it was a case made by someone who actively sought the spotlight and the potential power that came with it. In that sense, Lomax's Stanford speech reflected the broader scope of his life. He was a publicity-seeking provocateur who did what he could both to report on the news and to keep himself in it. That effort made him one of the loudest and most influential voices of the 1960s civil rights movement and Black foreign policy journalism.

Domestically, Lomax tended to argue for integrationism as a viable civil rights goal, though that position vacillated throughout his career. Yet one of his closest friends and allies was Malcolm X. Their relationship was built on the reciprocal benefits they could provide, each the ideological foil for the other at various moments, but they were also real friends, and Lomax's classical southern understanding of integrationist civil rights evolved over the years because of his proximity to Malcolm, the Nation of Islam (NOI), and Black nationalist thinking. His thinking took a circular trajectory, beginning at the classical rights understanding of a Black southerner from Valdosta before finding a more nationalist position after his long association with Malcolm. Though he never abandoned his admiration for the NOI's leader, Lomax's public thinking about race rights turned more pragmatic in the last five years of his life, following Malcolm's 1965 assassination, and his philosophical evolution ultimately took him back close to where he had begun. That play of Malcolm on Lomax also worked in reverse, with the journalist accompanying Malcolm at his most seminal and career-defining moments.

Lomax was a study in contradictions. "We need a revolution in this country," he declared in the late 1960s. Then he demurred by describing what he called a "revolution by education," emphasizing Black studies as a strong start that needed to filter down to primary and secondary education. He insisted that he was in favor of nonviolence but then explained, "The American white man—like all white men—only understands violence." The white man was "the epitome of violence." Whites in general were "a racist, violent people." Even with such an assessment, he supported integration, while at the same time calling for a total restructuring of the American economy. "Some will no longer be able to luxuriate with four automobiles and five garages while others have nothing," he said. "You can't tell a man work is virtue but there are no jobs so he goes to hell by default." Lomax predicted a new revolution in 1976, two hundred years after the first one. Although the revolution never occurred, and Lomax did not even live to see the bicentennial, it was not an unreasonable prediction. For all of his bravado, he possessed a pragmatic willingness to shift positions in response to changing situations and in pursuit of his own success, as well as a keen ability to diagnose the problems the country faced. "America is fundamentally a country of style rather than substance," he said. "I'll bet we could walk out of here, into the parking lot, and find that nine-tenths of the people flying the flag have no intention of doing what the flag stands for."[3] His dual mission, as he saw it, was to call out that nine-tenths while playing a game of style over and against one of substance. Lomax's life was an argument that you could not do the former without doing the latter.

His foreign policy thinking was much the same. If Pan-Africanism existed on one end of the ideological Black foreign policy spectrum and noninterventionist calls for peace in Vietnam existed on the other, Lomax found himself moving between those two poles. His most consistent message in this regard—and the one that seemed to bridge the ideological divide—was an opposition to colonialism that pushed back against resource extraction and economic hegemony in Africa and Asia. Lomax tended to avoid comparative models in favor of analyzing individual regions and leaders in their specific cultural context. That said, Lomax was a popularizer of anticolonial movements, a freelance journalist with an ideological and financial interest in his presentations, but he was a layperson, and his accounts of conflicts in various parts of Africa, Thailand, and Vietnam often lacked the nuance of scholars steeped in the history of those regions and their relationships with the West. Continuing his general inconsistency, he advocated peace while defending indigenous military action as a salve against colonial intervention; continuing his bent for sensationalism, he often ignored detailed intricacy in favor of wide-scale conclusions to make his arguments. Such was the nature of a self-promoting novice with deep-felt concerns about the well-being of the people he covered.

Lomax's consistent efforts to find this ideological third way would be both a blessing and a curse. He was consistent in his contradictions but not in his analysis of events. By using a broad-brush approach to paint the symptoms of systemic racism rather than more nuanced but less interesting causes, Lomax kept himself in the public eye, thereby making himself an effective mainstream advocate for Black issues. But despite his central role in that advocacy—his position at the forefront of so many of the civil rights movement's pivot points—those contradictions left his legacy at the historical margins. They made his role in the movement harder to interpret and eventually harder for historians to see at all.

Thus, while he is almost always featured in a tertiary role in accounts of the 1960s civil rights movement, he has never been given pride of place. The same can be said for accounts of American foreign policy in Africa and Asia during the decade. But Lomax was central to the era's civil rights movement, and while he was not central to American foreign policy in any way, he was decidedly influential in popularizing the situations in sub-Saharan Africa and southeast Asia. Lomax was also one of the most important journalists of the decade, helping to cement the career of Mike Wallace, setting precedents for Black journalism in radio and television, and maintaining a literary profile that included newspaper reporting, long-form magazine journalism, and the best-selling books *The Reluctant African* and *The Negro Revolt*.

This volume moves Lomax to the center of the civil rights narrative of the 1960s, describing his particular "art of deliberate disunity" and the influence it had on the decade's journalism, its civil rights activism, and its public thinking about foreign policy. He was in many ways both created by the national tumult of the 1960s and a creator of many of its seminal moments. His thinking would always be pragmatic, willing to change with perceived necessity to remain influential or controversial or to support rights activism. The trajectory of that thought was riddled with inconsistencies, but it mirrored the inconsistencies of a country in the throes of dramatic change, as the hypocrisy of America and of Lomax worked in a reciprocal relationship to create a nation more open to Black journalism, more willing to provide racial equality, less tolerant of global colonialism, and ultimately (and ironically) less hypocritical.

His inconsistencies were his own, as were his lies and crimes. But they were also, in their way, America's inconsistencies. And they never stopped him from his consistent and beneficial advocacy for Black rights. Lomax's story is unique, but it is also representative—a contradiction that the controversial journalist would surely find fitting.

1   From Privilege to Prison

Thomas A. Lomax was born to be a preacher. The North Carolina native heard the call early, and in 1880, at the age of twenty-one, he and his new bride, Rozena, traveled west to find a new mission field. Ultimately, Thomas took the pastorate at Macedonia First Baptist Church in Valdosta, Georgia, the seat of Lowndes County. A small city in southwest Georgia with a population of fewer than twenty thousand, it was the moderately urban hub of a decidedly rural region. Macedonia was the city's oldest Black church, founded by the Reverend Charles Anderson as Macedonia First African Baptist Church in 1865. At times, Thomas also preached at St. James Baptist Church. He and Rozena—who found her own calling as a successful religious playwright—became the parents of two children: James, born in 1899, and Sarah, born in 1901.[1]

Valdosta was founded one month after the election of Abraham Lincoln and four months before Georgia's secession. After the war, the town emerged as a cotton farming hub for southwest Georgia, as most former slaves in the region turned to sharecropping to survive. To help farming and industry develop and thrive, it also became the convict leasing capital of the area: Kinderlou Plantation, located just outside Valdosta's city limits, was a particularly brutal prison labor camp and staging ground for the leasing of thousands of victims of the white South's new version of slavery.[2]

It was a galling, overtly racist use of the criminal justice system, and it was a standard of the Deep South white supremacy that enveloped the

Lomax family. But in cases where race was ancillary to the outcome of a criminal decision, Valdosta demonstrated that it could be at least occasionally responsive to Black voices. Historian Bill Boyd describes a 1905 murder-for-hire trial where the prosecution hinged on the testimony of Alf Moore, a Black farmworker from Tennessee. Moore had been asked to commit the crime, refused, and then watched the machinations that ultimately led to the murder. Though he was not the only witness, Moore provided the sole eyewitness account, which proved to be convincing even after he was cross-examined by defense attorneys who tried to use his race to invalidate his testimony. The defendants—a white father and son—were convicted of capital murder and hanged in the prison across the street from the Lowndes County Courthouse, just blocks from the pulpit at Macedonia. "It may have been the first time in Georgia history," Boyd explains, "that the testimony of a Black man put a white man on the gallows."[3]

Valdosta's version of Jim Crow, though oppressive and overarching, still left spaces for the testimony of a witness like Moore and the growth and development of a family like the Lomaxes. As a teenager, Sarah traveled to Macon to begin teaching at Central City College, an institution founded in 1899 by Georgia's Missionary Baptist Convention, which provided high school and collegiate education, as well as religious instruction, to Black students from the central and southern parts of the state.[4] There Sarah met and fell in love with Emanuel Curtis Smith, a native of Warren County, Georgia. Although the Lomaxes disapproved, the two had a whirlwind romance and were married in Macon on 18 May 1920, when Sarah was nineteen and Emanuel was twenty-two. But two years later, when a pregnant Sarah returned to Valdosta, she was alone.[5]

The pregnancy was difficult for Sarah, in poor health and abandoned by her husband. She died on August 25, nine days after giving birth to a son. She named the child Louis Emanuel Lomax, combining a masculine version of her own middle name—Louise—with his father's first name. Yet that father had already run away, back to his hometown, before moving to Abbeville, Georgia, where he worked in the Wilcox County school system. His firstborn son never mentioned him publicly or in correspondence, and there is no evidence that the two ever had any contact. Louis's last name was that of his mother's family, which took over the responsibility of raising him when he was just days old.[6]

Four years before Lomax's birth, southwest Georgia had permanently earned a national reputation for white supremacist violence. After plantation owner Hampton Smith was killed by one of his debt peonage workers for poor treatment, a manhunt instigated by civilians and law enforcement generated a ruthless race riot in both Lowndes and neighboring Brooks counties, with white mobs killing at least thirteen people and no one held accountable for the rampage. One of those murdered was the husband of Mary Turner, eight months pregnant, who threatened to swear out warrants against her husband's killers. The NAACP reported that in response, another mob captured her, took her to the county line, and hung her by her ankles. They poured gasoline on her and lit the flame. They cut open her abdomen, pulled out her fetus, and stomped it into oblivion, before riddling the body with bullets. Three days later, the police found and killed the murderer of Hampton Smith, leaving the body for another mob to remove its genitals and drag it to a neighboring town, where they held a public burning.[7]

The legacy of this violence hung heavily over the town and helped to make Valdosta a cloistered, racially restrictive place for a boy to grow up. Young Louis was raised in the Lomax home with his grandparents; his Uncle James, now Thomas and Rozena's only living child, also lived on the property while beginning a teaching career (figure 1.1).[8] "Humor and sorrow are allies, opposite sides of the same coin," Lomax wrote as an adult;

> Three incidents of my early youth made me painfully aware of this ambivalence. There was a deacon in my grandfather's church who used to break into gales of laughter while shouting. I would watch his face as he shouted, "Hallelujah, ha, ha, ha," and saw in its contortions the betrayal of inner stress.
>
> And there was also the day my Uncle James (who was a Baptist minister and principal of the Negro school) lectured us about the fact that Negroes "laughed at the wrong time." Uncle was irked because we had laughed during the film "Imitation of Life." What tickled us was Peola, the light-skinned Negro girl who passed for white and then confessed all at the funeral of her dark mother whom she had mistreated.
>
> The third incident involved turnabout but the motivation was the same. I was delivering groceries; my bicycle turned over, threw me to the ground, and my hand was badly crushed by the loaded wooden box. The accident sent a white woman into hysterical laughter—perhaps not unlike that of the shouting Negro deacon. She called to her next door neighbor to come out and see the bleeding nigger![9]

FIGURE 1.1 — Lomax's grandfather standing in front of the family home in Valdosta, Georgia. COURTESY SPECIAL COLLECTIONS AND UNIVERSITY ARCHIVES OF THE UNIVERSITY OF NEVADA, RENO. ITEM 82-30-8-4-1-1.

Such was the climate as Lomax grew up in Depression-era Valdosta. African American urban unemployment rose to 50 percent in the early 1930s. Black unemployment hovered at twice the full national average throughout the decade. Those who did have jobs were paid substantially less than their white counterparts for the same work. In the North, approximately half of all Black families received some form of Depression relief. Conditions were even worse in the South. Throughout the first decade of the Depression, one-fourth of all southerners were tenants or sharecroppers, as were half of all southern farmers, and by June 1932, farm prices had dropped to 52 percent of the 1909–1914 average. At the same time, farmers paid taxes that were 166 percent higher than in 1914. Southwest Georgia fell squarely along those statistical lines, exacerbating both the poverty and the racial animus that existed in the region. Lynching numbers declined in the 1930s, but only because white southerners used less noticeable methods of racial control.[10]

"When I was eight years old," Lomax recalled, "a white man ordered his bulldog to attack me simply because I was a Negro." A wealthy white family came out of a nearby house and chased away the white man, demonstrating the class divisions in the town and the politics of respectability that governed Deep South relationships. "Valdostans, like most people, are children of fixity; as individuals and as a tribe they find a crag, a limb, a spot of earth—physical or emotional or both—and they cling on for dear life," Lomax explained. "They change without growing, and the more they change the more they remain the same. What frightens them, as with most people, is the sudden discovery that what they are—how they have lived all their lives—stands somehow in the path of history and of progress."[11]

Valdosta did, however, have space for Black success. Rozena became a prominent figure in Valdosta, the wife of a well-known minister. Along with authoring religious plays, she had more political duties, as her grandson later explained:

> On that day, almost thirty years ago, when my grandmother was placed in charge of issuing Federal relief to Negroes in our small South Georgia town, I began to understand our national purpose.
>
> As an eight year old I watched that long line of black people snake its way across our front porch in search of food, clothing and comfort, and I did not need erudite scholars to spell out our national goals; after a day of passing out relief bundles I went to grandfather's church and heard people sing, "I know God's got the power because we're eating government flour," and I knew once and for all that God, whatever he is, and government, whatever that is, somehow fuse in the destiny of a people.
>
> Then, ten years later, I covered my first major story: The funeral of a lynch victim. With that, my concept of our national purpose was complete.
>
> Now that I look at a world pained by hunger and troubled by aggrieved black men it is as if the sorry scenes of my childhood and early manhood are set again—this time on a worldwide canvas.[12]

Lomax was shaped by the distinct nature of the racism of southwest Georgia, and that racism became the lens through which he viewed the national and international injustices upon which he would comment throughout his life.

Another time during his Valdosta youth, Lomax "attended the church of a Negro minister who had been cornered by a group of young white hoodlums and made to dance in the street" because the whites were offended that the minister was so well dressed. It was the common kind of incident that reinforced notions of inferiority and difference, both in the preacher and in the young man who witnessed the ordeal.[13]

In November 1933, just after Louis's eleventh birthday, after years of relief work and religion, the family matriarch and the woman who had raised him for his first decade, Rozena, died at the age of fifty-eight. Because her husband, Thomas, was already seventy, young Louis was left in the care of his Uncle James and James's wife, Fannie.[14]

Having previously worked as a Pullman car porter, James Leonidas Lomax began to follow his real passion, education, in the early 1920s, just before the birth of his nephew, when he became a teacher and principal at Magnolia Street School in Valdosta. Fannie was also a public school-teacher. In 1929, the city opened Dasher High School, and Lomax became its principal. He was described as "a stern disciplinarian, yet a kind and gentle humanitarian." When he wore "a dark blue suit to school, teachers and students stayed out of his pathway." James brought that same combination of discipline and empathy to the job of raising his nephew.[15]

He and Fannie devoted themselves to Louis's education, privately tutoring him in addition to his regular schoolwork, instilling in him an interest in literature and writing and requiring him to memorize Bible passages and classical poetry. "The sin in the Lomax home," Louis remembered, "was to use bad English."[16]

Such sins were part of a politics of respectability that helped define educated middle- and upper-class Black families in Georgia. In Atlanta, for example, organizations developed such as Lugenia Burns Hope's Atlanta Neighborhood Union, a group of upper- and upper-middle-class Black female volunteers who provided social work services for those in need. At the same time, however, such groups demonstrated a clear separation between the social classes, an insulation of those in Black Atlanta who did not need monthly relief checks. Hope was the wife of Morehouse College president John Hope. Her Neighborhood Union performed necessary work to assist underprivileged people, but that aid provided its own version of paternalistic control. In teaching home care to working-class citizens, sponsoring health classes, and fighting against prostitution, the group set the terms by which they offered assistance and thus drew significant distinctions between the classes. The economic gap between classes was less stark in Valdosta than in Atlanta, but the politics of respectability nonetheless succeeded in creating separations. In the absence of money, education and manners served to draw such lines for families like the Lomaxes.[17]

Those lines could and did cause problems. Lomax related that a Black woman who attended Macedonia was once "slapped by a white chain-store manager because she picked over some fruit and then refused to buy it." There were discussions in the community about boycotting the store, "but there was never any suggestion that we take our trade to the Negro merchants, whose prices were a third higher than those in the chain store."[18]

As a teenager at Dasher High School in the mid-1930s, Lomax entered a "contributors' contest" in the *Valdosta Daily Times* that asked readers to submit interesting stories about south Georgia history. Lomax wrote a story about a group of "pranksters" who panicked the town by dousing a vulture in gasoline, setting it on fire, and freeing it to fly over town. It was his first byline.[19]

In his strict, disciplined household, however, bylines were not enough. Louis also had to work. "I shined shoes and mopped the floors in a barber shop where the white owner used to pat his feet, chanting, 'Mop, Nigger, Mop,' when I was fifteen years old," Lomax recalled in 1965. "But I was earning money for college, and the barber's sons were eighteen years old and couldn't read or write. I made up my mind, then and there I would come back to Georgia one day. Last November I did, as the only man, black, blue, green, or yellow from that city to be listed in 'Who's Who in America.' And the mayor was at the airport to meet me."[20]

Among Lomax's classmates at Dasher High School was Charlie Mae Knight, who attended Macedonia Church along with Louis and other future leaders, including Ossie Davis, five years older than Lomax, from nearby Clinch County. Knight credited Macedonia and Thomas Lomax with instilling in all three of them a strong social conscience that would play out in different ways through the course of their lives. "Many were the times white people would come to our church," Lomax remembered. "We would give them the front seats and they enjoyed themselves as our ministers held forth about Moses using the rod to part the waters of the Red Sea. More than once the minister would go on to suggest that there were some 'black Moseses' in the making and I wondered even then if white people knew what we were really talking about."[21]

Their environment required the kinds of performances that created actors and journalists. "During the summer between my freshman and sophomore years in college, I worked as an orderly at the Little-Griffin Hospital in Valdosta, Georgia," Lomax later explained.

> My first duty each morning was to put chairs in the hallway leading to Dr. Griffin's office. By nine-thirty these chairs would be filled with white ladies seeking the services of the best known gynecologist in

south Georgia. For a Negro woman to be treated by Dr. Griffin, and in his office at that, was unthinkable.

I was out in the hospital yard raking leaves one morning when Sister Lucy—a woman of middle age and a stalwart member of my grandfather's church—came strolling up carrying a Jewel lard bucket filled with fresh eggs.

"Mornin,' Louis."

"Howdy, Sister Lucy."

"That Dr. Griffin," she said pointing to the hospital, "he there?"

"Yes, ma'am."

"Thank you, Jesus," Sister Lucy intoned, "cause I needs treatin'."

This I had to see. I followed Sister Lucy as she made her way through the back door of the hospital and into the corridor leading to Dr. Griffin's office.

"Mornin,' daughter," Sister Lucy beamed to the first white woman in line. "Why you here? You gonna have another baby?"

"Ain't three enough, Lucy?" the woman asked, beginning to laugh.

"Honey, I had two and that enough for me!"

The corridor rang with laughter and Sister Lucy walked past the next eight women in line.

"How's that husband of yours?" Sister Lucy asked, leaning over a woman at the head of the line.

"He's fine, Lucy. How you?"

"Praise God, I'm fine! You know, I brought that husband of yours into this world."

"I'm gonna tell him I saw you, Lucy."

"You do that and the Lord'll bless you." With this, Sister Lucy had made her way to Dr. Griffin's secretary-nurse.

"Is Dr. Griffin in there?" Lucy asked, widening her eyes with expectation.

"Yes, Lucy, he's there. How you?"

"With the help of Jesus, I'll make it."

Dr. Griffin's office door opened, a patient walked out, Sister Lucy walked in. Whatever was wrong with Sister Lucy, Dr. Griffin fixed it. He was paid with a Jewel lard bucket full of eggs. Sister Lucy made her way back down the hall laughing and joking with the waiting women.

"Give the preacher my prayers when you get home," she said to me, once we were again out in the back yard. Then she added, almost in an undertone, "Lord, honey, white folks sure are foolish!"²²

The anecdote demonstrates the aspirational models in Lomax's early life. Racism was a cudgel but could be turned around on its perpetrators with cunning and guile. It was a lesson carried over from slavery, Brer Rabbit getting one over on Brer Fox. "Remembering our way of life," wrote Lomax, "I am convinced that, for the most part, Negroes were not really afraid. Rather, we were clever; canny, actually, for that was the way to stay alive and get ahead."[23] Using racial assumptions or the politics of respectability to improve your own situation was always allowed, and such lessons would carry Lomax into problematic territory after he left home and began his college career.

The story that Lomax always told of his life after he left Valdosta fit the narrative of strict discipline and a strong social conscience: after graduating from his uncle's Dasher High School, he attended Paine College in Augusta, where he edited the college newspaper, *The Paineite*; pursued graduate studies at American University and newspaper work with the *Baltimore Afro-American*; moved to Savannah to teach at Georgia State College as an assistant professor of philosophy; and then was off to Yale for additional graduate study before becoming a feature writer for the *Chicago American*.[24]

It was a story of ascension, one that gave Lomax a strong academic credential when selling himself and his expertise, fitting the expectations set by the academic home of his aunt and uncle. It was repeated by multiple media outlets. "He studied at King College and did graduate work at Yale," the *Chicago Defender* reported. "He was a member of the faculty of Georgia State College where he was assistant professor of philosophy." Historian Manning Marable claimed that Lomax graduated from Paine in 1942, then earned a master's degree in sociology from American University in 1944 and one in philosophy from Yale in 1947.[25] It was a good story, but it was untrue.

After he graduated from Dasher in 1938, Lomax actually entered Georgia State College (GSC) in Savannah, where he would later claim to have taught. There for the 1938–1939 school year, he was a mediocre student, earning a C average. He decided to leave, according to his uncle, because of "some dissatisfaction that arose relative to the housing of a visiting football team."[26]

Whether his absence was related to football or poor academic performance, Louis would not return. J. L. Lomax talked in early November to GSC's president, Benjamin Hubert, telling him that his nephew "assures me he left voluntarily." Lomax was "anxious that he continue his work.

He is dependent entirely upon me for support, as I have had him since the death of his mother at his birth." The family then turned to a more religious choice, Paine College in Augusta. Affiliated with the Christian Methodist Episcopal denomination, it was a private college founded in 1882, one of the most prominent and well-established institutions outside of Atlanta. J. L. Lomax asked the Paine registrar to "assist me in giving him work, or otherwise helping with him," and cited Louise Ross, a Paine graduate who later taught in Valdosta, as an additional recommender for his nephew. The Paine registrar, H. L. Graham, was receptive. He could not admit Louis for the fall, as the semester was halfway complete, but agreed to admit him in January 1940.[27]

Despite his troubles in Savannah, Lomax jumped confidently into his new life at Paine. In his first semester, he took English, religion, psychology, mathematics, biology, and French. He would continue to overload himself with coursework each semester. The heavy loads took a toll, and Lomax never made an A in his undergraduate career at GSC or Paine. After his transfer, he continued to be a C student. He later claimed that it was during his college years that he formed a relationship with Martin Luther King Jr., who was a junior in high school at the time.[28]

Before his junior year at Paine, Lomax worked for the summer as a handyman in a white-owned shop in Valdosta. His boss "would entertain his customers with dramatic descriptions of lynchings he had attended." The stories finally became too much, and Lomax left the store in anger. When the son of the shop's owner came to the Lomax home to ask Louis to return, his family replied that Louis would not work in a place where he was subjected to lynching stories. The owner's son assured them that the behavior would stop. Lomax went back, and the owner put his arms around his employee's shoulders. "Louis, I wouldn't hurt *you*!" It was, for Lomax, a perfect example of the stifling attempts at racial civility that existed in his hometown, another reason to escape Georgia altogether.[29]

For one brief collegiate year, from 1942 to 1943, Lomax began officially using his father's name, referring to himself as Louis Lomax Smith. There is no evidence of any contact with Emanuel Smith, but perhaps Louis was experiencing some sort of identity crisis.[30] While he registered for courses in the spring semester of 1943, Louis never completed them, and he left that winter for Washington to begin a career in journalism. There did not seem to be a specific reason for his exit. He was even set to be the editor of the school's newspaper, *The Paineite*, that year. Rather, he may have simply been demonstrating the restlessness that would mark the rest of his life.

A year later, in January 1944, he would claim that he had been enrolled at Howard University while working in Washington, even explaining to Paine's president, Edmund Clarke Peters, that he had earned twenty hours of credit there. The school, however, had "so reduced my work that it would take me two or three years, if ever, to finish," even though he needed only twenty-two hours to graduate from Paine—the same number of credits for which he had registered in spring 1943 before dropping out. "What I should like to do," he told Peters, "is have my work transferred to Paine and take my degree from there. I should like to know if the college will accept the work I am doing at Howard and permit me to take the comprehensive and graduate." He assured Paine's president that he had "a very nice job in government" and that he was leading "a very fine congregation of people" as a minister. He was, in essence, asking in January to return to Paine with his Howard hours and graduate in May.[31]

Peters was unmoved by the request and decided to call his bluff. He told Lomax that he had not talked to the college's executive committee, but "my first reaction is against this. Now that you are in Washington with a good job it would seem to me that even though it would take a little longer the better plan would be for you to complete your work there at Howard." It seemed unlikely that an average Paine student would have accumulated a strong record at Howard while working a full-time government job and leading a congregation. Apparently Lomax's lifelong reputation for embellishment was already well established. Contrary to the claims he made throughout his life, which were repeated in virtually every historical account about him, he never graduated from Paine College— nor, for that matter, from any college at all.[32]

This element of the con, of duplicity in self-presentation and a willingness to skirt the rules, were not present in those who raised him. They seemed out of place in a biography of upper-middle-class propriety. For Lomax, such deceptions were a broader version of Sister Lucy's cunning, a way of moving to the front of a line dominated by white people and white supremacy. It was the work of Brer Rabbit, his belief that being clever and canny was the key to success. It was also a way to compensate for failure when measuring yourself against a group of successful relatives who raised you but were not your parents. So it was that despite a decidedly respectable upbringing, Lomax maintained an element of the unrespectable, of the confidence man, throughout his life, even while he was engaged in projects of real civil rights value.

For all of the fabrications about his early academic achievement, Lomax actually attended American University in Washington, DC, for the 1945–1946 school year.[33] During that time, he also served as minister of Washington's Bethlehem Baptist Church. The church had been led since 1926 by Virginia minister James C. Banks, but upon his retirement in 1945, Lomax was one of several pastors who served relatively short stints at the church until another Virginia minister, Willie B. Allen, took over the congregation in 1954 and stabilized its leadership. In April 1946, Lomax returned to Augusta and spoke—as a representative of Bethlehem and at the invitation of President Peters—at a student chapel service at Paine.[34]

A development that was perhaps even more important came in June 1945, when Washington radio station WWDC gave a weekly forty-minute program to Lomax, who was still in school at American University. "It will mark the first time," explained the *Chicago Defender*'s Charlie Cherokee, "a Negro has written and presented dramatic skits over the air in DC."[35]

The program aired on Sunday nights and was called *The Negro Speaks*. The *Defender*'s Alfred E. Smith wrote about one episode wherein Lomax described the world in "a new idyllic state of perfection," where there was neither intolerance nor hatred and "white, brown and black peoples lived together intermingled in perfect harmony." After the show, WWDC was inundated with calls and letters from angry white listeners, upset with the "implied race equality" depicted on the show. As Smith told the story, Lomax explained, "But it was only a dream," to which his white critics replied, "Well, Negroes have no business even dreaming race equality in public."[36]

In another tale about Lomax's time in Washington, Smith claimed that the "newsman and ordained minister" made a long-distance call with the aid of an operator with a deep southern drawl. She was very friendly, and during a delay in the connection they discovered that they were both from Valdosta. They shared memories of different places and streets in the town until the operator asked, "You're colored, ain't you?" "Why yes," said Lomax, "I am." "Well, that's all right," she responded. "We're both up North now."[37] While the incident seemed innocuous, it meant something. The operator seemed to indicate that her bigotry, the bigotry of Valdosta and of the South, could stop at the water's edge of the Mason-Dixon Line (though Washington was below the line and still a southern city), making it an attitude based less on principle than on regional custom. The fierce southern devotion to the racial line was at once completely baffling and open to negotiation. Regional identity could change and indeed had changed, nearly continuously, since the end of the Civil War. It was malleable in a way that moral conviction was not, providing a legitimate hope that the institutions built on racism could somehow be toppled.

This notion affected Lomax's thinking for much of his professional life, and until that mythical toppling could take place, he continued to rely on the media. In September 1945, for example, he used *The Negro Speaks* to raise money for Black victims of polio and infantile paralysis, raising more than two hundred dollars by the end of the first month of the fund drive. Despite scattered white racist anger, the show was successful. In October, the Mutual Broadcasting System purchased *The Negro Speaks*, moved it to a new time on Sunday nights, and syndicated it under a new title, *The Tenth Hour*. For the first time, Lomax, however briefly, had gone national.[38]

Throughout his life, Lomax claimed that after leaving Washington he became a visiting assistant professor of philosophy at Georgia State College before moving on to further graduate work at Yale. Both, however, were fabrications. Perhaps the first was an exaggeration of his freshman year at Georgia State, about which he never spoke. He was not qualified for the job of visiting assistant professor, as he had not received a degree from Paine, Howard, or American, and there is no evidence that he spent any time at GSC from 1946 to 1948. Similarly, there is no record of him enrolling at Yale. These were stories that aligned with his aspirational upbringing in Valdosta and with his obvious intelligence, but as Brer Rabbit knew, sometimes aspirations require a measure of duplicity.[39]

Instead of Savannah, Lomax traveled to Chicago, where he began work in 1948 at the *Chicago Herald-American*. He was the first Black journalist hired by a Hearst newspaper.[40] At some point, he married his first wife, Dolores, who worked for Chicago State University. Northern racism was different from that of Valdosta, but it was still ever present. Not only did realty prices keep Lomax and his wife on the south side of town, but he was the only Black writer in an almost completely white space. At the same time, the cost of living was higher in Chicago than it had been in Washington or Georgia. So Lomax fell back on old habits and decided to start scheming again.

On 21 November 1949, using the alias Dr. Robert J. Frost and a phony New York driver's license and claiming to be a graduate student at the University of Chicago, Lomax entered the Gary Auto Livery in Gary,

Indiana, and rented a 1947 Chevrolet sedan from Joseph Cheramonte. He then drove the vehicle to Chicago and, by means of a forged registration, sold it to a used-car dealer. Two days later, Gary Auto Livery reported the car missing. On 5 December, Lomax returned to the used-car dealership to present a bill of sale and ask the dealer to cash the check he had provided. But the police were waiting for him, and he was arrested.[41]

Later the authorities discovered that Lomax had committed a similar crime a month earlier, renting a 1949 black Ford sedan from an agency in Evanston, Illinois, and then selling it in Chicago with the help of a New York registration for a 1948 Ford Tudor. In light of this new information, the United States attorney in Hammond, Indiana, deferred to his counterpart in Chicago, who in turn deferred to state charges. On 7 December 1949, Lomax was indicted on two charges of running a con game and one of larceny and was held on ten-thousand-dollar bond.[42]

Adding to his troubles, Lomax had passed several bad checks to Chicago State, totaling $175. Officials at the university chose not to press charges since they knew that he was accused of more serious crimes and that his wife, who worked for the university, would pay them back through her wages.[43] It was another stage in a difficult education, as the kid from a strict disciplinarian upbringing continued to falter after leaving home. Just as he had been too smart to earn only Cs in college and to run cons on his guardian and on Paine's president in a failed effort to complete his degree, he knew better than to be involved with car theft schemes. But he did so anyway. His lack of a degree and his criminal record would haunt him for the rest of his life and motivate him to work even harder in an effort to compensate for his early mistakes.

But failing to get a college degree and then lying about it were far less egregious than stealing cars. Despite poverty and the pressure to live up to a lofty standard set by one's family back home, it is hard to imagine any scenario where Sister Lucy or Brer Rabbit would engage in felony criminal acts. There is no known explanation for Lomax's behavior in Chicago. He had never found himself in trouble with the law prior to his December arrest, and while he would be accused of financial misconduct later in life, he would do nothing as immediately fraudulent as stealing cars. While his willingness to engage in confidence scams remained a relative constant, car theft was an anomaly, and Lomax's consistent attempts to hide his criminal record left no clues as to his specific motivation.

Lomax was arraigned on 16 December 1949, convicted on 18 January 1950, and sentenced two days later. The indictment charged Lomax for attempting to sell Mose Banger a car that he did not own (under the alias of Robert J. Frost). He convinced Banger to write him a check for three hundred dollars for the car.[44] The multiple charges stemmed from the different entities hurt by Lomax's confidence scam. One charge was generated by Banger, who bought one of the cars Lomax rented in Gary. A second was generated by the Litsinger Motor Company after the manager of the used-car dealership, Marion Casey, agreed to buy another of Lomax's rentals for one thousand dollars. The court issued subpoenas for twelve different witnesses in the case to demonstrate the connected facets of the scheme. The third charge stemmed from Lomax's theft of the car he attempted to sell to Litsinger, which was owned by Lawrence Lannan of Evanston.[45]

After being convicted, he entered Joliet State Penitentiary as Prisoner 29305, and Lomax and his wife—who was now pregnant with his only child, Hugh—began almost immediately to press the court about mistakes made in his sentencing.[46] He had been convicted on the first charge, which carried a sentence of three to ten years, following the testimony of Cheramonte. He then pled guilty to the remaining charges, each of which carried a sentence of one to ten years, in return for concurrent sentences. The *3* on the first mittimus document, however, was blotted out and a *1* put in its place, causing confusion about potential parole on which the Lomaxes sought to capitalize.[47]

Throughout his motion to correct the record, Lomax was insistent that he did "not wish to be represented by the Public Defender," stubbornly choosing to represent himself instead.[48] The complaint he drafted— along with the individualism and obstinacy that led him to be his own attorney—presaged the attention to detail and willingness to provoke that would define his later career. From prison, he argued that there was a discrepancy in documentation, as the verbatim record by the shorthand courtroom reporter quoted the judge as stating, "The sentence will be to the penitentiary" and "I will sentence him to three to ten on the first one and let the other two run concurrently one to ten each." The official report, however, said that Lomax was "sentenced to the Illinois State Penitentiary" for no less than "three years nor more than ten years" on one charge and no less than "one year nor more than ten years" on the other two.[49] Lomax responded by filing "a writ for relief from illegal confinement," arguing that he had "already served thirty three months pursuant to what he believes to be illegal confinement" that was "due to the imperfect Record in the causes here identified."[50]

Life in Joliet was difficult. It was the prison of Leopold and Loeb, of Baby Face Nelson, and, for a short time during Lomax's confinement, of James Earl Ray, whose later actions would weigh so heavily on Lomax. An aging facility, it had few modern amenities and exceedingly small cells that housed two prisoners each. Joliet remained in use even though Stateville Correctional Facility had been built in the 1920s to replace it. The frenetic Lomax, who changed schools, jobs, and cities regularly, must have been miserable.[51]

In October 1951, he took his case to the Federal District Court, submitting a motion for an order of restraint against the clerk of court of Cook County, the court reporter, and the criminal court itself, cataloging his frustrations with the official record and the difficulty he had in getting records, even though the clerk of court had made it very clear that the files would arrive after a twenty-dollar fee was paid. He argued that the transcription mistakes made it reasonable to assume that one year was a legitimate minimum sentence, rather than three. The confusion about his sentence was not actually rectified until April 1953, and even then, a frustrated Lomax tried to get the charges expunged because he was not notified of the changes prior to their filing.[52]

He was finally paroled and released from prison on 28 September 1954. It had been a humbling experience, but the ever-hustling Lomax was quick to recover. After leaving prison, he stayed at the YMCA on South Wabash Avenue, where he attended and contributed lectures to various "writer's workshops." He then found work as a nightlife reporter for *Club Chatter* magazine. The job did not last long, however, after his parole officer advised him to quit when he discovered that the shady periodical was not publishing advertising that had been paid for in advance. The officer also expressed concerns to the FBI about Lomax's potential for Communism, admitting that he had no evidence but was struck by Lomax's high level of education, and it was "his thinking that highly educated members of the different races are not drawn together except on some ideological basis such as Communism."[53]

Dolores divorced him while he was in prison, the strain of the separation and constant appellate setbacks finally taking their toll. From May 1955 to early 1956, Lomax worked as a paper salesman at the Bankers Printing Company and lived in room 604 at the Sutherland Hotel on Chicago's Drexel Boulevard, originally registering as single but later living with Suzanne Avery, whom he claimed was his wife. Lomax had struggled to keep up with his rent payments as a paper salesman, though Avery, it was said, had money of her own. The daughter of neurologist Loren W. Avery, a citizen of relative renown in the city, she was described by the FBI as "white, 5'3", natural medium blond hair, wears glasses, 21–25 years old, not attractive." Lomax claimed that she worked for the *Chicago Daily News*, but the bureau was unable to corroborate that assertion. During the brief affair, Lomax traversed both a racial and a class line in the wake of his first marriage and release from prison.[54]

By January 1956, Lomax had begun working for Reliable Insurance Company on Michigan Avenue. After a divorce, abandonment by Avery, and an extended prison sentence that set back a promising journalism career, however, he was not satisfied with being a lonely insurance salesman in a city where his closest family member was his cousin, Edmund. Particularly in the tumultuous first month of the Montgomery Bus Boycott, Lomax knew that he was not living up to his own expectations, that there was more he could offer.[55]

So he started over. His parole officer allowed him to take a job with the Associated Negro Press in Washington, DC. Lomax thrived in the new setting, and over the next several years he published in such major newspapers and magazines as the *New York Daily News*, *Pageant*, and *The Nation*.[56]

His journalism experience prior to his prison sentence allowed him to get his foot back in the door, and he would use it to report on the racial realities he had experienced growing up in the South and falling down in the North. Ultimately his coverage of public school desegregation would translate into new opportunities and an association with the prominent journalist Mike Wallace, who in turn provided the break Lomax had been waiting for.[57] At last, he could put Valdosta, college, Dolores, and prison behind him. Life in the spotlight was calling.

2 The Hate That Hate Produced

Lomax's first major newspaper byline came in the *Baltimore Afro-American* on 3 February 1945 with a story about the Georgia Senate's repeal of the poll tax. The Supreme Court had upheld the law eight years earlier, but Governor Ellis Arnall pledged to abolish it when he was elected in 1942. Lomax's entree into journalism built from his devotion to the performative. He had early won a writing contest for his local white newspaper. He had preached, like his grandfather and guardian. And he had grown up under the same Jim Crow system that had allowed the poll tax in the first place. Ministerial work was the family business, but journalism provided a method of performance that allowed him to actively push back against the sins of Valdosta. The *Afro*, founded in 1892, was one of the largest and most significant Black weekly newspapers in the country, led by publisher Carl Murphy, who had a history of taking chances on inexperienced, sometimes troubled journalists. Lomax fit that profile and was able to write for the paper during his time in Washington, DC.[1]

When he resumed his journalistic career in early 1956, following his time in Chicago and at Joliet, Lomax traveled to Mississippi to cover the tense race relations that followed the acquittal of Emmett Till's murderers. He then became public relations director for the Mississippi Council of Negro Leadership, which was led by the controversial activist and doctor T. R. M. Howard. An eccentric, wealthy, and influential civil rights leader and early mentor to both Medgar Evers and Fannie Lou Hamer, Howard had founded the council in 1950. He came to national prominence in the wake of Till's 1955 murder when he used his home as a command center for activists in and around Mound Bayou.

Till's death demonstrated how little the state of white supremacy had changed since Lomax left Georgia. He had entered prison eighteen months after President Harry Truman's executive order integrated the military and exited four months after *Brown v. Board of Education*. In between those two events, *Shelley v. Kraemer* (1948) struck down racially restrictive housing covenants, while *McLaurin v. Oklahoma State Regents* (1950) and *Sweatt v. Painter* (1950) ruled that the intangibles of higher education could not be achieved in a state of segregation. The decisions were important milestones, but the on-the-ground racial intransigence of white southerners kept many of those gains theoretical. By the time he made his way to Mississippi, the Montgomery Bus Boycott was in full swing, beginning what Lomax would later call the Negro revolt. At the same time, the death of Emmett Till had shaken the nation and bred Howard's activism.[2]

Though he had previously been lauded by the white press for pushing a Washingtonian self-help agenda, Mississippi papers turned on Howard after Till's death, labeling him "Public Enemy No. 1." After Till's murderers were acquitted by a local jury, Howard castigated J. Edgar Hoover's FBI for failing to protect vulnerable Black citizens and for not opening a federal investigation into the Till case. "It's getting to be a strange thing," he said in one of a series of public talks around the country, "that the FBI can never seem to work out who is responsible for killings of Negroes in the South." His condemnation was so scathing, in fact, that Hoover denounced Howard in a January 1956 open letter, refuting the charges and castigating Howard as an attention-seeking charlatan who demonstrated a "complete disregard for the facts." "We advised him that we were deeply concerned over this serious charge," read one FBI description, "and in effect, called on him to 'put up or shut up.'" Howard responded with his own public letters excoriating the bureau for its denunciation and with private letters attempting to prove his charges. (He claimed that he knew locals who had complained of discrimination to the FBI, only to be confronted by local law enforcement and threatened for making such allegations.) Lomax, frustrated by Hoover's response to Howard and hoping to write about the story, sought meetings with the bureau, the Justice Department, and the White House. In response to Lomax's advocacy, and in retribution for it, Hoover initiated an investigation into Lomax's "credit and criminal" history. "This should be handled in a most discreet manner."[3]

Lomax's letter was aggressive but not confrontational. "I represent a group of free lance writers who research and distribute articles to the Negro Press under the name ASSOCIATED FEATURES," he explained, arguing that his goal in writing was to gather information that would allow an in-depth account of the government's responses to Howard's charges, which were extensive. He explained to Hoover that Howard "has proof—by documents and witnesses—that your office has received complaints by Negroes that certain federal rights have been denied them by local officials, and that your office has 'leaked' these complaints to the local officials who have, in turn, terrorized the Negroes making the complaints." He also objected to Hoover's unwillingness to initiate a federal case in response to the murder of Emmett Till. More generally, he noted that Howard was claiming "that members of your office are of the southern 'hue'" when it came to race issues. Still, after reciting the complaints against the bureau, Lomax agreed with Hoover "that these charges ought to be proved or withdrawn." His only aim, he argued, was to present a fair governmental response to readers of the Black press.[4]

Lomax's letters to the president and the FBI director made it into the hands President Dwight Eisenhower's cabinet secretary, Maxwell Rabb, who then worked with the bureau to develop a profile of the troublemaking advocate, hoping "to really make it crystal clear that the irresponsible agitation on the part of some of the Negro leaders was hurting their cause." Rabb planned to respond to the letters, to "talk rather frankly with Louis Lomax, the colored writer, and urge caution."[5]

Rabb ultimately decided not to see Lomax. Instead, officials began doing more clandestine research, reporting back to Rabb that Lomax was formerly a Valdosta preacher, mistaking him for his uncle or grandfather. They reported on a 1947 civil rights complaint, "wherein a police officer was alleged to have used too much force on a local Negro for which the Department ruled did not constitute a civil rights violation," and on Lomax's criminal conviction and parole. "Lomax still reports to his Parole Officer," an FBI memorandum reported, its author advising him "not to marry a white girl (Suzanne Avery) although there was some indication that the two were living together without the benefit of matrimony."[6]

Armed with that information, the FBI decided to participate in an interview but to do so cautiously, an internal memo noting that because of the "identification of Lomax as an ex-convict and the impression he gives as being a 'confidence man,' the Bureau should be most circumspect in furnishing material to Lomax." Louis B. Nichols, the agent charged with speaking with Lomax, jotted a note to himself in response to the memo: "We will keep our guard up."[7] Hoover, for his part, responded positively to Lomax, assuring him that Nichols would be "very glad to explain to you this Bureau's responsibilities in connection with the investigation of alleged violations of the Federal Civil Rights laws." These preparations, however, were for nothing: Lomax never appeared in Washington for his interview, claiming illness kept him away. He hoped to reschedule, but the bureau declined further contact.[8]

Though he was never able to talk to the FBI, Lomax sold stories on the Mississippi crisis to both the *Afro* and the *Chicago Defender* and continued to do so after returning to Chicago. Through the summer he covered civil rights and the 1956 Democratic National Convention for both papers, culminating in reporting on the pretense that convention delegates were arguing over a civil rights platform plank, when in fact the disagreement had been resolved months earlier by compromise between northern and southern factions to keep white southerners from hijacking the convention. While the platform as adopted called for "full rights to vote," "full rights to engage in gainful occupations," and "full rights to education" and acknowledged the existence of the *Brown* decision, it denounced "all proposals for the use of force to interfere with the orderly determination of these matters by the courts." The language was intentionally vague and designed to provide cover for the party's white southern constituency. "The Democratic national convention's civil rights fight," Lomax reported, "was a sham."[9]

After the Democrats nominated Adlai Stevenson, the hustling Lomax again ventured south, this time exclusively for the *Afro*. He covered the desegregation of the white high school in Sturgis, Kentucky, where white mobs formed to stop a group of Black students from entering. Sturgis had no school facilities for Black students, who instead had to travel twenty-two miles to Morganfield. After local authorities would not disperse the mob, Kentucky governor Happy Chandler deployed state police and National Guardsmen to escort the Black students into class. More than half of the school's white students responded by refusing to attend, so the state attorney general halted the desegregation until the school system could develop a formal plan. The Black students, now barred from the school they had already begun attending, chose to stay home for the rest of the year rather than return to Morganfield. Lomax stayed with the story until the father of one of the students—a mechanic working at a garage owned by the mayor of Sturgis—was fired for his role in the fracas.[10]

Sturgis was an example of mass resistance in microcosm. Lomax was in prison when *Brown* was decided, but he was free to witness most of the white racial intransigence that followed. He covered a similar drama in Clinton, Tennessee, when twelve Black students registered at the local high school and white supremacists responded with mass action and, eventually, an all-out riot.

> I was in the center of "colored town," perched on the side of a mountain overlooking Clinton, Tennessee. Mob violence over school integration was into its third night. The Negro community was an arsenal; we stood in knots looking down into the center of town as John Casper ranted before a crowd in front of the courthouse. Negro citizens voluntarily stayed out of town and the sheriff advised me, the lone Negro newsman on the scene, against being on the downtown streets after dark. Had the segregationist mob decided to storm the mountain road leading to the Negro sector, it would have been a massacre.

Black men in the town, "many of them war veterans," were hiding in wait for potential attacks. Lomax, meanwhile, was waiting for the Western Union clerk to arrive so that he could file his news story on the situation. Lomax recalled, "Shortly before eleven o'clock, a small Negro boy came running up to me," Lomax recalled, " 'Mr. Lomax,' he panted, 'there's a white man down at the foot of the mountain in a car. He's a-honking his horn and a-blinking his lights and he shouted and tole me to tell you he's as scared to come up here as you are to come down there where he is." Lomax walked down to an area of neutral ground, where "the Western Union man met me. He took my copy, we shook hands, laughed, and said good night."[11]

Lomax published a feature in *Pageant* magazine on Bobby Lynn Cain, one of the Clinton students who integrated the white school and was among the first Black students to graduate from it. "Lord Help Me Not to Be Scared!" emphasized the plight of Cain and the other courageous Black students who agreed to engage in such advocacy. "As I write, I am remembering twenty years ago when as a member of the graduating class of a deep south high school I marched down the aisle on commencement night," Lomax wrote about his time at Valdosta's Dasher High. "School integration a thing undreamed and bus desegregation a thing unthought, I am remembering how with reckless spiritual abandon we sang, 'God moves in a mysterious way, His wonders to perform.'"[12]

The National Guard would stay in Clinton through the end of September 1956. Massive resistance was happening all over the South, but the incidents in Kentucky and Tennessee were the first Lomax saw up close and were formative in his thinking about race. The attacks on children were more coordinated versions of his own experiences as a youth in Valdosta and demonstrated the lengths to which white southerners would go to maintain the racial line.[13]

The North, however, was no place of refuge. In 1957, Lomax covered a series of racially motivated murders of teenagers in Chicago. In one, a group of fifteen white youths beat a Black seventeen-year-old to death with hammers. In another, a white teenager, wrongly assuming that a Black youth had thrown a rock at his car, pulled out a shotgun and killed him. The cases had a dramatic effect on Lomax. "I damn the fact that words cannot bear the burden of telling this story. It is a tale of the soul, a story that can only be communicated by a common fear of the future of man," he wrote of the shooting of Curtis Bivens, the young man wrongly assumed to be the rock-thrower. "How is it that men have lived through Dunkirk and Korea while Curtis died in Chicago?" Or, more immediately, "What is the reason for the short tragic life of Curtis Bivens. I don't know. If I did I would write no more." The gut-wrenching reality of such violence, combined with the prospect of greater professional opportunities, led him that summer to move to New York, which became his new journalistic base.[14]

From there he hoped to publish his first two books, *The Grimes Case*, an outgrowth of his coverage of the particularly salacious murder of two white teenage girls in Chicago, and *The Wheel and the Cistern*, a novel. Lomax optimistically claimed that they were scheduled for publication, but neither book was ever published.[15] He had more success with magazine journalism. Another of his *Pageant* articles tackled the subject of interracial marriage, offering a defense of the practice despite its overwhelming unpopularity: "The inter-racial couple is constantly reminded that it is thrusting against the tide," which manifested itself not only in "the scowling frowns" of white people on the street but in "the subtle jibes of those who fight for racial equality—yet abhor mixed marriage." The issue mattered to Lomax, as he had already been in one interracial relationship and would later marry a white woman. "It should not be too much to ask," he argued, "that a democratic people grant the request of one inter-racial couple and 'Please, just leave us alone!'"[16]

Meanwhile, Lomax began a new radio program, *Reporter's Searchlight*, on WLIB in New York, with plans for interviews with Adlai Stevenson, Eleanor Roosevelt, Thurgood Marshall, and Senator John F. Kennedy.[17]

Lomax followed such broadcasting pioneers as Clifford Burdette, an impoverished Atlanta native who moved to New York and began hosting a weekly program, *Those Who Have Made Good*, on WNYC radio in May 1941. Sponsored by the NAACP, the interview program emphasized the talented tenth of Black New York and featured, among others, actors Paul Robeson, Canada Lee, and Kenneth Lee Spencer and musicians W. C. Handy, Bill "Bojangles" Robinson, and Count Basie. Also appearing on the show were Countee Cullen, Adam Clayton Powell, Walter White, Black aviator James Peck, and radical activist Max Yergan. "My program is dedicated to the progress of the Negro people," Burdette explained, "to acquaint all of America with our achievements and to promote the cause of true democracy in the United States." Like Lomax, Burdette did his early collegiate work in Georgia, attending Morehouse for one year, but then struggled with various small-time jobs in and around Depression-era Atlanta until finally moving to New York.[18]

Burdette's big guests drove the success of his show, but Lomax's big guest never materialized, and he spent the next two years doing space-rate newspaper work, usually for the *Afro-American*. From October 1957 to December 1958, he covered a variety of stories, from civil rights to politics to scandal to crime. He wrote about movie stars such as Sidney Poitier, interviewed Joe Louis, and reported from the United Nations. He covered the desegregation crisis in Little Rock and the attempted assassination of his boyhood acquaintance Martin Luther King Jr. by Izola Curry at a Harlem book-signing event for *Stride Toward Freedom*. Curry stabbed King in the chest with a letter opener; King nearly died and required surgery to remove the weapon. It was also Lomax's first interaction with King since their youth. Both had been raised by Georgia Baptist ministers. As president of the Georgia Baptist Training Union Convention, J. L. Lomax gave the teenaged Martin Luther King his first big speaking stage at the convention's "Christian Youth Night." Although the younger Lomax also spoke at the conference, he was seven years older than King, and it was his coverage of the attack on King that initiated their long-standing friendship.[19]

While rekindling acquaintances in New York, Lomax was also forming new ones, and in February 1958 he married his secretary, Beatrice Spencer. The marriage would be a rocky one and relatively brief, perhaps partly because Beatrice continued to do secretarial work for her husband. It was the second of several marriages for Lomax, as the man born of a short, unstable relationship struggled to find stability in his own interactions with women.[20]

Other connections, though, would be more lasting. Soon after his new marriage, Lomax wrote in the *Afro* about the "Hitleresque Saturday night harangues" of a street-corner Black nationalist in Harlem. He described a short, bald man who mounted a ladder and began to draw a crowd by proclaiming, "Gather round. I want to tell you about the white man. He is a natural born liar and thief. And I want all of you to hear." Lomax wryly compared the scene to Valdosta. "Down home, Saturday night was bath night," he wrote. "In Harlem Saturday night is the night you go out and lay all your burdens at the feet of a ranting black nationalist." At the same time, he appreciated the joy, relief, and empowerment that came to the corner audience, "relieving themselves of all the tensions that afflict the disadvantaged," and he began to "realize that this, too, is a part of America growing up."[21] On another occasion, Lomax wrote about being with a Black friend and his white wife when they were accosted by a street speaker for the transgression of interracial marriage. As both a writer and a former preacher, he was fascinated by speakers who could draw out strong emotional reactions from simple storytelling. And it was his growing professional interest in groups such as the Nation of Islam that led to his break in the business.

After Lomax wrote a profile of him for *Pageant*, influential television journalist Mike Wallace was so impressed that he hired Lomax as a writer and interviewer for both radio and television. Meanwhile, after immersing himself in Harlem's Black nationalist thinking and spending time with Lewis Michaux, Carlos Cooks, and James Lawson, Lomax finally met Malcolm X. He then persuaded Wallace that the Nation of Islam would make a worthy subject for *News Beat*, Wallace's program on New York's WNTA.[22]

Malcolm recalled that Lomax "asked me one morning whether or not the Nation of Islam would cooperate in being filmed as a television documentary program." He was receptive but told his friend that "anything like that would have to be referred to The Honorable Elijah Muhammad." According to Malcolm, Lomax flew to Muhammad's headquarters in Chicago and convinced the NOI leader to participate, while Lomax claimed that it was Malcolm who did the convincing. Either way, Muhammad was swayed by the promise of publicity and his shared background with Lomax (though Muhammad had been born a generation earlier, in 1897, both came from small Georgia towns and were the sons of Baptist ministers).[23]

Press materials for the show explained that "Wallace retained Lomax to follow through on the story and he put the resources of the *News Beat* staff at Lomax's disposal." Lomax began attending meetings and tape recording various events before "four weeks of negotiations" finally resulted in the NOI giving him "permission to film their Washington, DC rally. There was also a tentative promise that [Elijah] Muhammad would consent to an interview after the meeting. That interview materialized."[24]

Lomax himself interviewed many of the subjects for *News Beat*. Others he interrogated as preparation for Wallace's interview. "I practically had to live with some of them," he said. "Those papers Mike held during the sessions had everything on them. The questions were printed in lower case, the answers were in caps. If the answer he got on the show didn't match the one written down, there was trouble. I made a pact with the Good Lord that if I ever got through that chicken wire I would remember everything I learned with Wallace." Jackie Robinson and Roy Wilkins, both of whom later had contentious relationships with Lomax, participated in the project, and Robinson provided blurbs for the publicity campaign. That campaign described the Nation of Islam and James Lawson's United African Nationalist Movement as "Black Supremacy" groups—sometimes referring to them as cults—that were "anti-white, anti-Christian, anti-semitic and anti-integration" and posed "a serious threat that will amaze Negro and white." Lomax, explained a press release, "has been covering this strange story with a special camera crew for the past two months." The documentary "was the result of a joint investigation" by Lomax and Wallace (figure 2.1).[25]

On 13 June 1959, the first episode of Lomax's collaboration with Wallace appeared. Titled *The Hate That Hate Produced*, the five-part documentary series introduced the country to the Nation of Islam. The show featured interviews of Malcolm, with gratuitous clips of him calling white people "devils." While Elijah Muhammad liked neither the emphasis on Malcolm X nor the focus on "hate," the program actually spurred growth in the faith. Three weeks after the first episode the group's Los Angeles mosque inducted five hundred new members, with similar additions across the country. At the same time, the program frightened many viewers from the time of the first episode through the final installment, which aired on 17 July.[26]

The opening episode started with Wallace delivering a scathing editorial on "a group of Negro dissenters" preaching a "gospel of hate" while "city officials, state agencies, white liberals, and sober-minded Negroes stand idly by." The NOI was "the most powerful of the black supremacist groups," a frightening example of "organized hate." Malcolm described the

FIGURE 2.1 — Lomax working with Mike Wallace on *The Hate That Hate Produced.* COURTESY SPECIAL COLLECTIONS AND UNIVERSITY ARCHIVES OF THE UNIVERSITY OF NEVADA, RENO. ITEM 82-30-2-2-1.

white man as the embodiment of the biblical serpent in the Garden of Eden. As Graeme Abernethy explains, the Black Muslims "were framed as the realizable inversion of King's contemporary demands for justice and equality for African Americans by nonviolent means. The sizable African American minority appeared, as if more clearly than ever before, as a potentially murderous revolutionary mass."[27]

That impression was created not only by the words of the radical leaders themselves but also by Wallace's framing. He began the series with a sensationalized introduction, which was followed by Lomax's interviews of such figures as Muhammad and Malcolm X. Commentary by Wallace was interspersed with the discussion and again at the program's conclusion. Lomax's questions to Muhammad and Malcolm allowed them to explain the Black Muslim position. "Can a white man join your temple?" Lomax asked Malcolm, who responded that he could not. "What do you think of the NAACP?" "Islam is a natural religion, and it is difficult to find a black body with a white head and classify that body as something natural." Immediately after this answer, the documentary cut back to Wallace: "We have, thus, seen Muslim leaders in reflective moments and as they talk to members of their own flock. But what about their approach to non-Muslim Negroes?" The show then played a supposedly anti-white speech made by Malcolm. "The film was made under adverse circumstances," Wallace ominously warned his audience.[28]

The documentary also featured speeches by representatives of the United African Nationalist Movement and an interview with its leader, James Lawson. In response to a question from Lomax, Lawson said that he did not support the NAACP, claiming that Arthur Spingarn, an influential member of the group's board, was a Zionist. This led to a discussion of Ralph Bunche, a devoted civil rights advocate who had also mediated the 1947 Arab-Israeli conflict, whom Lawson called "the George Washington of Israel." The program again cut to Wallace, but instead of contextualizing Zionism and the problems Black radicals might have with it, he provided a different kind of coda: "One of the rallying cries of these black extremists is the alleged failure of Christianity." With this statement to his largely white audience, Wallace directly associated Black rights with opposition to Israel and Christianity. He asked, "Is this Black Supremacist doctrine making headway among New York Negroes?"[29]

At the end of the program, Wallace turned the tables and interviewed Lomax about his experience with the project. It was the only time Lomax provided any editorial comment. "We Negroes have invested quite a bit in America," he said:

> It's not my fault that we're here. It's not your fault as a white man that the race problem exists. America was born with a race problem. And we've helped to eliminate it. Our backs have borne a great deal of the burden, and the general feeling is that America is on the upbeat—that we're going up—that our country is getting better, and I see no point in turning our backs upon America now. It's like pushing the wagon up the hill and then refusing to ride down, and I think this is the attitude of most Negroes. I hope so, anyway.

It was a mild, measured rebuke, one that seemed incongruous with Wallace's talk of anti-Christian Black Supremacy cults. "It is a terrible indictment of America," said Wallace as he closed the documentary, "that even a small part of our Negro population—even a small part—is willing to pay heed to the racist declarations we have heard here tonight."[30]

In addition to conducting interviews for *The Hate That Hate Produced*, Lomax helped write the show and was a credited producer. After the production, Lomax continued to do interviews and special interest segments for Wallace's *News Beat*. But the title and editorial commentary for the documentary series were Wallace's. Lomax compiled all of his footage and delivered it to Wallace, who edited the reels and added narration specifically to sensationalize the coverage for maximum impact. The Nation of Islam understood this, and when it held a New York City rally soon after the documentary's debut, Mike Wallace and all other white journalists were banned from the event. Lomax, however, did attend and watched as Elijah Muhammad charged that Wallace was trying to destroy the NOI: "Does he classify the truth as Hate? No enemy wants to see the so-called American Negro free and united. He wants to use you as a tool."[31]

For his part, Lomax managed to escape Muhammad's blame and maintained a good relationship with the group. Later that year when Malcolm began publishing an early version of *Muhammad Speaks*, the newspaper of the faith, Lomax helped him collect news stories and lay out the first issues. Malcolm was frustrated that so few of his Black Muslim cohort were able to write and edit. "I was torn," Lomax recalled, "between my deep disagreement with Malcolm's philosophy and my commitment to the notion that one should seize every opportunity to provide training-skills to young Negroes." The galleys for that early attempt, titled first *The Islamic News* and then *Mr. Muhammad Speaks*, were edited by C. Eric Lincoln, a friend and ally of both Malcolm and Lomax, who was then a doctoral student writing a thesis on the Nation of Islam.[32]

Muhammad's denunciation of Wallace was to be expected, but the documentary was a sensation, as were its subjects. Although Malcolm also complained about the negative reaction to the series, he understood that all publicity was beneficial. As Abernethy explains, the documentary "initiated the mass media campaign that Malcolm would sustain" until his assassination. "More than any other single factor, Malcolm's iconic emergence was accelerated by" the documentary. The Anti-Defamation League's Arnold Forster even claimed that Wallace exaggerated the group's size and influence, giving it an "importance that was not warranted." After the program appeared, exposés on the "black supremacy cults" appeared in newspapers throughout the nation. An extensive investigation of the organization of the Nation of Islam by *U.S. News and World Report* and an endorsement of the program by Jackie Robinson in his nationally syndicated column provided additional coverage. *Time, Cosmopolitan, Reader's Digest*, and the *New York Times* followed with their own analyses, and the *Detroit Free Press* launched an independent investigation of its hometown organization. Letters and telegrams poured in to WNTA from around the country, praising the coverage.[33]

The documentary was light on the Nation of Islam's place in the long history of Black nationalist thinking, thanks largely to the editorial work of Wallace, but it also neglected the kinetic nature of Malcolm's ideation as he grew as a thinker. His "gospel of hate" was necessarily tethered to the society in which he lived and that created the need for such revolutionary ideologies in the first place. It bred an understandable call-and-response pragmatism that left Malcolm adjusting his views as new manifestations of white supremacy appeared in response to Black agitation. In *The Hate That Hate Produced*, Wallace was unwilling to convey such nuances. Nuance, in fact, was the opposite of his intent. But the series did make a sensation of Malcolm, Elijah Muhammad, and the faith.[34]

It was a Rubicon crossed for the NOI, and it was also Lomax's biggest success. He had hustled to convince Wallace and *News Beat* that he had an inside angle on the group, sold them the concept, spent two months preparing interviews and footage, and written and produced the program. A triumph in self-promotion, it would set the standard for much of his career. The year after the documentary aired, he introduced Malcolm to photographer Eve Arnold, who was commissioned by *Life* magazine to photograph the Black Muslim leader. The shoot produced a famous picture, ultimately published in *Esquire* rather than *Life*, of Malcolm in profile, hand behind his neck, hat slightly cocked. It was a stylish picture, one that helped make Malcolm famous, and it was facilitated by Lomax.[35]

Despite his protestations to the contrary, Lomax was dramatically influenced by his time with Malcolm. He never became a Black Muslim, nor did he take an unambiguously nationalist position on American race issues, but his time with the NOI gave him a different lens through which to view the leadership and focus of classical civil rights organizations. The movement was becoming more confrontational, less willing to acquiesce. As the 1950s became the 1960s, the NAACP continuously demonstrated to many younger, more radical activists that the civil rights movement had passed it by. When the students from North Carolina A&T who initiated their 1960 sit-in campaign sought legal aid, for example, the NAACP declined. The shift between the old and new guards was growing, and as historian Osha Gray Davidson has noted, Lomax "was one of the first to understand the dimensions of this shift and to describe its significance." His first major national effort after *The Hate That Hate Produced*, an article in the June 1960 issue of *Harper's* called "The Negro Revolt against

'The Negro Leaders,'" became another controversial sensation, this time almost exclusively in the Black press. "This revolt," wrote Lomax, echoing the critique of his friend Malcolm, "swelling under ground for the past two decades, means the end of the traditional Negro leadership class."[36]

The revolt, Lomax said, would be all-consuming: "This new gospel of the American Negro is rooted in the theology of desegregation; its major prophets are Christ, Thoreau, Gandhi, and Martin Luther King. But its missionaries are several thousand Negro students who—like Paul, Silas, and Peter of the early Christian era—are braving incalculable dangers and employing new techniques to spread the faith. It is not an easy faith, for it names the conservative Negro leadership class as sinners along with the segregationists." For the bulk of the previous century, Lomax argued, "a small 'ruling class' has served as spokesman—and has planned the strategy—for all American Negroes." But the younger generation were overturning that leadership, claiming that "the NAACP is far too conservative and slow-moving."[37]

The article clearly reflected the negative views of the NAACP that Malcolm X and Lawson expressed to Lomax during interviews for *The Hate That Hate Produced*. Lomax had no intention of painting the group as a Zionist cabal, but he recognized the frustration with the results achieved by the NAACP. When he wrote about "a good deal of foot-dragging by moneyed Negroes in high places," he was coming to the same conclusions as the United African Nationalist Movement and the Nation of Islam: "Negro leadership organizations know what the revolt means and are about to be reconciled to being servants rather than catalysts."[38]

In May 1960, syndicated columnist Harry Ashmore examined Black leadership in the North, using as his guide Lomax's article "The Negro Revolt against 'The Negro Leaders,'" set to appear in the following month's *Harper's*. He argued that Lomax's piece was "an epitaph for the National Assn. of Colored People" to coincide with "the prior demise of the Urban League." The sit-ins had demonstrated that younger activists were no longer taking their cues from more conservative, calculating civil rights hierarchies. The revolt, "swelling underground" as it had been, would perform a kind of coup by proxy against traditional leadership. Ashmore agreed with Lomax: "Local organization leaders were caught flat-footed by the demonstrations; the parade had moved off without them." Lomax believed that in Black organizations, "there will never again be another class of white-oriented leaders such as the one that has prevailed since 1900." Ashmore was less confident in that conclusion, noting the moral compromises of leaders such as Roy Wilkins, A. Philip Randolph, and Martin Luther King Jr. and what he saw as the failed legislative agenda of "phony liberals" such as Adam Clayton Powell. Still, it was Lomax's work that allowed white commentators like Ashmore a starting point to critique Black civil rights leaders.[39]

Black columnists such as George Schuyler also found fodder in Lomax's *Harper's* article, though Schuyler, as was his wont, was far less impressed. "With the evident relish of a parson surveying a platter of steaming neckbones, Br'er Lomax pulls up to his chair, licks his chops and digs in with might and main, but the bones he forks up are pretty bare." Schuyler pointed out, for example, that the four students who held the Greensboro sit-in were members of the NAACP, making it hard to believe that their actions could spell the death of the organization. "The Negro's war will always have to be directed by some leaders, and the more experienced, the better," he wrote. Gandhian nonviolence was an "asinine pretense" in Schuyler's view, but organizational hierarchy would always be necessary.[40]

The *Harper's* article drew so much attention that *Coronet* approached King, another leader who was critical of the NAACP, to collaborate on a piece about the group with his friend Lomax. King, however, declined. "While I privately agreed with many things that Mr. Lomax said in the article," he explained in a letter to *Coronet*, "I feel a moral obligation to preserve a public image of unity in our organizational work." And Lomax had little interest in unity.[41]

Columnist Louis Lautier was more critical, defending the NAACP and claiming that Lomax's piece was "riddled with errors of fact." Lomax reported on 1958 complaints that the association's convention was held at a "white" Detroit hotel, but Lautier pointed out that the 1958 national gathering was at Cleveland's Municipal Auditorium. Lomax described a split between the offices of the NAACP and its Legal Defense and Education Fund, but Lautier explained that the separate offices were the result of tax exigencies: contributions to the defense fund were tax-deductible, while those to the association itself were not, due to its lobbying activities. Lautier also pointed out errors in Lomax's timeline concerning negative reactions to King's acquiescence on the milquetoast Civil Rights Act of 1957, as well as errors in quotation about King's trip to the White House for the bill signing.[42]

Jackie Robinson's criticism was also withering. The former ballplayer, now an activist and columnist, noted Roy Wilkins's support for the sit-in participants, the Legal Defense Fund's pledge to defend all those arrested, and a successful NAACP convention in Minneapolis as proof against Lomax's claims. He compared Lomax's critique to one made in 1959 by broadcaster Chet Huntley, who argued that "the NAACP might have outlived itself" by pushing too hard for integration. Lomax was making the same essential criticism for opposite reasons, Robinson argued, and was just as wrong as Huntley had been. Robinson also pointed out that Wilkins and Lomax had a feud in 1959 following *The Hate That Hate Produced* when Lomax tied Wilkins to "hate groups," noting that he had been photographed alongside a Black Muslim, in addition to other Black leaders. At the time, Wilkins blasted Lomax for smearing him and several other rights leaders. "I don't know how much of Lomax's current article has been influenced by this occurrence last year," wrote Robinson.[43]

Lomax was, his critics argued, practicing what he would later call "the art of deliberate disunity," first providing the Black Muslims a national platform over and against civil rights groups who were fighting for equality every day, then turning around and criticizing the old standards such as the NAACP. Many joined Robinson in assuming that Lomax's article was the result of time spent with the Nation of Islam. That may or may not have been so, but the journalist's career would demonstrate a continuous ability to befuddle his critics and stir up controversy. His next effort would venture into foreign policy, provoking an entirely new group to find themselves properly befuddled.

3   *The Reluctant African*

The British colonial Kenya that Louis Lomax visited in the 1950s was a brutal place, with blatant inequality that resembled conditions in his native south Georgia. For example, public bathrooms were segregated for Europeans and Asians, although those designated for Asians were nothing more than holes in the ground, while Africans were forced to find relief in the streets—a phenomenon that led Ralph Bunche to refer to the capital city as "one big pissory." There were stories of atrocities, including those committed by William Baldwin, an American who joined the Kenyan police force and openly boasted of killing more than a "dozen native terrorists," whom he referred to as "diseased animals."[1] That blatant bigotry and its similarity to home intrigued Lomax about the politics of the place and its potential for revolution.

Historical interpretations of African American foreign policy thinking in the 1960s tend to emphasize a growing Black nationalism, one that had been present in Black thinking since antebellum separatist movements but that experienced a rebirth at the 1955 Bandung Afro-Asian Conference at the onset of the Non-Aligned Movement. In 1959, Malcolm X and the Nation of Islam received their first major national publicity with Lomax's help, as *The Hate That Hate Produced* embellished the message that the Black and Brown peoples of the world had a legitimate anticolonial argument that cut against the bipolar politics of the Cold War. Two years later, the Bandung ethos was synthesized for African American readers in Frantz Fanon's *The Wretched of the Earth*, which described the alienation and dehumanizing effects of colonization and the psychological liberation of revolutionary efforts. Such thinking metastasized in the 1960s during the Black Power movement when leaders developed the theory further, arguing that Black America itself was a foreign colonized culture living under the thumb of the imperialist white United States. At the other end of the political spectrum was Martin Luther King, who, among many others, argued against American imperialism in a different way, emphasizing the immoral use of violence in the country's Vietnam policy and the existence of any conflict in general.[2]

At the same time, there was a long tradition of Black foreign journalists—mostly operating within the realm of the Black press and writing for a Black audience—who reported from the areas that Fanon and others theorized about. As early as the 1840s, African Americans such as Mary Ann Shadd Cary and Frederick Douglass reported from overseas, linking the conditions abroad to the United States. George Washington Williams reported from King Leopold's Belgian Congo in the late nineteenth century. W. E. B. Du Bois convened the Pan African Congress after World War I, and reporters of the Black press chronicled the colonial emancipation of African nations after World War II. As Jinx Coleman Broussard has argued, Black foreign reporting "saw the world primarily through the race lens" but often did so in an attempt to "elevate the standing of people of color by highlighting their accomplishments and refuting the negative stereotypes in the mainstream media."[3]

An early example of Black foreign reporters who ventured from this traditional pattern was George Padmore, London correspondent for the *Pittsburgh Courier* and *Chicago Defender*. For much of the period from the 1930s to the 1950s, Padmore covered the anticolonial Pan-African movement on the continent, and his vigorously anti-imperialist stance and strong writing gave him a measure of national renown that allowed his work to seep beyond the pages of the Black press and into the mainstream. During World War II, his reporting on the movements and successes of African American soldiers fit the Broussard paradigm but also emphasized the efforts of other Black and Brown peoples in helping to win the war. While he was not alone in this kind of reporting during World War II, his work was especially prominent, and his intense focus on anticolonialism laid the groundwork for his postwar advocacy, including a role as personal political adviser to Ghana's Kwame Nkrumah until his death in 1959.[4]

Among those who were influenced by Padmore was Louis Lomax. His ideology, though inconsistent, sought to provide a Bandung-style Third

Way between the poles of traditional thinking about African American foreign policy positions in the 1960s.

His ideas were built most consistently on opposition to colonialism. Like Black nationalists, he saw the United States as part of the broader imperialist problem and occasionally made a comparative American race analysis with regard to foreign lands, but like George Washington Williams in the Belgian Congo, he more often sought to interpret foreign political actors on their own merits and within their specific contexts. Since Lomax was a freelance journalist without any real foreign policy expertise, his understanding was necessarily filtered through his own racial experience, intentionally or not, and therefore his coverage lacked the nuance of those who studied the various regions more intently and for longer periods of time. Nonetheless, a devotion to national self-determination was a hallmark of Lomax's thinking. Though the areas he covered were incredibly violent, he never bent to a King-style antiwar stance, claiming that indigenous military action was often the only way to secure freedom from colonial yokes. Unquestionably, his ideas came with a measure of sensationalism absent in those of traditional Black correspondents or proponents of Black nationalist theory. While certainly both of those groups wanted the most eyes on their reporting and their advocacy, respectively, attracting personal attention was a tertiary motivation, at most, and was not given priority over careful treatment of the intricate details. Lomax, however, was prone to sweeping generalizations in aid of conclusions that would garner eye-catching headlines.

Lomax's "The Negro Revolt against 'the Negro Leaders'" in *Harper's* may have drawn some negative publicity from Black critics who supported NAACP leadership, but it had the benefit of establishing his relationship with the Harper and Brothers publishing house. In May 1960, as he was planning a trip to South Africa for a *Life* magazine story on apartheid, he had in mind a larger project, so he sent a book proposal to John Fischer, editor-in-chief of *Harper's*. In the proposal, titled "Africa South: The World's Newest Dilemma," Lomax claimed to have "established contact with the South African 'underground,'" which he described as stretching "from America to London to Buchanaland to Basutoland into South Africa," though most of its leaders in South Africa were in prison. His plan was to contact the "second string leaders," the "skeleton 'contact organization'" throughout sub-Saharan Africa.[5]

After talks with South African expatriates in the United States, Lomax was convinced that the region was "on the brink of a bloody revolt" against "colonialism and/or white domination" once more money and arms could be secured. He proposed to interview Arab financiers seeking to bankroll such a revolt with a view toward spreading Muslim hegemony to the Atlantic Ocean, as well as Soviet leaders who could be convinced to provide financing to hurt western colonial powers. Those colonial powers were not the only problems, however. "The rebels from Africa south hate Tubman, of Liberia, Selassie, of Ethiopia, and Nkrumah, of Ghana, second only to colonialism," wrote Lomax, arguing that the rebels "feel it nothing short of ethnic treason that these men will not allow their countries to be used as bases from which attacks on established governments can be made."[6]

Such sweeping generalizations would become common in Lomax's foreign interpretations. As with most generalizations, he was both right and wrong. William V. S. Tubman had instituted a capitalist economy in free Liberia and was intent on gaining international influence and support. Using his country as a staging ground for radicalism did not necessarily correspond with that goal, despite Tubman's legitimate standing as an anticolonial hero. Haile Selassie had a similar standing, but postwar paranoia had turned him toward autocracy to protect his political position. Two years after Lomax's memo, in 1962, Selassie would take over Eritrea and Ethiopia, his iron fist and austerity bleeding much of the countries' resources. Nkrumah, however, did not lose favor with southern rebels until 1963. He was at the time of Lomax's memo facilitating military camps in Ghana. As historian Matteo Grilli has argued, Nkrumah's influence waned after 1963, partly because of distance and logistics, but predominantly for political reasons, as many southern armed revolutionaries interpreted his Pan-Africanism as too conciliatory and passive. Perhaps Lomax saw the early signs of such a rupture, but his generalization remained, at the time, too broad to be significantly edifying.[7]

He proposed to interview, among others, representatives of Kenya, Tanganyika, Rhodesia, and Mozambique. He claimed without reservation that the revolutionary leaders of Africa "are not communist. They are openly anti-communist. But they are bitter toward the West," and that bitterness virtually assured that "Christianity is doomed in Africa south." Therefore, "Africa south looms as the crisis battleground of the next decade. If the free world is as moral or as defense minded as it says it is then it has precious little time in which to reappraise its position toward people who are determined to become free."[8]

The proposal was overly broad and full of promises and conclusions about the state of modern Africa. Lomax never really described how he would fulfill those promises, nor did he provide any evidence for his conclusions. In addition, he claimed, "I still must raise about two thousand dollars" to make the trip. He maintained that he was trying to get the money together, but the proposal was clearly an effort to get some or all of the total from Harper. A skeptical Fischer showed the proposal to Cass Canfield, chairman of Harper's executive committee, who thought it was "pretty hot stuff" but wondered, "Can't we see some chapters before committing ourselves?" He initially did not know who Lomax was, but after reading his *Harper's* magazine articles, he concluded, "He's a good journalist. My only doubt is that I feel Lomax may exaggerate some of the more newsworthy aspects of his subject. I am not completely confident of his objectivity."[9]

Canfield's criticism was fair, but the subject matter convinced the publishing house to take a risk. Evan Thomas, director of Harper's general books department, proposed paying Lomax "a sum of $300 for the guarantee that we would have first offer of any book length material which may be written as a result of [the] trip." If Harper decided not to publish, Lomax would be required to pay back the money. "We are not at all clear what form a book would take but we think it should be a combination of personal narrative and observation," Thomas wrote. He cautioned against outlines or preliminary hypotheses, urging Lomax to let the research guide his conclusions. "Does this interest you?" It did, and by the end of May, Lomax signed a contract granting him $300 in exchange for right of first refusal for Harper on whatever the author came up with after his trip to Africa.[10]

Lomax was a motivated, swift worker. In less than three months, he traveled to a variety of countries in Africa, chronicled his experiences, and delivered a manuscript, now titled *The Reluctant African*, to the press. The copy, he said, was "about how I felt during the entire trip. I have rendered the material in narrative form and without chapter breaks. I wanted you to see it as I felt it." He told Harper that "the final draft will be more than twice this in length, but will contain nothing that has not been adumbrated here."[11]

The book told the story of Lomax's two-month sojourn down the eastern coast of Africa and his interviews with those seeking the continent's liberation (figure 3.1). After meeting with exile and rebel groups in Egypt, Ethiopia, Kenya, and South Africa, he described a Black radicalism willing to do whatever it took to extricate colonial powers from the continent, including violent, bloody revolution, and accepting aid and advice from

FIGURE 3.1 — Lomax in Africa discussing issues of African colonial independence with unidentified leaders. COURTESY SPECIAL COLLECTIONS AND UNIVERSITY ARCHIVES OF THE UNIVERSITY OF NEVADA, RENO. ITEM 82-30-1-2-5-2.

countries of any economic bent. That willingness, along with Lomax's conclusion that the bulk of the 1960s would be consumed with uprisings linked with Cold War ideological battles, served as a warning to his American readers that there was more at stake in these movements than the country might realize. He argued that the best the United States could do was to dramatically change its stance on race and sponsor racial awareness events around the world. This suggestion, however, seemed like a small paean to national interest in the face of Lomax's doomsday prediction of Africa as a particularly volatile storm that would suck the entire world into its vortex.[12]

His narrative propped up an uncompromisingly integrationist message, one that fit into a classical civil rights paradigm. "Africans are totally unwilling to accept whites as coequals and partners in a free government, yet they have no qualms about accepting money from both East and West," he wrote. Lomax went to Egypt and met with President Gamal Abdel Nasser. He attended the Second Conference of Independent African States in Ethiopia, where, he observed, representatives merely nodded in the direction of nonalignment: all of them accepted support from colonizer countries in the bipolar world, as long as they could convince themselves that the aid was coming on African terms. At the same time, however, he remained solidly against colonialism and its mentality. "I detected a tendency by the world press not to take African politicians seriously," he claimed, with certain frustrated accuracy.[13]

In Kenya, he parsed the issues of land reclamation, emphasizing in particular the controversy over the nation's "White Highlands," a massive, largely unused stretch of land set aside for white settlers, and the Mau Mau rebels who fought for its redistribution. The culmination of his trip was a secret sojourn into South Africa, where he was predictably horrified. South Africa was, of course, the endgame of the white supremacist state and thus the apotheosis of evil for everyone along the civil rights spectrum.[14]

But Lomax's position clearly fit into one station along that spectrum. "As an American Negro who is committed to integration," he wrote, "I am disturbed by African politicians who say white people must get out of politics." Though that stance sounded good in principle, he argued, "the shattering moment comes when one realizes that the Africans are saying that the ethnic majority should form the government in its own image." Lomax found such a notion to be "egregious." After all, he argued, it would mean "that Europeans who have been in South Africa longer than Negroes have been in America have, at best, only squatters' rights."[15]

His solutions to the problems he found were those of the educated novice. He predicted that "the major African revolt is yet to come," proposed "an all-out stand against racism," and suggested that "private American foundations would do their country and the world a great service if they would underwrite a World Conference on Race Relations." The United Nations, he believed, should be more involved on the continent in an anticipatory role, rather than responding to each new violent outcropping. Finally, "the world states must put their economic and political power behind individual freedom and national sovereignty for all peoples."[16]

Black American discussion of African colonialism primarily emphasized and even celebrated nonalignment and the relationship between the situation in Africa and the struggle against white supremacy in the United States. It was largely a radical conversation and would become more so in the years to come. But Lomax hewed to the integrationist line, even pushing back against calls by the ethnic majority in South Africa to create a government "in its own image." His understanding of civil rights and its relationship to foreign policy would evolve over time, but his first real entrance into the public discourse after *The Hate That Hate Produced* was halting and conservative in the face of his trip to Africa. It was, living up to its name, reluctant.

Harper planned an initial print run of ten thousand copies. "This is a startling and threatening book," wrote production manager D. F. Bradley to Thomas, "and if we are going to publish it I feel that we ought to do it in a hurry, not only because the American public needs real information on Africa but because things will probably change so quickly that by March or April the book may well be far out of date."[17] It was the inherent danger in books that tracked current events, but Thomas, for his part, did not need to be convinced. "I think this is the most sensational thing I've read since the newspaper accounts of the dropping of the first atom bomb," he wrote. "It's a really terrifying story." He proposed a $1,500 advance against royalties, minus the $300 the press gave Lomax to help fund his trip. "I really think this is as important as all hell," he told his staff, and he planned to rush publication. By mid-November, Harper press materials announced the coming book as "an American Negro's subjective report on the people and forces now at work in Africa: a story no white reporter could get."[18]

To ensure accuracy, Thomas sent the book to the Council on Foreign Relations and to Richard H. Sanger, foreign service officer for the State Department in Lebanon, Jordan, Saudi Arabia, and Africa, to check the clearly subjective work for factual accuracy. Speed was of the essence, he urged Sanger, because "we're trying to get it out in a hell of a hurry." Acquaintances had asked Thomas "whether this man is a responsible reporter," and State Department validation would ease many of those concerns.[19]

There were also questions involving libel. The law firm of Greenbaum, Wolff, and Ernst reviewed the manuscript with Lomax to help him edit some of his own words to keep them in line with libel laws. Potentially more problematic were comments made by those he interviewed. "If any of them chose to disavow the statements attributed to them, much of the material might be actionable," the law firm explained. "Many of the interviewees admit, and indeed advocate, what may well constitute conspiracy, sedition, and even treason under the laws of the regime in power in their respective countries." Lomax countered that many of the interviews reflected openly acknowledged facts and that the opinions and goals of his sources were often "open and notorious"; they were "official policy of the

Pan African Congress in South Africa and of other anti-colonial movements." The one possible exception was the material credited to South African journalist William "Bloke" Modisane, who had heard about the forthcoming book and protested the portrait that Lomax drew from his interview. Greenbaum, Wolff, and Ernst worried about statements credited to Modisane, such as "We are going to launch a full scale revolution" and "We'll have to shoot every white man who comes within our gun sights." Lomax eased the attorneys' fears by agreeing to contact Modisane with an assurance that the text would not appear in a "distorted form."[20]

A native who moved to England in 1959 in response to apartheid, Bloke Modisane had worked as a reporter for South Africa's legendary *Drum* magazine and as a jazz critic. He also acted, wrote fiction and screenplays, and attempted throughout the 1950s to use his standing in the artistic world to bridge racial divides and make art and theater performances available to Black audiences. When Lomax interviewed him, Modisane was working on his autobiography, *Blame Me on History*, which would be published in 1963. His stake in the ongoing struggle against apartheid and his strategic place in the South African mainstream made his statements to Lomax all the more problematic.[21]

Lomax's attempt to reassure Modisane prior to the book's publication did little to curb the South African's adamant refusal to "acknowledge the accuracy of any part of the interview." He had certainly made similar or even more radical statements elsewhere, but because of his objections, Harper removed the more revolutionary parts of his quotes. "We believe," the law firm told the press, "that by these changes we have eliminated from the interview any advocacy of unlawful violence by Modisane and that as the interview now stands it is well within the contours of views previously expressed by Modisane for publication." For example, in speaking about the strategy used by Americans to address civil rights, Modisane was quoted as saying, "You Negroes made it by going to court," adding, "but we Bantu will have to do it another way." When Lomax asked him about guns, Modisane told him, "Such things are always available if one really wants them," but his statement did not include threats to harm white South Africans. It was a description of Bantu aims that was far more vague and measured than in the book's first draft.[22] Even with the editorial changes, the press remained concerned about the portrayal of ongoing conflicts by an author who overtly centered his political opinions. "We must not present the Lomax book as impartial journalism," Thomas concluded. "Everything we say about it should make it clear that it is a highly subjective view or interpretation."[23]

That emphasis, even after the near-universal positive response the manuscript had received, proved prescient in October, less than a month before publication, when Robert Coughlan of *Life* magazine sent Thomas his thoughts on the manuscript. "I found it very interesting as a personal report," he wrote, "but I'm afraid that the conclusions suffer from lack of knowledge about Africa, both in general and especially and acutely in regard to the places he didn't visit and which, in fact, disprove his most important points." Coughlan disagreed that "anti-white racism" existed in Tanganyika, Uganda, Ghana, Nigeria, and other areas: "They want the white man's technical and financial help, and will for a good long time to come." Even in hubs of radicalism such as Kenya and the Congo, he wrote, "there are men of moderation among the African leaders." It seemed to the *Life* author that Lomax had taken his experiences in Rhodesia and South Africa and jumped "to an unjustified generalization about the rest of black Africa." He urged caution as the book went to press. "As an interesting personal encounter and emotional diary it has merit," he told Thomas. "As a serious piece of reporting on contemporary Africa it has really none."[24]

To be fair, Lomax made it clear that he was a novice in a strange land, a nonexpert making broad conclusions. The first story in *The Reluctant African* describes Lomax being castigated by African colleagues to "never call Africans 'natives.'" His interviews openly included the questions of a neophyte American. "Would you say 'amen' to Communism?" he asked Joshua Nkomo. "Where do you stand in the East-West struggle?" "Will you accept aid from the Russians?"[25]

Coughlan's emphasis on reporting was specifically a critique of Lomax's tendency to generalize rather than of his subjective approach to the African situation, as the Black press traditionally and of necessity did not adhere to strict standards of objectivity. In describing the efforts of the *Atlanta Daily World* at the time of Lomax's writing on South Africa, for example, historian James Buford Murray explained that the paper attempted "to develop racial awareness among its readers to insure the psychic stability of the Negro in the face of racist theories of inferiority." It "worked for the realization of a state of security for Negroes by informing readers of their rights and of the procedures by which they were deprived of those rights." Although historian Charles Simmons describes the *World*'s editorial policy as an attempt at objectivity, there is no such thing when a journalist has a stake in the game. Rather, Simmons is referring to a pragmatism that judges each situation independently, after gauging the possible outcomes for both the situation and the paper's best interest. "I think sometimes that when the scholars in the profession talk about objectivity they mean something else altogether," notes Percival Prattis. "I think they mean dignity. I think they mean that we should fight like gentlemen and not brawl."[26] Lomax's style was that of a brawler, and it bothered Robert Coughlan.

"Well, I'll be damned," Thomas responded to Coughlan. "We had that Lomax book checked in manuscript by a presumably responsible officer at the State Department." Though he was troubled by Coughlan's concerns, Thomas concluded, "All I can do now is try and temper the tone of our advertising. I'm surely glad the anti-white feeling is not as high as Mr. Lomax gives us to understand. But aside from that I'm feeling rather low in my mind, to put it mildly."[27]

Nonetheless, later that day Thomas sent a copy of the Lomax manuscript to Martin Luther King Jr., hoping for a comment he could use in the press's publicity materials. "Since you are now again honorably in jail," he told King, "you may have some leisure for reading." Lomax also solicited his own endorsements, sending the manuscript to Lorraine Hansberry, who called the book "a superior piece of journalism" and "a splendid accomplishment—I got to shouting a little 'uhuru' up there myself in my living room." South African author Stuart Cloete also provided the press with positive commentary.[28]

Such praise clearly worked. The book appeared in print in mid-November 1960, and by the end of the month *The Reluctant African* had sold more than 7,500 copies.[29] But for Lomax, it was not enough. As Thomas and the press had learned early on, prior to his trip to Africa, the author was constantly looking for cash. After the book's publication, he called Harper and Brothers "desperate for money," claiming that a check he was expecting from an NBC interview had not come through. By mid-November, Lomax's newly signed agent, Marie Rodell, asked if Harper might be interested in a Richard Wright anthology edited by Lomax, which might draw an advance for her perennially hard-up client. Such would be a theme through the rest of the author's life. Harper was "not keen on the Richard Wright anthology idea," but with the early success of *The Reluctant African*, the press was able to "try to blast some money out of our bookkeeping department for you know who" (figure 3.2).[30]

The *New York Herald Tribune* devoted two reviews to Lomax's new book. Henry Winslow recounted the author's trip from New York to

FIGURE 3.2 — A Lomax publicity shot prepared for media appearances related to *The Reluctant African*. COURTESY SPECIAL COLLECTIONS AND UNIVERSITY ARCHIVES OF THE UNIVERSITY OF NEVADA, RENO. ITEM 82-30-6-10-1.

London to Cairo to the Sudan and down to Johannesburg. The crux of Lomax's frustrated observations, argued Winslow, was that "American State Department people are sitting 'laced to their swivel chairs watching the greatest freedom explosion in human history occur in an anti-American, anti-white, anti-capitalist, anti-Western context.' All else he heard and saw underscored this central, ugly impression." While the story was interesting, Winslow claimed, it was neither novel nor enlightening, for "there is no new thing under the African sun."[31]

Maurice Dolbier noted that the book was rushed into publication, appearing only months after Lomax's trip concluded. Such haste was required because in African politics, "men and situations alter before anything written about them can possibly get into print." Dolbier found Lomax's account of sub-Saharan Africa's political, social, economic, and racial upheaval "vitally necessary" as a primer for events that would surely continue to change, his narrative made possible by access granted by his Blackness and therefore fundamentally different from the efforts of white American journalists.[32] It was also different fare than would come from traditional foreign correspondents at historically Black newspapers, who hewed more to facts and domestic comparisons than to conclusions wildly flung at readers based on somewhat limited observations.

"*The Reluctant African* is a disturbing book," explained the *Baltimore Afro-American's* Saunders Redding, "and one is left with the impression that it would have been more disturbing had Lomax seen more." Yet Redding believed that despite its pessimism, the book made necessary arguments about the primacy of racism in African relations, the ultimate need for war to rectify such racial imbalances, and the consequences of that racism in apartheid South Africa "as being a bellwether for civilization."[33]

In May 1961, Lomax's *The Reluctant African* was named a joint winner, along with E. R. Braithwaite's *To Sir, with Love*, of the *Saturday Review's* Anisfield-Wolf Award for books that dealt "most credibly with social and group relations." The award, which was presented by *Saturday Review* editor Norman Cousins at a luncheon at New York's Pierre Hotel, came with a plaque and one thousand dollars, which Lomax sorely needed. The *Review* then publicized the book, leading to various radio and television appearances, including Lomax's first interview on Jack Paar.[34]

Pearl Buck, Lillian Smith, Ashley Montagu, and Oscar Handlin were the judges for the award. Smith saw Lomax's work as the best of the offerings that year, saying that he "writes very well; with disarming simplicity, but the simplicity that is the result of much thinking about many facts whose significance he knows well and understands with his heart." She was impressed with both the book's brevity and its immediacy. "He speaks of segregation, multiracialism, plain old racism, and integration, and speaks to the point and with a precision of thought that I found myself respecting very much. He clarifies the fact that the young African leaders are, in a sense, exploiting both Russia and the United States, playing them against each other as if they were two old jealous men, while she (Africa) rakes in the money from both." At the same time, "he says these things gently, with soft laughter, and you smile with him, seeing the shrewdness of these young leaders but at the same [time] realizing the danger to all of us of a racial holocaust." Because she had a niece living in southern Rhodesia, Smith tended to keep abreast of news from the continent. "I believe Lomax is right in what he says," she wrote. "I think it outlines the situation in a very clear way."[35]

In his acceptance speech for the Anisfield-Wolf, Lomax noted that since he began working on the book, "upwards of two dozen independent African states have been born," and "they have forged a new balance of pressure in the United Nations and have named racism the Achilles heel of the embattled West." After expressing hope for those nations and their fight against the racism that had so dogged them, he drew parallels between Africa and the United States. "This then is our national purpose," he told his audience, "to admit the verdict of destiny and assume our role as the westernmost outpost in man's Odysseyan [sic] journey from tribalism and divisiveness to an open yet unified society." He closed with an even greater flourish. "Let us set aside the cynicism and inaction that tend to beset us and write with faith of the responsibilities and glories that are just ahead," he implored. "For if we can stay the deluge of racism for a little while longer, man's instinctive desire to survive will yet make brothers of us all." It was far more hopefulness than Lomax normally displayed, but awards can make optimists of even the most cynical. It also fit with the message of his book, the "brothers of us all" line reflecting his frustration with the desire of Black South Africa to form a government in its own image.[36]

During the ensuing tour to promote the book, Lomax spoke at a fundraising dinner for the Jersey City NAACP. While he repeated some of his critiques of Negro leadership, he also argued that fewer leaders and more actors were necessary for positive change. "We of the NAACP must realize that we are servants of the people," he told the crowd. It was shifting sand for a pundit who had previously been so at odds with the association. He also spoke about the ideological concept of the ghetto, which he claimed needed to be eradicated not only physically but "mentally and spiritually," and about desegregation, claiming that "all integration means from a Negro's point of view is that he has the opportunity to advance in accordance with his ability."[37] When viewed through the lens of the chaos and colonialism he had witnessed in Africa, Lomax could muster at least a brief détente with the NAACP's leadership and policy objectives.

He was powerless, however, to manufacture other, more local efforts at rapprochement. Harper sent information about the book to Jet's Book Shop in Valdosta, Lomax's south Georgia hometown. But Jet's was a white bookstore and told the press that since no customers had asked for the book, "they did not want any stock." Valdosta State College's bookstore was also uninterested, advising "that they handled only textbooks and inexpensive reprints." The response demonstrated Lomax's fraught relationship with his hometown and his hometown's fraught relationship with race. Valdosta State in early 1961 was still more than two years away from desegregating. When the book derided colonialism, apartheid, and Jim

Crow, and the bookstores were controlled by small-town southern whites, the author's birthplace was beside the point.[38]

Elsewhere, though, interest in the book was still acute. The African Historical Research Society ordered seventy-five copies in February, and the press was pleased with continued sales in far more cosmopolitan hubs such as New York and Chicago. By April, *The Reluctant African* had sold more than ten thousand copies. Lomax was an integral part of those sales, doing multiple speaking engagements and even giving talks at local high schools in Queens.[39] That kind of hustle would only redound to his benefit as he began a new project closer to home.

4   The Negro Revolt

By early 1961, *The Reluctant African* was a Book-of-the-Month Club selection, and its success, combined with Lomax's two years of broadcast
experience with Mike Wallace, landed him a job writing the news program
and producing occasional news specials for New York's WNEF-TV. He was
hired by Ted Yates, director of creating programming for metropolitan
broadcasting for WNEF. Yates had worked with Lomax before as a reporter
and producer on the WNEW-TV program *The Right to Sit*, which docu-
mented the burgeoning sit-in movement. Lomax's television credits continued to expand nationally as well, as he wrote several episodes for NBC's
long-running *Frontiers of Faith* program that were set to air that year.[1]

In April, bolstered by *The Reluctant African*'s prize and his work on
the NBC show (figure 4.1), an opportunistic Lomax pitched another
book proposal to Harper: an edited "selection of the National Council's
TV plays" to be titled *Frontiers of Faith*. It was essentially an effort to take
his own episodes and combine them with several others in the format of a
book. "The plays are competent works, and many of them are very good,"
wrote Harper's Genevieve Young, "but they are not as a whole inspira-
tional or even religious. Lacking such a sales 'handle,' we don't see a market
for the book."[2]

Lomax was undeterred by the failure. In March, "Three Gentlemen
from Africa," his second *Frontiers of Faith* episode, made its debut, and
with his profile growing, he and Malcolm X debated the problems in Black
America and their potential solutions on New York's WINS radio program

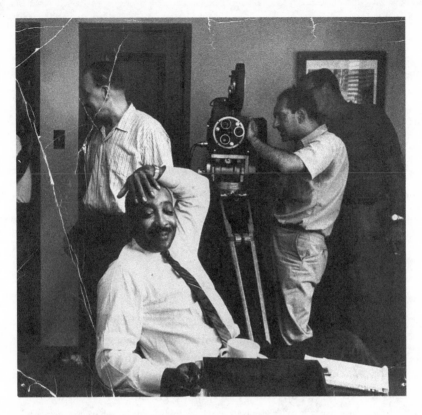

FIGURE 4.1 — Lomax while working at NBC in 1961. COURTESY SPECIAL
COLLECTIONS AND UNIVERSITY ARCHIVES OF THE UNIVERSITY OF
NEVADA, RENO. ITEM 82-30-8-4-4-3.

Open Mike. In April, they debated at Yale. Lomax defended integration as
a viable civil rights aim and nonviolence as a method, though he continued his critique of movement conservatism. Though Malcolm X and he
were on different sides of the lectern, the events cultivated their friendship
and influenced Lomax's thinking.[3] In the April 1961 edition of the new
magazine *The Urbanite*, Lomax published a scathing piece, "The Act and
Art of Being a Negro," in which he argued that Black America had so long
presented itself as whites expected it to that individuals eventually bought
into the charade. Black nationalist thinking offered a potential answer.
"What a sweet shock it is," he wrote, "for a Negro who has been imbued
with a sense of inferiority all of his life suddenly to hear a doctrine which
holds that he, the Black man, is superior, of God's own choosing," and that
the white man, "the serpent who lost his legs through sin," is inferior,

"lost, doomed, living on borrowed time." Lomax wondered, "Could it be as the black nationalist charges that your mind has been enslaved?" It was the inherent danger in Du Bois's double-consciousness, that the less authentic self would win out, to the detriment of a legitimate fighting spirit. "Being a Negro in America is not an easy state," Lomax wrote. "So much of your time, energy and creative efforts are consumed with just being *Negro*." Only a rekindling of the original authenticity could provide real momentum in the civil rights effort, and Black nationalism provided at least one useful method of rediscovery.[4]

In June, his article "The American Negro's New Comedy Act" appeared in *Harper's* continuing the same theme. "Negroes and white people are beginning to laugh together about the most serious affliction of American society," he wrote. "True, we Negroes have been laughing at white people for years. I suspect—in fact I know—they have been laughing at us. But until recently the laughters have not been mutual or the same: our comic response was born of hurt; theirs, I regret to say, of malice." Things, however, were changing. "Those of us who are laughing about racial matters are making a game of serious issues. This is the way of comedy: its essence is sacrilege. Nothing destroys racism more effectively, for laughter is a criticism, not an endorsement, of things as they are." And it was not simply flippant. "There is seriousness in this comedy act and we who laugh about it are neither nihilists nor clowns," Lomax argued. "We are, rather, men afflicted with the passionate faith that man can be better than he is and with the equally passionate conviction that honest laughter underscores the need to close the gap between human aspirations and human performances. This is not to say that the Negro will save modern society, only that he is a part of it."[5]

The *Amsterdam News* ran a response by Gertrude Wilson, "a white Park Ave. mother with a keen perception of today's world." Wilson launched a scathing critique of Lomax as a "professional Negro" who was "making hay on Negroism. I think it's nauseating." None of the humor Lomax described was new at all, she argued, and many of the "facts" he cited were not accurate. "I'd like to know what would inspire Mr. Lomax to say he was 'the lone Negro newsman on the scene' at Clinton, Tenn. He knows that isn't true." Lomax was able to sell the narrative, Wilson maintained, because he was playing to a white audience that did not know any better. "If this is what he wants to shovel up for gullible whites he may make a few dollars, but he won't last as an expert observer."[6] Such a critique, coming from a white resident of Park Avenue, was likely to only bolster Lomax's credibility. Wilson claimed to be "sick of the 'professional Negro,' and sick of the 'hep cats' who spend their time laughing at white people," but such complaints may have hurt her standing as a keen observer of the world before a predominantly Black reading audience.

Others received Lomax's article more positively, and that summer he pitched yet another idea to Harper, this one a book about Black revolutionary attitudes that would eventually become his next hit, *The Negro Revolt.* "I have delayed this until I could talk to people across the country and make sure I was on solid ground," he told Young. "With a month or so of travel and interviews I will be ready to write." He had no chapter outlines but was confident that the work would be a short process: "I hope we can get a late winter or Spring pub date."[7]

The Negro revolt he described was the new 1960s turn in the civil rights movement. The early movement had largely centered around education, from *Brown* to Little Rock to Prince Edward County, Virginia. With massive resistance to school integration still going strong in 1959, it was no surprise that students would help lead the way in fixing it. On 1 February 1960, four Black students at North Carolina A&T College in Greensboro sat down at a Woolworth's lunch counter and asked for service. Although it was not the first such action, it launched what would become known as the sit-in movement, where young activists challenged local segregation laws by demanding equal access to public facilities. The students in Greensboro were members of the NAACP, but they were acting independently.[8]

The Greensboro of that era was an interesting place. The white population was obsessed with its own progressive identity, which resulted in a stifling moderation. A focus on "civility" subordinated civil rights gains and fostered among whites a paternalistic sense of responsibility and a desire for consensus. This emphasis on etiquette also stifled honest debate, maintained the public display of Black deference, and cloaked the budding protest movement from progressive white eyes. Because such a restrictive atmosphere was not rooted in overt atavism, a new willingness to engage, to force the white South to show its racist fangs, would be necessary.[9]

The sit-ins were inordinately successful. Greensboro integrated its lunch counters, as did restaurants in Nashville. In Atlanta, the protest expanded to include all public facilities, and in September 1961, municipal Atlanta gave in and integrated. Thousands were arrested in these protests, and the willingness of the college students to be beaten and arrested without fighting back won them national support. It also trained an entire generation of activists unwilling to give up such protests.[10]

The sit-ins led to the creation of the Student Nonviolent Coordinating Committee (SNCC) and ultimately to the Freedom Rides, where activists from SNCC joined with those from the Congress of Racial Equality (CORE) to take buses across state lines, thereby putting their actions within federal jurisdiction and forcing the Justice Department to respond. The Freedom Rides prompted even more violence and further demonstrated that there was a new militancy among younger activists in the movement. It was that radicalism to which Lomax was responding.[11]

Even with the recent rejections and the relatively limited prospectus, Young expressed confidence in Lomax's proposal. "This is a book which can only be written by a Negro," Young wrote to him, "explaining the Negro point of view and the reasons for it. Unlike THE RELUCTANT AFRICAN, this is not news, but the story behind the news." Nonetheless, she expressed concern about statements in the proposal such as "American capital is in league with the segregationist," which she saw as far too broad to be edifying. "Shouldn't this be heavily qualified? Don't you mean that a few such instances have played a large part in Negro attitudes, perhaps a larger part than the actual facts deserve?" Lomax was prone to broad exaggeration, and Young was right that in such instances he needed to provide further explanation and evidence. Still, it was an easily defensible statement. Lomax meant it without real qualification and would continue to make such claims, in the book that became *The Negro Revolt* and throughout his life. Young had more advice for making the proposal more digestible and evidence-based, as she wanted "to have all the ammunition before I present the book at our editorial meeting Wednesday."[12]

That meeting went well, and by the end of July, Harper offered the cash-strapped Lomax a contract for the new book. "This will be a first-person story which will put the current racial unrest in America into context," Young told her colleagues. It would be a narrative that "could only be written by a Negro telling what other Negros think and say and do today, and why."[13]

To complete the manuscript, Lomax went to Washington to interview political leaders, and his publisher tried to help where it could. Harper's editor-in-chief, Evan Thomas, asked Robert Kennedy to meet with Lomax. After the author spoke with assistant press secretary Andrew Hatcher, Young wrote him a note of thanks, inquiring if Hatcher might help "arrange for interviews between Mr. Lomax and other White

House officials involved in the field of civil rights" and even if "there is a possibility that Mr. Lomax can see the Attorney General and perhaps the President."[14]

Those political relationships would yield dividends in other areas, as well. In the summer of 1961, Lomax telegrammed his friend Lorraine Hansberry, telling her that he had convinced three congressmen to fly down to either Florida or Mississippi to participate in a Freedom Ride, "provided some Negroes of stature fly with them." It was the kind of program Lomax loved, providing him publicity and allowing him to hobnob with celebrities and politicos while still aiding the cause of civil rights—and doing so in the manner that younger activists were dictating.[15]

But all was not well for Lomax. His marriage to secretary Beatrice Spencer, which began in 1958, ended in June in a "Mexican divorce" in Juarez. Spencer told the press, "We are still friends, but our personalities are so different we just could not get along as husband and wife." That may well have been true, but during the previous weeks Lomax had been publicly courting Betty Frank, a disc jockey and commentator on *The Home Show* on New York's WLIB radio, and the *Amsterdam News* reported that "friends believe they are serious." Frank was, in fact, serious about her new beau, and the couple wed in August. It was Lomax's third marriage. Though he was the child of a brief romance, he was raised in a stable household, so his proclivity to marry (and then divorce) was not a product of upbringing. Instead, it may have been that his aspirational nature, which continually urged him on to the next professional project, carried over into his personal life, and that his many relationships demonstrated a different kind of deliberate disunity. Ultimately, there is no definitive evidence for what caused either his serial womanizing or his penchant for graft. But his divorce from Spencer would not be his last, and future splits would prove more violent and less amicable.[16]

In early July, Lomax and Frank emceed a special telethon variety show featuring Lena Horne, Nina Simone, Diahann Carroll, and others to raise money for the Freedom Riders. Held on New York's WNTA-TV and sponsored by CORE, the telethon lasted more than five hours, from late Friday night into early Saturday morning, and raised roughly thirty-six thousand dollars. Manhattan borough president Edward R. Dudley declared 7 July to be Freedom Riders' Day and personally presented his proclamation to Lomax. He also sent copies to the NAACP, the Southern Christian Leadership Conference (SCLC), and Freedom Rider Diane Nash. "The Freedom Riders have conducted themselves with dignity in the face of vileness," the proclamation explained, "character when confronted with the greed of those wishing to maintain customs of privilege and courage in the face of grave personal danger." It was, in proclamation form, the kind of sentiment that Lomax was working to express while writing *The Negro Revolt*.[17]

Later that month, the *Amsterdam News* theatrical editor, Jesse Walker, reported that Lomax was writing "an American Negro series" for ABC that was currently shooting "in Harlem and over the country." The project was actually a documentary, an episode titled "Walk in My Shoes," that would be the season premiere for ABC's *Closeup* program. Focused on "the role of the Negro in American life," the program discussed the Nation of Islam, Martin Luther King Jr., Dick Gregory, and others. According to *Herald Tribune* television editor Richard K. Doan, Lomax was "helping script the story." He also conducted many of the on-camera interviews. The episode opened with Lomax telling his audience, "There is no single voice for the American Negro today. Some of us are disillusioned, some of us are frustrated, many are angry. We're difficult to know, harder to understand. I know, because I am a Negro. The only way the white man can know me is to walk in my shoes." The program then featured a taxi driver, a garment worker, a "slum-dweller," a suburbanite, representatives of the Nation of Islam, CORE, the SCLC, and the Freedom Riders, and finally Dick Gregory.[18]

The taxi driver expressed his frustration with life in an impoverished neighborhood. "We stay in hock from day to day," he said. A woman who complained of rat-infested dwellings and difficult conditions explained to Lomax that she did not have enough money to move and that housing prices were fixed to keep people like her stationary. "Some of the people who might have an opportunity to move," Lomax explained in a voice-over, "have been so beaten, so destroyed by the constant pounding of prejudice, segregation, discrimination, and bigotry that they no longer have the will to walk through a door which may be open to them." The Black population was concentrated in poor neighborhoods with low-paying jobs.[19]

The program, which was sponsored by Bell and Howell, highlighted the work of various civil rights groups to effect change, as well as cultural incursions that could influence white minds. For example, in a bit from his stand-up comedy, Dick Gregory quipped that baseball was "a great sport for my people. That is the only sport in the world where a Negro can shake a stick at a white man and it won't start no riot." Other scenes showed relative Black wealth, particularly in Los Angeles, but warned that continued waves of the Great Migration were revealing racism in that city, as well. Integration, the program pointed out, was a goal not because Black citizens wanted to eat or go to school with white people, but because there was no other way to gain equal access to resources. In sum, the episode took the everyday conversations that occurred within Black homes and workplaces and placed them before the nation, giving a largely white mainstream audience a sampling of both the opinions and the struggles of African Americans that were shaped by various manifestations of white supremacy. It gave a legitimate platform to many who previously felt they were merely screaming into the wind.[20]

In his book *Redeeming the Wasteland*, Michael Curtin contends that "Walk in My Shoes" "frames the available options on a continuum anchored by polar opposites: further attempts at liberal, incremental reform or militant, separatist revolt." The structure of the documentary makes the case that liberal reform is the reasonable default position but that the more militant approaches of the Nation of Islam are also viable, legitimate options given the country's racial problems. "The *reason* white viewers should press for further civil rights reform," Curtin explains of the documentary's argument, "is that without it, militant black movements will continue to grow." It was a pragmatic case that presented liberal civil rights reform as the better choice, even for those viewers predisposed to like neither of them.[21]

Some broadcast affiliates in the South refused to run the program. Chattanooga's ABC affiliate aired a Billy Graham program instead. In Miami, the local station broadcasted a House Un-American Activities Committee film, *Operation Abolition*, about Communist infiltration of youth protests of a committee hearing in San Francisco. Of ten different southern affiliates, eight preempted the show with something else, with only the Atlanta and Richmond markets choosing to present the program.[22]

The *Amsterdam News*, the *Pittsburgh Courier*, and the *Chicago Defender* had positive reviews of the program, acknowledging the power of such stories when given a national audience. Wendell Green of the *Los Angeles Sentinel* was less enthusiastic. "The tragedy of the hour long show was more of the missed opportunity, rather than its complete negative mirroring of thinking in Negro communities across the nation," he wrote. Lomax, he believed, was "a Negro writer who strives for the provocative" and who utterly failed. "A taxi driver driveling about Africa. A Jackleg preacher spouting race hate. The emotional segregation pleas of the Black Muslims. Chicagoans concerned about color. Angelenos concerned about

Negro migration. A Freedom Rider berating his elders who layed [*sic*] the foundation and opened up the way," complained Green. "I have yet to find more than one person who had anything good to say about the program. What a pitiful waste!"[23]

Green's criticisms were different from those of white southern network affiliates afraid of a pro-Black message. Rather, Green maintained that Lomax's message was not pro-Black at all. His talk of "negative mirroring" and a lack of gratitude by younger activists for "elders who layed [*sic*] the foundation" would be attacked directly by Lomax in *The Negro Revolt*. Indeed, such arguments were the reason he was writing the book, but they would dog him for years to come. Though he would push back against being stereotyped as the Black provocateur with a negative image, one who was seeking fame on the back of a legitimate civil rights struggle, he sometimes made himself an easy target.

The night before the debut of "Walk in My Shoes," Lomax appeared on Jack Paar's *Tonight Show* to promote the show, even though Paar was on rival NBC. Lomax was becoming a media sensation. In late August, he reunited with an old colleague when he was a guest on *The Mike Wallace Interview*. In talking with Wallace about *The Reluctant African* and emerging African politics in general, he demonstrated a reluctance to embrace Black nationalist thought or even to engage with the message of his friend Malcolm X. Wallace pressed him on whether the anger among Africa's Black population was justified after centuries of white imposition, but Lomax refused to take the bait. Justifying any kind of violence or anger was detrimental and inconsistent, he argued.[24]

He would vacillate on that position throughout his career, but when it came to the ultimate goal of civil rights, he never wavered. In October, he and Betty were with a group of five protesters, all leaders of various New York chapters of the NAACP, en route to Washington, DC, for a workshop hosted by the American Council on Human Rights. The group stopped at the Double-T restaurant on Maryland's Route 40 outside Washington and staged a sit-in at the whites-only establishment. Restaurants along Route 40 had already been a national embarrassment when African diplomats were refused service, and the plan was to highlight the everyday inequalities that still existed in Maryland for everyone else. For Lomax, it was a chance to participate in activism, rather than merely commenting on it. Like so many actions in Lomax's life, it involved both provocation and publicity—self-promotion with the best of intentions. Before the protesters were arrested, Lomax left to call the press, but he returned to the scene. He explained that the demonstrators acted as individuals, not as representatives of the NAACP. "We've heard all that talk of moral suasion for years but the only way to accomplish what we want is direct action."[25]

Of course, that kind of talk would have made a far greater impact closer to February 1960, when the sit-in movement began. Although sitting in at segregated venues was still a vital part of the civil rights effort, grandstanding as a radical activist critical of the NAACP while participating in a protest that the association had supported for nearly two years seemed foolish. Nevertheless, this theme had been successful for Lomax in the past, and he would return to it again. In November, he spoke at the luncheon for the regional conference of Lambda Kappa Mu sorority in Newark, New Jersey. His speech, titled "The Twilight of Modern Negro Leadership," reprised some of his criticisms from his 1960 *Harper's* article, "The Negro Revolt against 'The Negro Leaders.'" He boldly predicted, "If the current crop of Negro leaders do not change their approach within five years they'll be out."[26]

He repeated the message during an address sponsored by the Forum and Forensic Society at Atlanta's Clark College. Arguing that "current Negro leadership" had "for all practical purposes lost contact with the masses," Lomax told his audience, "The great debate in Negro leadership is over legalism as the best means of change. Legalism is not the answer." He reminded them that segregation suits were still mired in the courts while sit-ins were actually generating real integration on the ground. "We must be ready to go out and suffer for the things we believe in."[27]

In late November, word leaked out that Lomax's new book, *The Negro Revolt*, was soon to be published by Harper. Genevieve Young was clearly pleased with the effort. "I find this book tremendously exciting, increasingly so, the oftener I read it," she told the author. "(The reverse is usually true.) There is real meat here, and I think you are writing better than you ever have before." She believed the biggest problem in the draft had to do with organization, particularly early in the text, and she made suggestions for revising the opening chapters to create a tighter, more concise text. Young's other concerns were more substantive: "You make several sweeping statements ('The Negro is the only true American . . .' etc.) which are not supported in the text, and which give an entirely erroneous air of irresponsibility to the book." She encouraged Lomax to "be very careful to distinguish when you are talking about Southern whites, and when you are talking about whites in general, at the times when you are castigating whites for their behaviour to the Negro." Racism existed across the country, but in the opinion of Young—a white northerner—regional variances of racism could not be swept into broad generalities.[28]

Despite the healthy advance on his new manuscript, just a month after submitting it Lomax found himself needing more money for a trip home to Georgia. Like his serial marrying, his financial struggles had no real precedent in his early years. Whether or not his constant overspending was another manifestation of his aspirational nature, it was a perennial problem for the rest of his life. Young was accustomed to Lomax's desperation for income and agreed to add a supplement to his contract for another $250 advance against future royalties.[29]

In return, Young presented Lomax with pages of detailed notes and suggested revisions for the manuscript in an attempt to streamline the narrative, clean up the often-unwieldy prose and broad generalizations, and moderate some of the unsourced radical statements to make them more defensible under scrutiny. In January 1962, she pressed Lomax further to supply two missing chapters and to make the requested revisions as soon as possible. The reason for the urgency was that *Washington Post* reporter Wallace Terry had signed a contract to write a book on emerging Black leaders in the civil rights movement for Robert B. Luce, a short-lived publishing house in Washington founded by the editor who would, in 1963, take the reins of the *New Republic* magazine. Harper feared that the two books—both evaluations of the state of civil rights by pioneering Black journalists—would be obvious competitors and wanted the earlier publishing date to gain the upper hand. Young encouraged Lomax to work "with all deliberate speed: deliberate because you must not rush on your thinking and writing of this revision, and speed because time is getting short. We must come out before Wallace Terry's book does." She worried that "the edge of the audience's appetite will be taken off for this book, not to mention the fact that you're likely to get less review attention." As it turned out, Terry's book never appeared, but its threat drove an often-disorganized Lomax to complete *The Negro Revolt*.[30]

Finally, at the end of February, Lomax produced a complete copy of the manuscript.[31] But Young knew that it had to pass muster with the Harper legal team before publication, so she sent a copy to Greenbaum, Wolff, and Ernst. Their report came back in early March, and their concerns anticipated all of the eventual criticisms from Black leaders after the book's formal appearance. "We assume that Mr. Lomax can substantiate that various factual assertions made throughout about the organizations involved, i.e., that the NAACP is losing membership; the program of the various groups (such as the Black Muslims); what they have done, etc.," the firm worried, explaining that any inaccuracies could create legitimate complaint from any of the groups. "We are most concerned on this score about the NAACP and Roy Wilkins, against whom an animus on the part of the author could be said to emerge. If facts stated about NAACP are inaccurate, or if inferences and comments are unfair, this apparent animus could be claimed to show malice on the part of the author." In an extended, detailed breakdown, the firm repeated its concerns about "the NAACP problem" in the text.[32]

At the same time, the firm questioned Lomax's claims that "Martin Luther King is not an intellectual," that the SCLC was "being run in King's name, but by somebody else," and that the Urban League had "lost the respect of Negroes." Such statements needed to be supported with evidence or to be removed. (Ultimately, though, qualifiers or explanatory footnotes were not added to the book, and Lomax's criticism of King, the SCLC, and the Urban League, along with his larger screed against the NAACP, remained.)[33]

Even while making (and fighting) certain revisions to the manuscript, Lomax wasted no time in moving on to his next project. By late 1961 he was working to recruit Black businesses to sponsor "The Man Thurgood," a television biopic of the NAACP lawyer who had sometimes served as his confidant. Earlier in the year, Jack Greenberg had succeeded Marshall as the leader of the NAACP's Legal Defense Fund. While most commentators did not question the move, Lomax worried that "Jews would die before they would let a Negro rise to the leadership of one of their organizations," so why were organizations such as the Legal Defense Fund willing to let a Jew, "or any white man," take the reins? His was largely a voice in the wilderness, as Marshall himself had chosen Greenberg, who was certainly capable and overwhelmingly approved.[34]

Lomax's response was less a public display of anti-Semitism than a plea for the kind of racial unity he saw in Jewish organizations, an idea he explained further in *The Negro Revolt*. Jews, he wrote, were "a people with a tradition, which, as both a theoretical and practical matter, offends Negroes." Historian Seth Forman has argued that Lomax's understanding of "Jewish 'togetherness'" was actually far more progressive than that of "other civil rights activists." Still, it did not translate into support for Greenberg.[35]

Meanwhile, the ambitious Lomax was looking past *The Negro Revolt*. Months before its publication, he sent Harper a treatment for a new novel he planned to write titled "St. Albans." He intended to base the fictional account on a sociological study he had already conducted on the changing demographics of St. Albans, Queens. It would reflect the ethnic transformation in the neighborhood over thirty-five years, "somewhat on the order of A TREE GROWS IN BROOKLYN," he explained. "This ethnic changeover will differ greatly from the current concern over Negroes moving into an all-white community. The latter cases almost always involve a Negro family moving into a community that is completely white and the rukus [sic] starts from there." The situation, while dramatic, was "abnormal" for most neighborhood demographic shifts. "After all, three Negro families—a la PEACEABLE LANE—do not make a slum. Twenty thousand Negroes almost always do make for a slum. Why? What happens to the people in the meantime? This is what ST. ALBANS attempts to come to grips with."[36]

Genevieve Young was detailed in her response, attempting to steer Lomax away from a novel into something more sociological in its presentation: "The technique of MIDDLETOWN, by the Lynds, might be studied with profit."[37] The St. Albans idea demonstrated Lomax's real desire to write fiction, but since he was again "strapped for money," he agreed to make changes, and Young gave him a $500 advance, "should your new outline for the St. Albans book prove satisfactory." If it did not, the money would be considered an additional advance on earnings from the forthcoming *The Negro Revolt*.[38]

Soon after receiving his check for the "St. Albans" treatment, Lomax and his wife, Betty, attended a White House dinner for Félix Houphouët-Boigny, president of Ivory Coast. Several other leading Black figures were invited, including Sidney Poitier and George Weaver, assistant secretary of labor. Less than a decade after leaving prison, Lomax was a national figure, dining with the Kennedys.[39]

Meanwhile, *The Negro Revolt* was being prepared for publication.[40] When it debuted in June 1962, Cass Canfield, longtime president and chairman of Harper and Row (which changed its name from Harper and Brothers that year), sent a copy to Martin Luther King Jr. "I think that this is an important book," he confided to King, "and would much appreciate any comment you care to make on it."[41]

In the book Lomax traced the history of the Black rights movement, reaching back into slavery before resetting the narrative with the Montgomery Bus Boycott and moving forward with the protests through the 1950s, the birth of the sit-ins in 1960, and the simultaneous evolution of a different ideological protest outside of the South. He described incidents of racial violence and police brutality and the failure of white liberals to rise up against the abuse. He interviewed his friend Malcolm X and described the growing influence of the Nation of Islam. An appendix disputed the myth of increased Black economic prosperity used by segregationists to push back against civil rights activism. The bulk of the story, however, was devoted to the "Negro revolt" against "Negro leaders," an expansion of his earlier article. The NAACP, he wrote, was inefficient and guided by wrong principles, "beset by dissension within and criticism from without." The Urban League had abandoned its role in aiding the transition of Black southern migrants to northern industrial hubs. The SCLC "leaves much to be desired." While he largely agreed with the group's integrationist ends, he saw the SCLC as overbearing, often criticized by younger, more mobile, and radical groups for swooping into local areas and stealing attention from local officials, only to leave without shoring up final settlements. In short, a new generation of militant activism was challenging the theoretical position of integration as a viable goal and the leadership of traditional groups as out of touch with the real problems and broader concerns of Black America.[42]

Lomax also included plenty of Green's "negative mirroring" in his narrative. He argued that "Negro businesses failed" in the late Gilded Age and early twentieth century not because "the Negro people lack a merchant tradition," but instead "because it was 'Negro'; it assumed that a separate Negro economy could exist within the white economy, and it reckoned without the ingenuity of the white merchant, who not only could afford to sell at a lower price than the Negro merchant but who also welcomed Negro money as long as his Negro customer stayed in 'his place.'"[43]

Lomax's early work in *The Negro Revolt* was in many respects in line with Malcolm's thinking. He took the "old guard" of rights workers—his principal target was the NAACP—to task for watching as a more activist contingent passed it by. In the process, his analysis clearly described the divisions within Black life. "First, there were the traditionally free Negroes versus those who had once been slaves," he wrote, "then there were the former house slaves versus the former field slaves; while among those who had always been free there were the aristocrats versus the common men." Describing the social stratification of Black life in the context of failed rights efforts or, at the very least, an unwillingness to adapt to new methods of advocacy was a rag well worn by Malcolm. Just months after the publication of *The Negro Revolt*, Malcolm spoke at Michigan State

University and gave his famous comparison of house Negroes and field Negroes. "So you have two types of Negro," he said. "The old type and the new type. Most of you know the old type. When you read about him in history during slavery he was called 'Uncle Tom.' He was the house Negro. And during slavery you had two Negroes. You had the house Negro and the field Negro." Malcolm's analysis would go much further than Lomax's. For example, Lomax saw the bureaucracy of the NAACP as a problem but never considered Roy Wilkins to be an Uncle Tom. And Malcolm's focus remained on those who actively benefited from the status quo. But the language of the two friends was still resonant.[44]

While Lomax was the first to use the slave metaphor in the public sphere, that does not mean he was not cribbing ideas from Malcolm. The NOI leader had such a dramatic influence on Lomax's thought, and the book's publication came so soon before Malcolm's speech, that it is entirely possible Lomax was echoing Malcolm, not the other way around. At the same time, the differences in their interpretation led them in divergent argumentative directions. "Whatever hope there was that Negroes would inherit a separate world was destroyed by the reign of terror and injustice visited upon that world by white people," Lomax wrote in *The Negro Revolt*. It was the language of Malcolm, but it brought Lomax to a different conclusion: "The clear determination to make us the white man's servant rather than his brother rendered every Negro father a weakling before his son, a limp reed in the eyesight of his wife. These—more than segregation per se—were the moral flaws that made the Negro world an anathema; and because of these moral flaws we embraced integration, thereby changing the social history of this nation." The notion that integration was built on moral flaws would meet with Malcolm's approval, but Lomax made the case that it changed American social history and was the only option left to a people suffering under a "reign of terror."[45]

The Negro Revolt also criticized school desegregation "as the cornerstone of a civil rights policy," arguing that it presented "a tight little drama carried out by a few Negro actors while a white mob throws bricks and epithets. Yet each of the embattled towns have thousands of Negro citizens who must become involved if total desegregation is to become a reality." Desegregation also took an inordinate amount of time, provided no relief for those who had finished school, and threatened to hurt the careers of Black schoolteachers. Whereas Malcolm's critique of integration ended in renouncing the validity of the concept, Lomax's concluded with a desire for a more holistic approach.[46]

The crux of Lomax's argument was that "instead of token integration making the mass Negro more content with his lot, more willing to suffer for the sake of the future then, it has made him more impatient," more disillusioned. And "with the Negro's deepening disillusionment also came widespread doubts about goals which had hitherto been unquestioned," such as school integration. There were also concerns about the leadership that had established these goals. Civil rights organizations were dominated "by middle-class Negroes and white liberals" and had "lost touch with the mood of the Negro masses," Lomax wrote. "The result was a concentrated attack on segregation that reflected 'class' rather than 'mass' concerns." Therefore "the current Negro revolt is more than a revolt against the white world. It is also a revolt of the Negro masses against their own leadership and goals."[47]

Lomax devoted a chapter of the book to the Black Muslims, who were part of the Negro revolt but aimed in a different direction. They "represent an extreme reaction to the problem of being a Negro in America today," he wrote, "turning their backs" on mainstream society instead of working to improve it. "Their one positive aspect is that they work to make Negroes proud of being Negro." He even worried that the failure of integrationist civil rights groups could turn the Black Muslims into "a potent and dangerous force." This would be a common trope for Lomax, praising and damning the Nation of Islam at the same time. Later, for example, when praising Whitney Young, Lomax argued that "Black Muslim leader Malcolm X is the only Negro I have met in recent years who knows the soul of Negroes as well as Young does." Theirs was disagreement about ends coupled with an agreement about the state of race relations and a genuine admiration.[48]

The book was undoubtedly an early success. Even Wallace Terry, unwitting instigator of the book's quick release, reviewed it positively in the *Washington Post*, arguing that it "should receive wide readership because Lomax is formidable on his subject matter."[49]

In the *New York Herald Tribune*, Ernest Dunbar offered a glowing review, calling *The Negro Revolt* "a hard-hitting, arresting, fact-studded volume which dissects the anatomy of the Negro's present position, laying bare the innermost tissues and exposing quite a few sensitive nerves." He described the book's theme, Lomax's criticism of the NAACP and of King, and his respect for the influence of Malcolm X and the Nation of Islam. The review also highlighted Lomax's description of Harlem as "the New World's Congo" (a place "occupied by black people but run by white people") and of the difficult balancing act maintained by presidents of historically Black colleges and universities, who, although they were in charge of seminal institutions, had to curry favor with white legislatures to maintain funding. (In one story Dunbar related from the book, a Black college president who had just made a fundraising presentation to white patrons was asked by a woman in the audience to sing the Negro spiritual "Swing Low, Sweet Chariot." The president was shocked but sang anyway, and he left the event with fifty thousand dollars.)[50] It was, the reviewer wrote, a "provocative book." This was high praise coming from Dunbar, who was himself a pioneering Black journalist, the first hired by a major magazine when he joined the staff of *Look* in 1954. He would serve as a senior editor at the magazine from the late 1950s until it shuttered in 1971 and would write his own provocative book, *The Black Expatriates*, about African Americans living "in exile" in Africa and Europe.[51]

Poppy Cannon White, the white widow of former NAACP executive secretary Walter White, also reviewed *The Negro Revolt*. Her commentary focused less on the book's critique of the association than on its conception of race. She noted approvingly that while Lomax had mentioned the scandal that resulted "when NAACP leader Walter White married a white woman," he maintained that the African American population had long ago ceased to be purely African and that race itself was a social construction that was largely man-made. His defense of interracial relationships was consistent with his earlier work and would not change.[52]

But not all praise was equally helpful. *Harper's* editor John Fischer published an article in the magazine, "What the Negro Needs Most: A First Class Citizens' Council," that contained suggestions that were just as problematic as the headline indicated. Fischer argued that the next step in the civil rights process "is full-scale participation, on easy and equal terms, in the ordinary operations of American society. It will be won only when the average Negro (not just the brilliant exception) is willingly accepted by the average white (not just the self-conscious 'liberal') as a reliable neighbor, a good colleague to have in the office or plant, a welcome addition to the local political club, bowling league, trade association and PTA," he claimed. "This obviously will mean the erosion of a lot of white prejudices; but it also demands some big changes in the habits, character, and ambitions of a lot of Negroes. The aim of the new Council would be to produce those changes." In service of that goal he called on Lomax and *The Negro Revolt*, citing Black reluctance to register to vote and the prevalence of Black crime. His argument angered columnists such as the

Amsterdam News's Gertrude Wilson, but it may have helped drive book sales among white skeptics.[53]

Lomax helped drive sales by engaging in the normal television and radio promotional routine for his new book.[54] In July, as part of his press junket, he moderated a symposium on "The Negroes in Our Cities" that included the NAACP's Roy Wilkins, the Urban League's Alexander Allen, the SCLC's Wyatt Tee Walker, Malcolm X, and Samuel W. Yorty, the mayor of Los Angeles. Yorty attacked "the Muslim movement" as "a Nazi-type organization preaching hate" and claimed that "inflammatory and ridiculous charges and lies are being fed daily to members of the Negro community by the Negro press." Faced with such statements, and called upon to interact with representatives of the very groups he had strongly criticized in the book, Lomax did what he could to keep the peace.[55]

In August, he appeared on Barry Gray's radio show on New York's WINS. During the interview, Gray lamented the absence of Black television hosts, and Lomax pointed out that his radio station also had no Black hosts. On the spot and on the air, Gray offered Lomax his seat during his September vacation.[56] The possibility of being more than an author and media guest looked more and more like reality.

5 Ambitions

In July, with *The Negro Revolt* selling well, Lomax changed directions again, pitching a book on poverty as told through a study of four families: "a city slum family; a sharecropper family in the deep South (these will probably be Negro); a white-collar family (probably from the lower echelons of the civil service) and a family that is the victim of technological unemployment—perhaps a West Virginia coal miner's family." Each would represent a different kind of poverty with its own expectations and devastation, he explained: "All of them have in some way failed to come to terms with the complexity of modern life; these are the people the Affluent Society has left behind." Genevieve Young was confident about the project, tentatively titled "Profiles in Poverty." "Lomax knows this world well," she told her colleagues. She hoped to offer him a contract with a $3,000 advance: $500 payable upon signature, $1,000 on completing a full treatment of one family, and the other $1,500 on completing a draft of the manuscript. The original plan was to have a 100,000-word manuscript delivered in January 1963 for a fall release date. "I'm *really* steamed up about this project and delighted that you are too," Young told the author. "It's a perfect Lomax subject and we'll sell a million copies!"[1]

Lomax was pleased with the interest and enthusiasm of the press but was adamant that the $3,000 advance be paid up front. He was chronically in need of money and made the case that preparation of the book would be a considerable expense for which the advance was necessary. He claimed that another press had offered a $5,000 advance for a different project if

Harper refused to pay the money up front. Young, ever Lomax's champion inside the press, encouraged the payment, saying that Lomax was "an indefatigable promoter of his own books and is much in demand as a speaker" and that he "accepts engagements only if books will be sold after the lecture." That kind of work ethic, she argued, made the full advance payment a worthy investment.[2] Lomax's aspirational mindset may have driven his ongoing financial needs and certainly spurred his consistent overspending. This particular instance of financial exigency in part reflected the fact that he had just moved into a new house that he clearly could not afford. Ostentatious purchases such as homes were almost always the result of a misalignment between Lomax's self-image and the reality of his financial circumstances, leading him to mismanage his money, a problem that had plagued him since he left Valdosta after high school.

Harper declined the full advance demand but was able to compensate for the impasse by signing a contract with New American Library for a paperback edition of *The Negro Revolt*, which provided Lomax a $2,500 guarantee, $1,500 of it due upon signing. The press could substitute an extra $1,500 of *Negro Revolt* money for an advance on Lomax's poverty book, for which he would have to wait. So in August 1962, Harper got a contract with Lomax for the book on poverty, and Lomax received his money.[3]

At the same time, Lomax was attempting to sell an edited autobiography of jazz composer and performer Charles Mingus, which Mingus had been writing for years and would require standard revision, and he was asking for another $5,000 advance. The press was polite but uninterested. "In view of the other irons you have in the fire, and the exciting television possibilities that seem to be opening up," Young told him, "I feel that you ought to think a long while before you commit yourself to a project as strenuous and time-consuming as this one." She added, "In view of the sales record of books about jazz and musicians—even the best of them—we doubt whether any publisher will be willing to make a $5,000 advance."[4]

But Young was wrong. McGraw-Hill did pay an advance for the manuscript, which Mingus claimed publicly to be $15,000 but was actually $5,500, still a respectable sum. "I think they're nuts," said Young of McGraw-Hill. Whatever that payment was, the bulk of it went to Mingus, and Lomax returned to Harper. "As usual," complained Young, "Louis Lomax is in need of money." The paperback contract would provide some cash, but the $500 advance from the "St. Albans" novel, which had never materialized, still had to be deducted. Still, she believed another $500 advance might be possible. At least, she thought, "this may lessen Louis's need for money."[5]

It did not. Mingus, like Young and so many others, realized that money was often Lomax's principal motivation and thus severed their relationship soon after the McGraw-Hill signing. Mingus was a savant but was also known as the "angry man of jazz," with a notorious and often self-destructive temper. With the advance in hand, he claimed he was retiring. He moved to Majorca to edit his manuscript without Lomax but was not able to finish it in 1962 or the following year. McGraw-Hill finally canceled the contract in 1964. For the next several years, Mingus unsuccessfully looked for a new publisher, claiming that his failure was at least partly because Lomax gave a typescript to people who then released it "on the fucking market." The Mingus autobiography, *Beneath the Underdog: His World as Composed by Mingus*, was edited by Ned King and was eventually published by Knopf in 1971, well after Lomax's death.[6]

Meanwhile, *The Negro Revolt* had sold more than six thousand copies by the end of August 1962. The press clearly attempted to use the events of the civil rights movement to generate sales, and that month Young announced, "We're flinging our advertising budget to the winds, and are taking another ad in next Tuesday's *Times* to hit the Albany issue while it's hot."[7]

Led by SNCC and the NAACP, the Albany Movement—which was making international news in a southwest Georgia town close to Lomax's Valdosta—had the goal of desegregating public facilities and registering Black voters. Though area whites opposed it, they did not turn to overt violence or make loud racist screeds. Police chief Laurie Pritchett had studied the movement and white reactions and developed a strategy to outwit the protesters. He used mass arrests but avoided the kind of dramatic, violent incidents that might backfire by attracting national headlines. Pritchett arranged to disperse the prisoners to county jails all over southwest Georgia to prevent his jail from filling up. What began as a local struggle for rights gained national publicity, but much of it cited Pritchett as a successful leader and Albany as a civil rights failure.[8]

Albany was a demonstration of the "Negro revolt" in practice. A local movement born of specific need and led by young activists willing to challenge the stifling status quo, it was co-opted after receiving national attention by opportunistic members of the old guard such as Martin Luther King Jr. (figure 5.1) and his Southern Christian Leadership Conference.

ready for the hecklers" and "as many who want to come to try to disturb us." On 18 August, with much of the nation's attention focused squarely on Albany, the New Jersey rally took place. The *New York Herald Tribune* estimated that roughly one thousand defiant protesters attended the rally, despite a small but vigorous counterprotest from white Englewood. The *New York Times* had a smaller estimate of five hundred people, of whom roughly one hundred were members of the press and police. The *Amsterdam News* challenged both numbers, arguing in a piece by James L. Hicks titled "White Liars" that the rally attracted roughly two thousand attendees and raised $540 for the cause. Whatever their number, the protesters were zealous. "Either you're going to give us equality or we're going to take it," proclaimed civil rights lawyer Paul Zuber. Lomax repeated that message while also countering criticisms that outsiders like himself had no business interposing themselves into the racial tumult of Englewood. Black equality, Lomax argued, was the business of all in Black America, no matter where the problems arose. He castigated what he called "slowism" in the civil rights fight. "Russians are going to the moon and America is keeping Negroes from going to the public library," he told the crowd, at a time when the country "needs every brain it can borrow, scrape up or steal."[9]

The rally led to a public school boycott to push for integration of the system, and Lomax was an integral part of this action as well. The *Amsterdam News's* Hicks credited Lomax with "sav[ing] the rally in August," describing pushback from some local Black ministers who called for calm rather than agitation. Again, the conclusions of *The Negro Revolt* were borne out. A strain of the Black ministerial community had always shied from activism, representing a stable middle class that had a stake in the racial status quo. One of these Englewood ministers was "a Morehouse man," so Hicks asked Lomax—whom he wrongly believed had also attended Morehouse, but who was certainly a fellow Georgian and a former minister—to talk to him. Lomax held a "closed door discussion" with the minister, "and when they came out, to our delight and surprise, Rev. Taylor announced he would stand with Zuber and support the boycott."[10] It was the Negro revolt in microcosm, Lomax pushing back against the old guard and paving the way for a more confrontational activism.

The summer of *The Negro Revolt's* release in 1962, Lomax took that activism further and moved more directly into local politics as he announced his candidacy for state assembly to represent the Eleventh District in Queens on the Liberal Party ticket.[11] Concern soon arose over

Lomax's campaign, as the Democrats planned on nominating Black assistant district attorney Kenneth Browne as their candidate, which would pit two Black men against the white Republican incumbent Alfred Lerner. As it turned out, however, Browne lost in the September primary, leaving Lomax to run against two white candidates.[12] In the election, Lerner won a narrow victory over Hyman Greenberg, 18,512 to 16,596, while Lomax came in a distant third with 5,501 votes.[13] His brief career as a political candidate was over.

In September, the director of New York's WUHF radio announced that Lomax would host his own program, *Louis Lomax Interviews*, focusing on publishing, theater, and special news items.[14] He also began working with the United States Information Agency, the government's Cold War propaganda arm, to write a film to be titled "Progress of the American Negro" and to be directed by Willard Van Dyke. George Stevens, head of USIA's film division, argued that the subject was one that the world "has been so badly informed about. What strides we have made, for all our failings. We have something to boast about." That was a debatable claim, and Lomax had certainly not been publicly boasting about it. For whatever reason, the film was never made.[15]

At the same time, Lomax served as cochairman, along with Jackie Robinson, of a massive voter registration drive targeting Harlem and sponsored by the New York branch of the NAACP. The effort, which began with a 26 September rally also cochaired by Robinson and Lomax, was another example of Lomax's collaboration with an organization that both his rhetoric and his currently best-selling book criticized for being stodgy and ineffective. Making the project even more unlikely, he had also previously clashed with his cochair over the original article that led to *The Negro Revolt*.[16]

In January 1963, Embassy Pictures president Joseph E. Levine announced that Lomax would write the screenplay for *Burn, Killer, Burn!*, a film to be based on the novel by Paul Crump and coproduced by and starring Lomax's friend Sammy Davis Jr. When a reporter asked why "such an angry young man" as Lomax should write the movie, Davis responded, "Because no white man could know how a Negro feels—only another Negro could do the job needed." Lloyd Richards, who had made his name as the stage director for *A Raisin in the Sun*, was scheduled to direct, with Ivan Dixon and Cicely Tyson to costar. Filming was scheduled to begin in September. The controversial novel—the first issued by Johnson Publishing's books division—was semi-autobiographical, written by a Chicago man on death row about a convicted killer who chooses suicide to the death penalty. After the book's publication resulted in national publicity, Crump was granted a reprieve and had his sentence commuted to life in prison.[17]

Soon after the announcement, Lomax hosted a special episode of the *Today* show on NBC, taking over for Hugh Downs for an examination of Black writers in America that included interviews with James Baldwin, Ossie Davis, Langston Hughes, and others. He also joined John Oliver Killens, Baldwin, Daisy Bates, and William Branch at a fundraiser for the NAACP's New York branch in conjunction with Negro History Week, again demonstrating his willingness to aid the association. On the occasion of Lincoln's birthday, the Lomaxes attended a White House reception followed by an evening of parties hosted by various members of Congress.[18]

Things, it seemed, were going well, as the former convict was becoming a legitimate celebrity. Yet in February 1963, he was again asking Harper for money. "Lomax has over $1,200 coming to him on April 1st," wrote Genevieve Young, "but is, as usual, desperate for money now."[19] The frustrated press took the step of creating a list of debits and credits for Lomax. "I don't think Lomax understands that we are set up to make payments just twice a year," explained one Harper accountant. If an author's account was in the black, which Lomax's was not, "we are willing to advance such monies as a reprint payment, on request. But we aren't allowed to do so if his account shows a debit."[20] Such debits only grew in December, when Lomax withdrew from the "Profiles in Poverty" project. "The contract will be formally cancelled," Young told him, "once that part of the advance paid you has been returned."[21]

There was nothing to do but move forward, continuing the civil rights effort while simultaneously making a name for himself, in the hope that such work would eventually solve his ever-present financial struggles. In March 1963, he gave a speech at Connecticut's Hartford College for Women, where he called New York governor Nelson Rockefeller a "capitalist without a conscience." The politician "preaches liberalism in Detroit, kisses babies in Harlem, and then gets money from gold mines in South Africa where Black men are chained to their beds at night. One day the Black Africans will revolt and cry their hatred at the United States and we will wonder why." Though caustic, it was a nuanced critique from someone whose time in Africa had given him an international perspective on the relationship between capital and race. The speech was also intended to cause controversy. Jackie Robinson was one of the first to take the bait, ending his temporary détente with Lomax by praising Rockefeller's philanthropy and his devotion in particular to Black colleges and churches in the South. Robinson made the absurd claim that "it would be just as unfair to attack Nelson Rockefeller for making money out of gold mines in segregated South Africa as it would be to attack A. G. Gaston, the prominent Negro business tycoon of Birmingham, Alabama, for making money in that hellishly segregated city." Less outlandish was Robinson's critique of Lomax for continually seeking publicity. He was "running true to form": "Mr. Lomax consistently attracts attention to himself by making sensational statements and charges which reflect on other people." Robinson used Lomax's earlier feud with Roy Wilkins as his example. It was the kind of charge that would always attach itself to Lomax, despite the veracity of his message.[22]

After speaking in Connecticut, Lomax traveled to Los Angeles to appear on a televised panel with Malcolm X and Norman Houston (figure 5.2). He and Betty were also the guests of honor at a daylong party at the home of James and Laura Hardon, a prominent family in the city's Black community. Also in attendance was their daughter, Nira Hardon, a law student and public schoolteacher who would become the director of equal opportunity programs for USAID and later chairwoman of the board of trustees for the University of the District of Columbia. The Hardons called it a "Pot Shot" party, where—as reported by the *Los Angeles Sentinel*'s Jessie Mae Brown—guests had a chance to ask Lomax questions about "why his claim to fame has to be built from criticizing leaders, churches, NAACP, etc." Lomax "answered with ease" before leaving the party to make the television appearance. The remaining guests watched the panel discussion on television before Lomax returned with his friend Malcolm to field more questions "into the wee small hours."[23]

The panel, part of *The Ben Hunter Show*, was itself a significant moment. Historian Louis A. DeCaro has argued that it was during the panel that Malcolm first "emphasized the traditional view of the submitted life according to Islam rather than the central tenets of Elijah Muhammad's black religion of separation." He also "equated Allah with the divinity of Christianity and Judaism, claiming that only the names for God are different." Although he was turning toward a more traditional view of Islam, in another segment of the show he parroted Elijah Muhammad's teaching that "the white race is a race of devils and what a white person should do if he is not a devil is prove it." At the end of the night, as Malcolm and Lomax left the studio together, Malcolm was confronted by a group of Arab stu-

FIGURE 5.2 — Lomax giving a speech to a largely white college audience at UCLA. COURTESY SPECIAL COLLECTIONS AND UNIVERSITY ARCHIVES OF THE UNIVERSITY OF NEVADA, RENO. ITEM 82-30-5-10-1.

dents from UCLA who challenged his "white devil" assertions. In Lomax's telling, Malcolm countered by arguing that it was pragmatism that made it necessary to "wake up the deaf, dumb, and blind American Negro." The students were dissatisfied, and Malcolm, frustrated, got into the car with Lomax, never to mention the incident again. The turn away from the NOI would come later, but DeCaro sees *The Ben Hunter Show* and its aftermath as an early indicator of Malcolm's philosophical change.[24]

Lomax's relationship with Malcolm was clearly strengthening. In May 1963, when Alex Haley interviewed Malcolm for *Playboy*, he noted that Lomax had said, "Eighty percent, if not more, of America's 20,000,000 Negroes vibrate sympathetically with the Muslim's indictment of the white power structure. But this does not mean we agree with them in their doctrines of estrangement or with their proposed resolutions of the race problem." Malcolm agreed with the general estimate, placing Black sympathy with the Nation of Islam cause at roughly 90 percent, but disputed that there was a foundational difference between the group's indictments and its proposed resolutions. "A Muslim to us is somebody who is for the black man," he told Haley. "I don't care if he goes to the Baptist Church seven days a week. The Honorable Elijah Muhammad says that a black man is born a Muslim by nature. There are millions of Muslims not aware of it now. All of them will be Muslims when they wake up; that's what's meant by the Resurrection."[25]

In June, Lomax traveled to Chicago to deliver an address to the Cosmopolitan Chamber of Commerce. At a luncheon devoted to "A Positive Approach to Race Relations in Business and Industry," he struck a decidedly Malcolmian chord, telling the audience that "the American Negro is as mad as hell" and that "the only things that will pacify him are freedom, justice and equality." He predicted a "long, hot summer" with "picket lines, demonstrations and noise in the streets." He also repeated his criticisms of "the old type Negro leader" but broadened his message to argue that "the white man should discriminate in our favor to atone for past abuse." He castigated Chicago's white business community as principally to blame for job discrimination and Black unemployment. "Must we have a race riot three times a day to go to the bathroom?" he asked. The speech was a success. "He came! He spoke! He conquered!" wrote A. L. Foster, the chamber's executive director. Lomax "won the approval of the slightly fewer than 350 guests who attended."[26]

Lomax appeared with CORE national director James Farmer that month on New York's WCBS program *Legislative Hearing* to discuss racial discrimination in that city. He made news again by announcing on the show that a deputy city commissioner, Anne Kelly, had told the state labor board that she did not want a Black secretary. "What good is it to have all these laws and hold hearings and deal in all of these platitudes when the city government and the state government itself are involved in this kind of thing?" Lomax asked. While he did not name Kelly specifically, his assertion that the deputy commissioner was a woman forced the city to identify her and admit that she was under investigation. Louis Broido, commissioner of the city's Department of Commerce and Industrial Development, under whom Kelly worked, hedged to the press while admitting that something similar to what Lomax described may have occurred, though not for nefarious reasons. Ultimately Lomax was subpoenaed by the State Commission for Human Rights but angered the panel by commenting on their secret internal investigation, about which the members of the commission were themselves barred by statute from making public statements. Lomax, explained commission chairman George H. Fowler, was "either ignorant of the law or personally and politically motivated."[27]

Meanwhile, the New American Library's paperback edition of *The Negro Revolt* appeared, and over the summer, Éditions du Seuil in Paris published a French edition of the book. But as some fronts opened, others closed. In May, reports emerged that the Sammy Davis contract for *Burn, Killer, Burn!* was never finalized. Literary agent Oscar Collier was instead trying to secure rights to the book to create a film starring Sidney Poitier and Cassius Clay and scripted by Robert P. Davis and James Baldwin. Davis planned instead to star in the Broadway production *Golden Boy* in the fall.[28]

In the summer of 1963 Lomax planned to join Elijah Muhammad, John O. Killens, Evelyn Cunningham, and others in traveling to Cuba to celebrate the tenth anniversary of Fidel Castro's July Revolution and to cover it for *Harper's*. Lomax was among fifteen Americans and a total of two hundred outsiders invited by the Cuban Institute of Friendship with the Peoples for a twenty-day visit to the island nation. The only other Black journalist to make the trip was Charles Howard, former publisher of the *Iowa Observer* newspaper and the National Negro Publishers Association correspondent to the United Nations.[29] In response to concerns that Castro was intentionally trying to curry favor with the Black population, Lomax argued that "some white writers were also invited" and that the vast majority of the delegation was white. Contrary to Lomax's protests, though, Castro was in fact trying to ingratiate himself to the American contingent. The group was feted around Havana, included in lavish parties, and given several opportunities to talk with the leader himself. What they were not granted was the chance to write anything groundbreaking about the state of Cuban life. Instead, the reporting from the trip led to either glowing descriptions of the hospitality the contingent received or mistrustful, though unsurprising, denunciations of those in power. Lomax fell into the former camp, not endorsing Communism in any way but interpreting radicalism toward economic equality as a pleasant, if unrealistic, goal for the Black population of the United States, as he would begin to demonstrate in his public commentary.[30]

The journey was not without drama, beginning even before the planned departure, when the State Department—which had endorsed the trip for most of the group—warned that neither Muhammad nor Lomax had valid passports for travel to Cuba and could be prosecuted upon their return. Eventually Lomax's passport was validated, but that did not mean that the government fully approved of the venture. (Muhammad's passport was not validated, and he did not make the trip.)[31] With no direct travel to the island, Americans first went to Mexico, the only nation in the hemisphere that had regular flights to and from Cuba, and applied for a transit visa. After Lomax arrived in Cuba, the Mexican consul in Havana announced that he was delaying transit visas for American reporters for at least forty days. The United States embassy in Mexico City responded that it had "no authorization to intercede with the Mexican government on behalf of American correspondents seeking Mexican transit visas out of Cuba" and added that the agency had, in fact, been ordered not to intercede. Lomax, stuck in Havana and waiting for his visa, sent a public telegram railing against the decision and "the treatment accorded me by the Mexican government allegedly at your (US) request." It was suggested that the State Department was using the delays targeted at American journalists to discourage such travel and thereby continue to isolate Castro and Cuba.[32]

The government denied the charge, publicly explaining that it had helped in every way it could and blaming problems on officials in Mexico. "Contrary to what Mr. Lomax alleges," said a State Department spokesman in an August press briefing, "the Department of State in no way hampered his return travel. Indeed, the facts demonstrate that the Department assisted Mr. Lomax in every practical way."[33] Whoever was telling the truth, Lomax's charges against the government cut against the traditional norms of Black foreign correspondents and moved him into an argumentative line with Muhammad and Malcolm, portraying the federal government as the activist cause of racial animosity rather than the potential solver of such problems and comparing it unfavorably to a more egalitarian Communist government. Lomax was not yet arguing for armed self-defense, though he would eventually get there, but his affinity for Castro's Cuba was revealing.[34]

More pressing upon his return home, however, was the March on Washington for Jobs and Freedom. Beginning in April 1963, the SCLC launched Project C in Birmingham to take advantage of the violent racism of Eugene "Bull" Connor, an official who the group knew would respond more harshly to its tactics than would Laurie Pritchett. The C stood for confrontation, and the marches and sit-ins in Birmingham that summer were designed to provoke Connor and local law enforcement into making mass arrests and engaging in other barbarous public behavior, which in turn would force the federal government's intervention into southern race relations and thus bring an end to segregation. And it worked. Police unleashed dogs and water hoses on peaceful protestors, many of them children. More than twenty thousand were arrested, and ten were killed. After King was arrested in one of Connor's sweeps and a group of local ministers criticized his presence in the city, King responded with his "Letter from Birmingham Jail." The violence that summer would make international news, and leaders sought to take advantage of the publicity by bringing Birmingham to the nation's capital.[35]

In August 1963, more than a week before the March, Lomax held a press conference in San Francisco and charged the Taconic Foundation with donating $1 million to the march with the goal of "defanging" its "original purpose." He argued that the event's initial plan was to have half a million "rough and tumble Negroes" descend on the Capitol for a sit-in that would "bring the government to a screeching halt," but after the Taconic gift the strategy shifted to a march to the Lincoln Memorial for a simple ceremony. Lomax's criticism seemed misdirected. Founded by financier Stephen Currier, the Taconic Foundation was dedicated to promoting social equality through nonviolent means. It had already given funds that year to CORE and the NAACP's Legal Defense and Education Fund, and in 1961 it had provided grants to SNCC while that group was engaged in the very sit-ins that Lomax claimed Taconic was trying to stop. To be sure, the foundation gave far more money to more conservative groups, such as the Southern Regional Council, which were critical of militant activism. Regardless, Taconic refuted the charge as "completely erroneous." A spokesman for the New York charity claimed that "not one cent of Mr. Currier's personal funds or of foundation money has gone for the march in any way, shape or form"—a statement that did not necessarily refute Lomax's charge.[36]

Lomax was in the San Francisco Bay area to give the John B. Russworm Lecture at the California Negro Leadership Conference at Stanford. "Negro leadership must lead the black masses from the state of Negro euphoria, that seizure of silly happiness and emotional release that comes in the wake of a partial civil rights victory," he told his audience, "and into the real world of hard work and continuing sacrifice that must be conquered before we schedule our victory celebrations." He argued against moderation, compromise, and "black bourgeois sophistication." He warned that Black activists needed to develop "the art of deliberate disunity. Only through diversity of opinion can we establish the basic prerequisite for the democratic process." There were, after all, "enough prejudiced white people around for each of us to have his quota. We don't have to fight each other for the right to fight the enemy." The speech exemplified both

FIGURE 5.1 — Lomax sitting with his boyhood friend and adult ally
Martin Luther King Jr. COURTESY SPECIAL COLLECTIONS AND UNIVERSITY
ARCHIVES OF THE UNIVERSITY OF NEVADA, RENO. ITEM 82-30-8-4-3-6.

They decidedly failed in negotiations with local white leaders, taking
Pritchett and others at their word, and left southwest Georgia after assuming victory, only to find that white leadership had been dishonest.
Meanwhile, the local activists who created the movement were left to continue fighting without the benefit of a national spotlight. Lomax's book
had predicted just this kind of outcome, as younger activists with a greater
stake in the game were only slowed by the imposition of an older generation of Black leadership. While King and his contemporaries would demonstrate that, in fact, the movement had not yet passed them by, Albany
gave credence to the conclusions of *The Negro Revolt*.

Lomax responded by continuing to participate in the revolt himself. In
August, he accepted an invitation, as did Malcolm X, to speak at a rally
in Englewood, New Jersey, designed to fight discrimination in housing,
education, and policing. As the date for the rally neared, Malcolm was
forced to cancel his appearance, and the Englewood police department
trained dogs to patrol the event. Organizers, however, were not dismayed.
"This doesn't bother us," claimed a spokesman, adding that they were "all

the debits and credits of Lomax's philosophy: he defended those at the extremes of the civil rights position with a call for pluralism but did so by denouncing moderation and compromise.[37]

Contradictions were often part of Lomax's rhetoric. His criticism of the March on Washington, for example, put him out front with Malcolm as public Black opponents of the event, though both of them privately saw value in what the SCLC and others were planning. Malcolm saw the march as "history that we should be a part of," though publicly he disparaged the event as an ineffective farce organized predominantly by white people. But Lomax actually attended the march with Malcolm X. Journalist Peter Goldman described being led by Lomax, "all busy mystery," to a hotel room, where Malcolm "was holding court, not trying to convert or to wound anybody but making gentle fun of the whole occasion." Malcolm watched the rally from the National Mall, and Manning Marable has estimated that several hundred Nation of Islam members followed him to the capital despite the group's official stance against the event.[38]

Organized by Bayard Rustin and A. Philip Randolph, who had originally planned a March on Washington for Jobs and Freedom in January 1941, the event brought together an integrated group of more than two hundred thousand people to march down the mall to the Lincoln Memorial, where speakers lamented the violence in Birmingham and championed a federal civil rights effort and passage of the Civil Rights Act, which had been introduced by the Kennedy administration in June. King gave his "I Have a Dream" speech, and after the event, leadership traveled to the White House to press Kennedy for substantive change, an effort that seemed to work, as the president spent his last months stumping for passage of the bill that would ultimately become the Civil Rights Act of 1964.[39]

But Lomax would continue his criticism of the protest. He said he was surprised by the turnout but disappointed in the "festive" atmosphere, which he thought did not demonstrate the righteous anger needed to influence policy. The original plans had called for civil disobedience actions that would continue the Birmingham efforts, but those ideas ultimately gave way to a simple march and rally. Lomax was complimentary of the speeches made by King and John Lewis and claimed to be proud of the effort but saw it as ineffective: "I hope I'm wrong, but I don't think it changed a thing." He believed that another march would be necessary for the certain filibuster of the coming civil rights legislation, and this one needed to be aimed at the Capitol. "Next time," he said, "we will have to go back to the other end of town."[40]

After the September bombing of the Sixteenth Street Baptist Church, that grim exclamation point on the sentence that was Birmingham 1963, the Committee of Artists and Writers for Justice sponsored a memorial service at New York's Town Hall, with proceeds from the collection to be used for gravestones for the newly deceased. Lomax served as a public spokesman for the group and made remarks at the service, along with James Baldwin and John O. Killens. Ruby Dee, Carol Brice, and Odetta performed. Killens argued that the bombing had made him doubt the efficacy of the strategy of nonviolence. Baldwin denounced President John F. Kennedy and American society more broadly as being complicit in the killings. While the service honored the victims, it also produced a radical message. Taken as a whole, the speakers argued that the Kennedy administration was at least partly to blame for the deaths of six Black children in the bombing and the resulting protests. They condemned Kennedy's slow caution and his refusal to get more directly involved in response to the rhetoric of Alabama leaders such as George Wallace and Bull Connor. They also questioned the policy of nonviolence, arguing that equality meant the right to armed self-defense. Lomax explained to the audience that nonviolence was a good tactic for certain protests, but "there is something immoral about the kind of non-violence that says you can get away with anything against me." By whatever method, however, something had to be done. "What difference does it make how high the standard of living is when the murderers of children can go free?" he asked. "Until there is justice all the rest is the tinkling brass of phony liberal lies." Lomax was not necessarily rejecting integration as a goal, but he was clearly questioning the mentality that led ministers—from his grandfather to King—to endorse turning the other cheek. Though his views would not remain entirely consistent, the Sixteenth Street bombing truly rattled Lomax and left him calling, at least subtly, for a position of self-defense rather than nonviolence.[41]

The previous night, Lomax had spoken at a Harlem meeting of James Lawson's United African Nationalists. He joined Adam Clayton Powell, James Farmer, Dick Gregory, Lewis H. Michaux, James Baldwin, Bayard Rustin, and others in addressing a Harlem Square rally sponsored by both the Pan-African National Association in the Americas and the Human Rights Political Association. Flyers for the 28 September event announced, "The United States racial pot is boiling! White America's democracy and Christianity is on trial. Is race hatred, white racism, brutality, murder, lynchings, bombings, rapings, all to go unpunished, forgotten, forgiven, or repaid? Compensated? Justified?" The leaflets reminded Black Manhattan that

"Kennedy said nothing about the six children in Bombingham Alabama, which is an insult to 30 million black people, but we will!" The audience was not predisposed to be receptive to Lomax's message. He did not have a specific constituency per se, but he had never been confused for a separatist, and he was vigorously booed and heckled for arguing for integration and an expanded place for the Black population in American society. "Regardless of how much you want to go back to Africa," he told the crowd, "you're not going." The booing was such that he stopped his speech early.[42] It was a strange display for someone who often argued against integration, who had been closely aligned with Malcolm, and who would make an argument against nonviolence the next night, almost as if he had a greater desire to provoke than to create beneficial alliances.

Regardless, the day after the memorial service, the Committee of Artists and Writers held a press conference at the Astor Hotel and announced a boycott of Christmas shopping to protest the events in Birmingham. Lomax, Baldwin, Killens, and Dee argued that Americans "have no right to celebrate Christmas this year" and said that they had contacted major civil rights organizations asking for their participation. "On Christmas morning," said Dee, "mothers and fathers will say to their children, 'Santa Claus didn't come because bombers came to Birmingham.'" The goal was less to promote self-defense or nonviolence than to keep the focus on the violence in Birmingham and on the Sixteenth Street bombing in particular. The group predicted that a successful boycott could reduce holiday revenues by up to $2 billion. When fifteen thousand protesters marched in Washington to protest the church bombing, Dick Gregory told the assembled crowd that he would participate in the boycott.[43]

Not all saw the benefit of such a move. The *Pittsburgh Courier's* Claude Hall believed the effort was futile, as "Negroes, alone, cannot wage a successful nationwide boycott, due to economic factors apparent, glaringly, to anyone who has taken the time to examine them. Secondly, it is unlikely that any substantial percentage of Negroes would follow such a national plan." Indeed, the Council for United Civil Rights Leadership— representing the SCLC, SNCC, CORE, the NAACP, the Urban League, and the National Council of Negro Women—announced that the country's major civil rights organizations would not participate in the boycott. Roy Wilkins made much the same point as Hall, adding that it would be unfair to Black children and would have no real impact on Birmingham. "That rotund bundle of joy, Santa Claus, just might wriggle down the nation's chimneys after all," reported the *Defender.*[44]

The *Courier*'s Izzy Rowe took particular joy in the rejection of Lomax, arguing that many leaders were applauding Wilkins for rejecting the boycott plan. "Some of them said that the well-known author-newsman had a heck of a nerve asking leaders to join forces with him after giving the back of his 'write' hand in magazine and daily newspaper articles," wrote Rowe. "Any number of the civil rights heroes have been trying to avoid Mr. Lomax."[45]

Such was not the case with Martin Luther King, however, as he broke with the Council for United Civil Rights Leadership and supported the boycott. Then the Chicago chapter of CORE broke ranks and also decided to join the protest. Not only would the effort show solidarity with those in Birmingham, but it also might "cause store owners that practice racial discrimination in their hiring policies to change them and hire Negroes." The group encouraged Black Chicagoans, "Don't spend your money where you can't work and show the power of the Negro dollar." Lomax, meanwhile, was adamant about the statement. "The white power structure is not going to yield until you're ready to move," he said. "What lies ahead of us is going to make Birmingham look like a tea party."[46]

The boycott was unsuccessful, never achieving any broad momentum. Christmas sales were up overall and in major markets across the country. Lomax, however, was clearly moving in a more radical direction, associating the actors in Birmingham not with the excess of Bull Connor or the white culture in the South but instead with the "white power structure" that made the Alabama city representative of the entire country, a microcosm of what Black Americans dealt with everywhere. It was a national indictment, as was the attempted boycott. Manning Marable has described Lomax uncritically as "an integrationist," but that is obviously not an adequate description of his growing ideological awakening, which really began in earnest in response to the ugly events of the summer of 1963. The deaths of children left him questioning nonviolence. His contact with Malcolm and with the Committee of Artists and Writers put him in more radical company and inspired him to rethink the ideological underpinnings of the movement, in much the same way that he had previously questioned an older generation of Black leadership figures and organizations. It was a development that would push Lomax in a new direction, one that would play out publicly in his next book.[47]

6   *When the Word Is Given*

In October 1963, Lomax published *When the Word Is Given: A Report on Elijah Muhammad, Malcolm X, and the Black Muslim World,* a study of the rise of the Nation of Islam that had been brewing since the author's first contact with the group in 1959. Lomax's friendship with Malcolm X and his closeness to many in the organization provided him an unusual degree of access. He also relied heavily on the research notes of his friends Alex Haley and C. Eric Lincoln, both of whom had published respected work on the NOI. More than half the book comprised the words of the Nation's leaders, with speeches by Malcolm and Muhammad printed in full, along with an interview Lomax did with Malcolm (figure 6.1).[1]

Still, Lomax's analysis was substantial. At times in the text he referred to Malcolm as the NOI's Paul of Tarsus, and at others he mused that he could be Muhammad's Charlie McCarthy. Of course, Malcolm himself compared his role to that of Charlie McCarthy. "Charlie is nothing but a dummy—he is a hunk of wood sitting on Edgar Bergen's lap. If Bergen quits talking, McCarthy is struck dumb," explained Malcolm. "This is the way it is with the Messenger and me. It is my mouth working, but the voice is his." Lomax was willing to accept the possibility but reminded his readers that "it was Charlie McCarthy who made Edgar Bergen rich and famous."[2]

Lomax described the organization's influence in northern urban industrial hubs as feeding from the discontent coming from residential segregation and urban poverty. At the same time, he traced the "scheme of

FIGURE 6.1 —
Lomax and
Malcolm X—
influential friends,
each with his own
constituency—carry
on a discussion
while posing for
photographs.
COURTESY SPECIAL
COLLECTIONS
AND UNIVERSITY
ARCHIVES OF THE
UNIVERSITY OF
NEVADA, RENO.

events, both economic and moral, that led to the formation of the Black Muslims" as beginning "on the west coast of Africa some five hundred years ago" with the advent of the slave trade. He provided biographical material on the religion's leaders and painted a picture of a faith whose adherents appeared more moderate in their thinking about race than those at the pulpit. Toward the end of his account, he mused on the future of the Nation, particularly in relation to the imminent death of the elderly Elijah Muhammad. "My prediction is that the Black Muslim hierarchy will gather in conclave and that they will come out with a new leader," Lomax explained. "That leader will not be Malcolm X." It was not a prediction of the eventual schism but instead an assumption that one of Muhammad's children would take over the group, leaving Malcolm in his current position. There were already signs of trouble. Lomax's book appeared as Malcolm was being censured by the faith in response to "intemperate remarks about the assassination of President Kennedy." The length of that silencing was at the time unknown, Lomax wrote, but "it had better not last very long if the movement is to maintain its impact."[3]

His concluded that "the Black Muslims will endure but they will not prevail. Rather, they will linger for years to come and be a constant reminder of what this republic did to thousands who sought its promise."

They would be a scarlet letter on the moral heart of the nation "and make us continually aware of what can happen if white men don't learn to love before black men learn to hate."[4]

The publication resulted in controversy that Lomax surely intended. The FBI in particular was concerned about the book because it noted that John X Ali, formerly John Simmons, had worked with the bureau prior to joining the NOI in 1957 and had a palpable influence on Elijah Muhammad, even maneuvering to gain more power in the organization. The FBI was fearful that one of its plants would be exposed in the book. Though Lomax would not reveal his sources, internal agency memos made it clear that his information came from the bureau. It was nothing new for the FBI to share tips with the Black press in an effort to influence narratives about the NOI and thus exacerbate its more radical elements. Lomax, however, had clearly discovered more than they were willing to give. Along with his bureau sources, Lomax was friends with Balm Leavell, publisher of the *New Crusader* and one of the first journalists to discover that FBI informants occupied high-level positions in the Nation of Islam. Leavell shared the information with Muhammad, who found it disturbing, and with Lomax, who used it in his book. After publication, Ali confronted Lomax and asked why he wrote about his FBI connection. Lomax replied that he had based his reporting on reliable sources.[5]

Manning Marable described Lomax as a journalist who always treated the Nation of Islam and Malcolm fairly. He praised *When the Word Is Given* as "the single best resource about the NOI's inner workings prior to Malcolm's split from the sect," noting that he "tried to present a balanced, objective critique of the NOI's strengths and weaknesses. He correctly identified the malaise among working-class blacks that several years later would feed the anger beneath Black Power."[6]

When the Word Is Given fully demonstrated Lomax's conflicted thinking. On one hand, he seemed to disapprove of the Nation's Black separatism and default to something resembling race supremacy. At the same time, he endorsed the majority of the Black Muslims' premises. "I know white people are frightened by Malcolm X and Elijah Muhammad," wrote Lomax. "Maybe now they will understand how I felt all my life, for there has never been a day when I was unafraid; we Negroes live our lives on the edge of fear, not knowing when or how the serpent of discrimination will strike and deprive us of something dear." Their activism was the result, if not of white devils, then surely of white people doing devilish things. This was the qualified endorsement of the academic, though the book was not a scholarly tome. While *When the Word Is Given* made nods to a socio-logical analysis of the NOI's actions and theory, it predominantly limited itself to surface descriptions that introduced Malcolm, Muhammad, and their contemporaries and worldview to a nation of curious novices, much like *The Hate That Hate Produced* but without the Wallace commentary and salacious title.[7]

"Chilling though it may be," Lomax admitted in the book, "the Black Muslims have erected their teaching on a group experience common to all American Negroes. Few of us concur in their conviction and sentencing of the white race. But none of us can question the accuracy of the indict-ment on which that conviction rests." He made the case that Malcolm and the NOI grew from the same ferment that produced the Birmingham activism in 1963: "They both emerged from a growing Negro consen-sus that old paths have led nowhere." They were both symptoms of his "Negro revolt."[8]

The *Chicago Tribune*'s Herb Nipson was generally appreciative of the text. He found it to be a valuable history of the Nation of Islam and of Black America's relationship with religion in general, fairly critiquing the credits and debits, successes and failures of both Islam and Christianity in attaining betterment for their people. Nipson paid particular atten-tion to the NOI's reception among non-Muslim African Americans, not-ing Lomax's argument that they tended to appreciate the denunciations of white behavior without accepting the broader NOI program. Nipson quoted this passage from the book: "In the end, the Negro masses neither join nor denounce the Black Muslims. They just sit at home in the ghetto amid the heat, the roaches, the rats, the vice, the disgrace, and rue the fact that come daylight they must meet the man—the white man—and work at a job that leads only to a dead end."[9]

The book provided more publicity for the NOI, without the editori-alizing of Mike Wallace, and again demonstrated that Lomax's thinking had progressed since the late 1950s. But historian Peter Goldman has ar-gued that the book's publication further drove the rift between Malcolm and Elijah Muhammad: "Malcolm's picture on the front jacket and Mr. Muhammad's on the back; Chicago was said to have been furious." In ad-dition, the book featured the first public instance of Malcolm breaking with Muhammad. "He was with Allah and was given divine patience with the devil. He is willing to wait for Allah to deal with the devil," Malcolm told Lomax. "Well, sir, the rest of us Black Muslims have not seen God, we don't have this gift of divine patience with the devil. The younger Black

Muslims want to see some action." The statement surprised Lomax and reflected Malcolm's initial pivot away from the Messenger.[10]

In November, just after the book's publication, Edwin C. Berry, representing the Chicago Urban League, criticized Lomax for giving "wide credence" to the notion that "there are no qualified Negroes" for skilled labor and white-collar jobs, which Berry flatly denied. Lomax had, in fact, made such a claim earlier that month, during a speech at Atlanta University. He seemed always to be courting controversy. For example, during a trip overseas, he spent a week in East Berlin with expatriate Paul Robeson. One of the most successful and prolific singers and actors of his day, Robeson had developed Communist sympathies and fallen victim to the McCarthyist paranoia of the postwar period, which ultimately drove him to Europe. Upon Lomax's return to the United States, he announced, "Robeson is coming home soon, and I don't mean just physically." His comment intimated that Robeson was considering abandoning Communism and drew a denial from Eslanda Goode Robeson, the wife and chief spokesperson of the ailing actor, who told the Associated Negro Press that Robeson was neither plotting a return to the United States after his five-year absence nor abandoning his political ideology. (Nevertheless, Robeson did return physically in late 1963, living in semiseclusion in the United States until his death in 1976.)[11]

Meanwhile, Lomax's ideological move toward a new radicalism opened him to new criticism. Early in 1964, James L. Hicks of the *Amsterdam News* questioned the role of Black leadership and the place of media creations such as Lomax in that category. Any Black leader who dared to question white people and not show deference and gratitude was branded "a 'new' kind of Negro," and then everyone labeled a New Negro was labeled a Negro leader, he charged: "Thus James Baldwin and Louis Lomax wrote a couple of books and essays giving white people more Hell than they have ever received before from Negroes and the white press, radio and TV immediately branded them as 'leaders.'" The same, he argued, was true of Malcolm X. "But ask a Negro if Baldwin is his leader, and he will immediately ask you 'leader of what'?"[12]

For his part, Baldwin wrote, "I had known Malcolm, crossed swords with him, worked with him, and held him in that great esteem which is not easily distinguishable, if it is distinguishable at all, from love." Baldwin's life in many ways was a mirror image of Lomax's. He grew up an urban northerner rather than a rural southerner, and instead of being in prison, Baldwin spent years away in France. Lomax was paroled in 1954; Baldwin returned from France in 1957. Whereas Lomax's journalistic career had taken him from rural Georgia to the North, Baldwin's took him, for the first time, to the South, "that Southland which I had never seen," after he left Europe. Baldwin made the same case about school integration that Lomax did in *The Negro Revolt*. "It was rather as though small Jewish boys and girls, in Hitler's Germany, insisted on getting a German education in order to overthrow the Third Reich," Baldwin wrote of the Central High School desegregation in Little Rock. Like Lomax, Baldwin met Malcolm X in the late 1950s, befriended him, debated him on television and radio, and commented on his thinking from afar. After Malcolm's death, Baldwin, like Lomax, was certain that "whatever hand pulled the trigger did not buy the bullet. That bullet was forged in the crucible of the West, that death was dictated by the most successful conspiracy in the history of the world, and its name is white supremacy."[13]

Hicks's critique of Lomax and Baldwin proved timely, as the same month, the Black Standard Publishing Company, a subsidiary of New York's African Jazz-Art Society, published a cartoon book by Cecil Brathwaite titled *Color Us Cullud! The American Negro Leadership Official Coloring Book*. It was a satirical look at many of the Black leaders who so bothered James Hicks. Among those pilloried were Martin Luther King Jr., A. Philip Randolph, Roy Wilkins, Malcolm X, Bayard Rustin, Dick Gregory, Baldwin, and Lomax. Born in 1936 to Caribbean immigrants, Brathwaite was raised in the multicultural Bronx and was a devoted student of the Pan-Africanism of Carlos Cooks. Through his early twenties, he was part of movements to reclaim jazz as a distinctly Black art and to eliminate the use of the word *negro*. A radical thinker, he was a gifted artist who took a job with the ABC television network in 1962, the year before *Color Us Cullud!* appeared. In his preface to the book, Brathwaite, now calling himself Elombe Brath, argued that "integration is a sociological farce, invented by white carpet-baggers and scallawags [*sic*], to use the black masses as a political football." The book was "a sincere critical analysis of twenty of the most publicized individuals or groups, who are often designated to speak for over twenty million black people, who reside in the United States."[14]

Of Martin Luther King, he argued, "We ought to call him King Sadim (that's Midas spelled backwards) because everything this king touches, turns to failure for his followers, but enriches him." His treatment of Lomax was equally harsh: "Lomax came into prominence, by helping a white television reporter spy on the Muslims, and trap a black borough president! How's that for credentials for leadership?... Huh? The white people continue to try to build him up, but he always goofs. . . . With everyone Africa conscious, he writes a book on his reluctance to be African. . . . He goofed again when he came to African Nationalist conscious Harlem, and told the people that they 'weren't going back to Africa.' He barely escaped in one piece! He's supposed to be against nationalism, but his biggest 'idea' to date, was a Xmas boycott, something the African Nationalists have been doing for over twenty years! By the way, didn't that Xmas boycott, turn out to be a goof? . . . Color him goofy!" The corresponding cartoon showed Lomax running away while a copy of *The Negro Revolt* is thrown at him.[15]

A. L. Foster, executive director of Chicago's Cosmopolitan Chamber of Commerce, hated the "puerile attempt to ridicule 20 public figures," but Brathwaite was not alone in his criticism, and similar complaints would dog Lomax throughout the 1960s.[16]

In February 1964, Lomax went to Boston to support the city's second Freedom Stay-Out. Inspired by a similar effort in Williamston, North Carolina, the first Stay-Out had occurred the previous year, when the Reverend James Breeden and Noel Day organized public school students to boycott classes to protest segregation. The event led to a year of organizing by the NAACP and local parents, ultimately coalescing into the Massachusetts Freedom Movement, which organized another Stay-Out for 26 February 1964. It was preceded by a rally on 10 February at which Lomax spoke. "We are very gratified to announce the presence at our second Freedom Rally of a national figure such as Mr. Lomax," Breeden said. "His coming here to address our Freedom Rally is an example of the growing network of communication and support between people in the Freedom Movement all over this country," he noted, adding that Lomax would be "the first of the national figures" traveling to Boston to energize protesters. Lomax told the rally audience of roughly four hundred that the boycott's purpose was to "dramatize our plight in such a way that decent men and women cannot ignore us." He declared, "The time has come for the power structure to stop using threats and scare tactics to stop us from using our freedom." The *Boston Globe* reported with awe that his speech was interrupted fifty-eight times by applause.[17]

Earlier that month, state attorney general Edward Brooke had ruled that the planned boycott was illegal. Statute dictated that only "physical or mental impairment" could justify a school absence, he maintained, which boycotters found particularly galling because Brooke was Black. Rights groups refused comment, but Lomax was defiant: "There is very little they

can do to us now that they haven't done before—we've all been to jail."
Potential fines could be as much as fifty dollars per child for anyone who
induced a student to stay out of school, but the community remained un-
daunted. King, the SCLC, and the NAACP backed the protest. Almost 180
faculty members at Boston University signed a letter of support for the
movement and were followed soon after by their counterparts at Brandeis,
Simmons, and Harvard Divinity School. Lomax returned to Boston for a
Freedom Rally the night before the boycott and to participate in Freedom
Schools scheduled as part of the Stay-Out itself.[18]

From Boston, he traveled to California for a conference on civil equality at Pomona State College, where he spoke alongside CORE's James
Farmer and John Doar of the Justice Department's Civil Rights Division.
"The FBI has been quite adept at catching kidnappers, train robbers, and
bank bandits," Lomax argued, "but why can't it run down church bombers
or other violators in civil rights cases?" Doar did his best to defend the bureau, claiming that failures of apprehension did not reflect a lack of effort,
and Farmer gamely defended nonviolence, but Lomax castigated both.
"Nonviolence is downright un-American," he argued—a radical position
that he did not express when playing the foil for his friend Malcolm. "One
of the reasons you don't respect me and you call me 'boy' is that I don't
defend myself." White violence and inaction by law enforcement would
continue, he said, but sometime soon, "the Negro will hit back when he is
hit."[19] Yet the rights movement as it existed in its current form was built,
at least in part, on "the debatable assumption that you're going to be better than your mothers and your fathers and extricate yourselves from the
bigotry you learned at home," he told his largely white audience. That had
not happened, and the result was a form of stasis. "We're a few hamburg-
ers and bathrooms down the road from where we were a few years ago," he
said. "Maybe we can eat in the hamburger stand now, but we can't work in
the store." More broadly, argued Lomax, the movement had been diffused
into a variety of localized movements, splintering leadership into what he
called an "articulate illiterati" and forfeiting centralized control.[20]

At times, though, Lomax's radicalism seemed negotiable. A week after
the conference at Pomona, he published an article in *Look* magazine praising new president Lyndon Johnson as the embodiment of "this nation
growing up. He is the white Southerner shaking off the shackles of his
beginnings; he is the Negro learning that he who would be loved must
himself not hate; he is the white Northern liberal realizing that prejudice,
whether it be racial or sectional, is wrong." It seemed an odd concession

from someone who had recently and publicly claimed that nonviolence was downright un-American.[21]

In January 1964, Lomax submitted a treatment for an autobiographical book to be titled "Parson Tom." "Louis keeps his agent in such a state of confusion that this was offered to Random House, who have offered $3500 for it," Young explained. "But we can have it if we want it. I don't think we want it." She believed that the outline did not show much promise and that even if it could be developed, there was no guarantee Lomax would actually finish the book. He had now fully abandoned the "Profiles in Poverty" project, and Harper was still attempting to get back its $500 advance. "Louis is so difficult to work with—unreliable, irresponsible, etc.," Young wrote, and the risk seemed far greater than the reward. The "Parson Tom" project would ultimately fall to Random House, which would discover all of the problems that Young predicted.[22]

As of March, Lomax had still not returned the money. "I was thinking about the PROFILES IN POVERTY book with regret last night," wrote Young, "wishing I'd pressed you a little harder on it. Poverty's gotten fashionable these days, and the timing would have been perfect for a book by you on the subject." As she had been doing since January, she encouraged him to sign an agreement allowing the publisher to deduct the advance from his earnings on *The Negro Revolt*.[23] When royalties were paid at the beginning of April, Harper held Lomax's and continued to press the author for a statement on his outstanding debt for failing to complete "Profiles in Poverty." Lomax responded later in the month from Cleveland, claiming, "I am here working on a TV documentary and writing three books—no less." He finally gave his permission for the debt withholding and promised to return soon after his work with Cleveland's KYW-TV was complete.[24]

"Profiles in Poverty," however, was not the only project Lomax had deserted after taking an advance. In July, McGraw-Hill garnished all of his Harper earnings on *The Reluctant African* and *The Negro Revolt*, a total of $3,051.50, after his relationship with Mingus ended and that book deal fell apart.[25]

The following month, the press had to take more from his royalty account after it tried to collect a debt from a Grand Rapids, Michigan, study group that had purchased copies of *The Negro Revolt* following a speech and book signing by the author. Harper discovered that it was Lomax himself, rather than the Michigan book group, who owed the money. "Lomax has been in the habit of taking cash for books sold in connection with his appearances," the press acknowledged, rather than turning the money over to the publisher. It was a small-time scam and could have been viewed as merely an oversight if not for Lomax's history of such behavior.[26]

Despite his financial troubles, Lomax remained committed to activism, and he soon became involved with a controversy involving the 1964 World's Fair, which was to be held in New York and spearheaded by Robert Moses, the city's parks commissioner. Moses was a leading advocate for slum clearance and gentrification; indeed, historian Alexandria Columbina Valera has argued that "it was felt by a number of architecture and development critics that Moses' approach to slum clearance was directly tied to the resulting social unrest felt in New York and beyond." During the summer of 1963, as the fairgrounds were being constructed (using private funding, so that Moses could avoid red tape), protests developed in response to employment practices at Harlem Hospital and housing restrictions at the Lower East Side's Rutgers housing project. Sensitive to those protests and to Moses's gentrification projects, Lomax responded the following year by organizing a "stall-in," an attempt to clog the roadways that led to the fair. "By having drivers run out of gas or stop their cars at key entrances and exits," Valera explains, "Lomax hoped to cause a significant traffic jam, reducing the impact and visitor count for the Fair's opening day." The action was largely ineffective, both because few drivers participated and because members of the highway patrol were on hand to ensure traffic ran smoothly. Yet the police presence demonstrated that Moses took Lomax's effort seriously.[27]

In February 1964, Lomax and Alex Haley were with Malcolm in Chester, Pennsylvania, organizing groups for the Boston public school boycott in response to continued segregation and congressional delay on the Civil Rights Act. Soon after, on 7 March during a lunch meeting to discuss the schism in the Nation of Islam, Malcolm confided to Lomax, "Somebody in the Chicago office is out to get me." He was referring to John X Ali, whom Lomax had warned Malcolm about more than a year earlier. Lomax had come into contact with Ali while researching *When the Word Is Given* and had learned about his history from conducting FBI interviews for the book. He told Malcolm to contact the New York Police Department and the FBI and to keep an official record if anything happened.[28]

Later that month, Lomax and Malcolm met up on Boston's WBZ radio program *Contact!* Malcolm had just left the Nation of Islam and was soon to make the hajj. Lomax told program host Bob Kennedy that he was confident that Malcolm would be successful without the NOI: "Malcolm X articulates for the majority of Negroes. He is much more of a threat to the white power structure now that he has become an activist," adding that he would "be more readily acceptable as a leader in the civil rights movement."[29]

Also that spring, Lomax gave a speech in Louisville, where he claimed that white people assumed that "the antithesis of nonviolence is violence. Not so. The antithesis of nonviolence is self-defense. And the black man is now the only American who does not have the right of self-defense." Nonviolence, in Lomax's new paradigm, described a response to violence, a form of passive defense. Violence, as a fundamentally offensive action, could be neither synonym nor antonym. Self-defense, then, was an active response to violence. It was the opposite of nonviolence but, perhaps more importantly, was categorically different than violence as a form of offense. It was Lomax's version of Malcolm's justification of self-defense as the appropriate response to white supremacy.[30]

On 3 April—less than a month after Malcolm's split with the Nation of Islam and in the middle of the fight for the Civil Rights Act—Lomax made perhaps his best-known appearance of 1964, when he spoke at a symposium sponsored by CORE at Cleveland's Cory Methodist Church. According to historian Manning Marable, Lomax gave "a pro-integrationist civil rights message that won respectful applause from the audience," which the FBI estimated at two thousand. It would, however, be forgotten as the opening act for Malcolm's speech, "The Ballot or the Bullet." Malcolm advocated using the power of the vote but warned that it could not be seen as a cure-all for Black America. He famously challenged President Lyndon Johnson to fight to pass the Civil Rights Act: "If he waits too long, brothers and sisters, he will be responsible for letting a condition develop in this country which will create a climate that will bring seeds up out of the ground with vegetation on the end of them looking like something these people never dreamed of. In 1964, it's the ballot or the bullet." In coming weeks, Lomax would echo Malcolm's sense of urgency and threat of more radical protest. But in that moment, Lomax took a more moderate position. "Nothing could be more fatal," he argued, than for the Negro revolt "to split white versus black." It was an issue that "goes to the moral root of the decay of Western civilization," but Lomax was uncharacteristically optimistic. "This Nation under God will have a new birth of freedom," he told the crowd. "White men and black men will one day settle their differences."[31] Lomax was playing the foil for Malcolm. He had clearly moved away from such a position in the previous two years but understood the inherent juxtaposition that would make the event, and Malcolm's message in particular, more effective.

Lomax was at the symposium because of his relationship with CORE and his history of engaging events with Malcolm. But Cleveland was a hotbed of radical organizing in 1964, and Malcolm, unlike Lomax, had close ties with many of the activists there. Lewis Robinson, for example, planned his announcement of the formation of the Cleveland-based self-defense organization, the Medgar Evers Rifle Club, on the night of the "Ballot or the Bullet" event.[32]

Rioting broke out in Cleveland in the aftermath of the symposium, but not because of anything Lomax or Malcolm said. A new public school was being built in a Black neighborhood with the specific goal of preventing Black students from enrolling in white schools. During a protest at the construction site, a minister was run over by a bulldozer. Although it appeared to be an accident, the climate in Cleveland was extremely tense, and citizens responded by taking to the streets. Malcolm, still in town, went on local radio and urged Black resistance to what had become a typical police response. Crowds finally began to disperse thirteen injuries and twenty arrests later.[33]

Days after the Cleveland event, Lomax was the featured speaker at the annual awards luncheon of the Bronx chapter of the National Association of Negro Business and Professional Women's Clubs, where he also received the organization's Achievement Award. His speech, however, was not a typical women's club address. Lomax rose to the podium and promised to make "the most important statement I will ever make in life," before launching into a fierce political tirade. "Roy Wilkins failed. James Farmer failed. Martin Luther King failed. Whitney Young failed. And Lyndon Baines Johnson failed," said Lomax, although the Civil Rights Act had already passed the House and was making its way through the Senate. "We haven't been able to achieve a thing. Martin Luther King wrapped his dream in love, and while it was ricocheting between Lookout Mountain in Chattanooga, Tenn. and the Gulf of Mexico, it turned into a nightmare." White leaders, he charged, assumed Black passivity as long as key Black figures were kept in check, but Black Americans "will no longer listen to the voices of moderation." He argued that nationally there would be "bloodshed and chaos" as a newer, more radical movement replaced the moderate Black leadership in the face of the white "conservative power structure."[34]

Clearly Lomax took up the radical mantle in Malcolm's absence but reverted to a more traditional counterargument in his presence. On 23 May 1964, for example, the two held a debate moderated by Irving Kupcinet at Chicago's Civic Opera House. Advertisers sold the event like a boxing match, with ads that announced, "DEBATE OF THE YEAR" and "See history made as the Rebel clashes against the Intellectual in the most controversial debate of our time." Backstage, Malcolm told Lomax to expect members of the NOI in the audience, telling him, "They are out to kill me." When Lomax stepped on stage, he saw, among others, John X Ali.[35]

"I propose," Malcolm said during the debate, "we lift the issue of civil rights to the level of human rights by bringing it before the United Nations." He argued that separation and integration, whatever their benefits and drawbacks, were "merely methods toward his real end—respect and recognition as a human being." He described the multiracial awakening that occurred on his hajj: "In the past, I committed myself to the indictment of all whites. But no longer do I subscribe to a sweeping indictment of any race." Malcolm had fundamentally changed his message. "Separation is not the goal of the Afro-American," he said, "nor is integration his goal. They are merely methods toward his real end—respect as a human being." Lomax seemed surprised, telling him, "I hate to admit this, Malcolm, but you've become a moderate."[36]

His views had not changed entirely, however. Historian Peter Goldman writes that Lomax pressed Malcolm on his earlier "white devil" claim. "Are all white men immoral, Minister Malcolm? Is there not one good one?"

"I haven't met all of them," Malcolm responded. "Those whom I have met are the type I would say are insincere. Now if there are some sincere whites somewhere, it's those that I haven't met yet."

"How about the woman," asked Lomax, "who took you in when you were a little boy and put you on the road to learning something," referring to the white foster family who took in Malcolm after the murder of his father. "My presence in that home was like a cat or a parrot or any type of pet that they had," said Malcolm. "You know how you'll be around whites and they'll discuss things just like you're not there. I think Ellison calls it the *Invisible Man* and Baldwin calls it *Nobody Knows My Name*. My presence in that home was not the presence of a human being."

"But she did feed you."

"You feed your cat."

"She clothed you."

"You clothe any kind of pet that you might have."

"And you impute to her no humanitarian motivation?" Lomax asked. "No. Not today."[37]

Along with such writers as Lorraine Hansberry, James Baldwin, John O. Killens, and LeRoi Jones, and actors such as Ossie Davis, Lomax was part of the Association of Artists for Freedom, which was similar to the Committee of Artists and Writers for Justice. "We meet from time to time to talk and argue," said Davis. "It grew out of the Birmingham bombings. We talk of what we as artists can do, how we can express the anguish for the moral situation we find in this country."[38]

In June 1964, members of the association debated a group of white liberals—David Susskind, *Fortune* editor Charles Silberman, and *New York Post* editor James A. Wechsler—at New York's Town Hall. The topic was "The Black Revolution and the White Backlash," and while the opinions of the various artists were by no means uniform, they were united in their assumption that white liberals were part of the problem facing Black America rather than part of the solution. Silberman himself said as much in his book, *Crisis in Black and White*, published that year: "When the struggle for Negro rights moves into the streets, the majority of liberals are reluctant to move along with it." Exasperated, Hansberry responded, "We have to find some way with these dialogues to show and to encourage the white liberal to stop being a liberal and become an American radical." But it was just that kind of frustration that whites feared. Wechsler, for example, claimed at the forum that the group was "ambushing captive white liberals."[39]

White liberal apathy was a common conceit for Baldwin, who did not participate in the Town Hall debate, but the ubiquitous castigation of white liberals by Lomax and his peers demonstrated that as of 1964, Baldwin was not alone in his frustration. The debate was described at length by Harold Cruse in his influential *The Crisis of the Negro Intellectual*. Cruse saw the artists' rejection of white liberalism as a consequence of the bifurcation between theory and praxis. The artists, he argued, failed to recognize that any group determined to do more than talk about racial equality would need to form pragmatic alliances with white groups to succeed. They were, in his mind, providing lip service to Black rights without understanding the work involved to achieve them. Nonetheless, Cruse was sympathetic to such rejection, rehearsing the historical progression of the white Left's often self-serving relationship with Black activists. It created a paradox that was, in fact, the crisis of the Negro intellectual. Much of Lomax's professional life, particularly through the rest of the 1960s, would occupy that liminal space between theory and praxis, between ideological purity and the pragmatic compromise of action. He would become, in his own way, the embodiment of the Black intellectual in crisis.[40]

Meanwhile, in the same month, June 1964, Malcolm announced the formation of the Organization of Afro-American Unity. Lomax was never part of the organization, though he had long supported Malcolm's split from Elijah Muhammad. He had a strong relationship with Peter Bailey, who edited the group's newsletter and would go on to edit *Ebony* magazine in 1968. He was also close with John Henrik Clarke and fellow author John Oliver Killens and would participate in a variety of author panels and events with each of them, even after the OAAU's dissolution.[41]

There were also personal crises afoot. During Lomax's busy summer of 1964, he and his wife applied to send his eleven-year-old son, Hugh, to Eastern Military Academy in Huntington, New York, which rejected the application. Hugh had been attending sixth grade at the Academy of St. Peter Claver in Jamaica, Queens, but wanted to go to a military school. The boy rated well on his entrance exams, but the superintendent, Carleton Witham, explained that he "wouldn't be comfortable" boarding at the school because of his race. Witham "thought Hugh was short on the worldly sophistication he would need," Hugh's stepmother told *Jet* magazine, "but said that could be easily overcome by turning him loose in Times Square with a shoeshine box." The charge of racism in a national publication seemed like fitting retribution. Even in family matters, Lomax understood that access to the press could be a source of retaliation for racist assaults and personal slights. Still, it was an ironic twist for someone who had previously told a Boston radio audience that he was not interested in sending his son to school with white children. Witham, for his part, tried to stanch the bleeding by claiming that the school had no policy against accepting Negroes and that in fact two had attended the previous decade. He explained that because of bullying, "it wasn't a happy experience for us or them," adding, "I don't think anybody ought to subject an 11-year-old to fighting grownups' battles." The Lomaxes asked the US attorney's office and the NAACP Legal Defense Fund for advice but seemed to have no legal recourse. "We want these people to suffer the same kind of hurt and personal humiliation that our son is suffering," said Betty Lomax.[42]

Meanwhile, much of the nation's attention was turned toward Mississippi and the Freedom Summer voting rights drive. Although passage of the Civil Rights Act of 1964 had been an unqualified victory for the movement, the legislation was not a cure-all, and it did not include voting rights provisions, for which workers had advocated. Significant voting registration drives had occurred in Louisiana and Florida, but outside activists had largely shied away from Mississippi, which was probably the most repressive of the Deep South states. Its racial intransigence, combined with its lack of major media markets, made segregationists in the state more violent and the consequences for rights workers more severe. In June 1963, for example, Medgar Evers, executive secretary of the Mississippi NAACP, was shot in the back in his driveway by a white supremacist. But the Civil Rights Act gave the movement the momentum it was looking for, and leaders decided to capitalize on it by moving into Mississippi. Known as Freedom Summer, the 1964 Mississippi voting rights campaign was supported by all of the major rights groups, who also invited the help of white college students under the assumption that racists would be more reluctant to harm them.[43]

It was not so. In Philadelphia, Mississippi, three rights workers—Michael Schwerner and Andrew Goodman, who were white, and James Chaney, who was Black—were arrested while driving to canvass the area and register voters. The Neshoba County sheriff, Cecil Price, then handed them over to members of the Ku Klux Klan, who shot and killed the whites and beat Chaney before shooting him as well. The murders garnered national and international headlines, but they largely served as symbols of a broader span of incredible violence. More than sixty bombings, more than one thousand arrests, six murders, and an untold number of beatings were part of a brutal response by white Mississippi.[44] Freedom Summer would dramatically affect Lomax. He and Dick Gregory addressed the closing session of CORE's annual convention in Kansas City on 5 July, a solemn event held even while the organization's workers Goodman, Schwerner, and Chaney were missing in Mississippi. Their bodies would not be discovered until August.[45]

Still, Lomax came in for more criticism from Jackie Robinson. "While hundreds of state and federal personnel were dredging waters and beating bushes in Mississippi to try to find the remains of two white youths and a Negro, evidently murdered by segregationists, Lomax was writing articles telling the Negro people to 'go slow' in the integration fight," Robinson charged. Lomax, like many others, had worried that Mississippi activism so soon after the passage of the Civil Rights Act would lead to violence and erode the will of legislators to act further on behalf of the dispossessed. For Robinson, conditioned by years of debate with Lomax, this was heresy. "From Lomax's point of view, Negroes should be so grateful for the new civil rights bill that he should not crowd the Southern white man," Robinson wrote. "Too often, it appears that Mr. Lomax is telling the white man what the white man wants to hear rather than what he ought to know." Robinson was clear about what he believed to be Lomax's motivation, noting that the author had "every right to advance his own career and to earn comfortable checks for his writing." This was unfamiliar territory for Lomax. He was no stranger to criticism and charges of opportunism. But being accused of accommodationism for personal gain was new and problematic to the author of *The Negro Revolt*.[46]

As if in response to Robinson's criticism, Lomax traveled to Berkeley for a summit of more than 350 Black leaders to form the Negro Political Association of California (NPAC), whose goal was to fight the state's Proposition 14, an initiative sponsored by the California Real Estate Association and designed to repeal the Rumford Fair Housing Act. Authored by Black state legislator William Byron Rumford, the act made it illegal for landlords to deny housing based on race, religion, disability, or gender, and Proposition 14 was a white effort to defend the right of landlords to discriminate. The new group also constituted an effort to unite rival factions of activists who had been split by a bitter Senate campaign between Pierre Salinger and Alan Cranston. Some pro-Salinger forces from Los Angeles boycotted the meeting. Lomax, however, urged California leaders to "unite for broader objectives." The group elected officers and produced a declaration of principles that called for a free housing market, fair employment, job training, integrated schools, antipoverty measures, and aid to small businesses.[47]

Lomax would ultimately join the staff of Californians against Proposition 14. In his new role as special community coordinator, he told the media that Prop 14 was "backed by extremists and racists who would be only too happy to see members of minority groups remain permanent second-class citizens."[48] In a speech, he called for unity in the face of such bigoted measures. Many "old line Californians," he argued, were "showing the same type of thinking as bigoted whites. Those of us living on the top of the hills, who cannot communicate with our people down on Central, Normandie and Manchester, will someday find themselves trampled, along with their neighbors, by their own people."[49]

He also led a meeting of more than fifty Black leaders called by Governor Edmund "Pat" Brown to generate a "unified and planned effort" to fight Prop 14. In his address to the group, he assailed Black leaders in Philadelphia for inaction in the face of recent rioting. "Where were the Negro leaders—who appear daily on television as the spokesmen of their people—when the riots started?" he asked. "Many of you got on the freedom train just in time to get on TV." He rallied his audience to action on Prop 14, charging that real estate agents from out of state were funding much of the campaign for passage. They were "peddlers of hate and bigotry" who would "unleash an ungodly campaign against Negroes the last two weeks of October," requiring the group to be vigilant. The last Sunday in October would be deemed Civil Rights Sunday. The Urban League would devote resources and manpower, and national leaders such as King, Wilkins, and Farmer would come to California to campaign.[50]

Lomax's interest in Prop 14 was inspired, at least in part, by his recent move to Laurel Canyon in southern California. He had been offered a television show contract after appearing on the Joe Pyne program on KTTV in Los Angeles to discuss an article he had published in *Ramparts* magazine. Pyne was one of the original confrontational media personalities, pioneering the strategy that would later be successful for hosts such as Rush Limbaugh and Bill O'Reilly. As a guest on the show, Lomax so dissected the right-wing hate-monger that KTTV offered him his own program at a salary of twenty-five thousand dollars per year. He took the deal and moved to Los Angeles—without Betty. It was another media opportunity and another marriage lost, and the move gave him more than a simply theoretical interest in Prop 14.[51]

In early October, he planned an event at his new house as part of the campaign against the proposition. The *Los Angeles Sentinel*'s Bill Lane reported that he had purchased the home "on one of the highest hills in Hollywood" in an effort to "get away from the smog" and mused that he "might find it easier gathering celestial thoughts to put into his widely read stories and books." He also "had in tow a beauteous California lassie named Wanda Baker, who he vowed will be his bride come Spring." The academy fight over Hugh's candidacy had happened only recently, but now that his son was settled at a boarding school, Lomax had quickly moved on.[52]

Late in September he was the guest of honor at a Prop 14 fundraiser at the home of Xenaphone Lang, a prominent Los Angeles attorney, where hundreds heard him speak. He helped the Delta Sigma Theta sorority canvass neighborhoods against the measure and later addressed a meeting of the group's Los Angeles alumnae chapter. In speeches around the city he urged "the leaders of the Negro community and others who are opposed to Proposition 14" to "get with the masses of Negroes to inform them and urge them to vote NO on 14."[53]

One such event charged seven dollars per person to raise money for the Prop 14 fight and was attended by hundreds, including actors and musicians. Lomax joked that the Alabama governor was trying to convince Saint Peter that Lomax deserved to go to heaven. He even claimed that he had been baptized by Martin Luther King in the Mississippi River: "He put me under the first time in the name of the Father, and the second time in the name of the Son—and, doggone, you know, that's the last thing I remember!"[54]

Despite the best efforts of Lomax and others, Proposition 14 passed overwhelmingly, and the NAACP responded by filing a petition for a writ to bar certification of the vote, citing the equal protection clause of the Fourteenth Amendment. Lomax joined CORE's Arthur Silvers and H. H. Brookins, chairman of the United Civil Rights Council, at a postelection flashlight procession that ended at Los Angeles City Hall, where they gave speeches denouncing the proposition. But the measure passed by almost two million votes, and stopping its implementation seemed like a lost cause.[55]

His one trip away from California during the Prop 14 fight was to Mississippi to report on the Freedom Summer murders. In October, as the Proposition 14 campaign was coming to a close, Lomax's account of the killings of Goodman, Chaney, and Schwerner appeared in *Ramparts* magazine in a special issue titled *Mississippi Eyewitness* that also included articles by Dick Gregory, John Howard Griffin, civil rights lawyer William Kunstler, and pathologist David Spain. The magazine's publisher and editor, Edward M. Keating, originally intended to turn over evidence that Lomax gathered from interviewed eyewitnesses to the Justice Department, but he refused when Judge Harold Cox of the Mississippi Federal District began seeking indictments against government witnesses in civil rights cases. In particular, Cox pursued indictments against two Black witnesses in a voting rights case that the Justice Department was prosecuting at the time. In response, Keating publicly announced that since witnesses to the murders would risk being killed if they were identified, the magazine would require guarantees of anonymity for them before turning over information from its investigative reports.

Lomax's article was a full history of the lives and deaths of Goodman, Chaney, and Schwerner, including background information on each of the workers and an hour-by-hour account of the attack that cost them their lives. Lomax described the aftermath, the anger, and the national and international scrutiny that descended on the state in the wake of the violence that permeated Freedom Summer. The special issue also included an interview with Dick Gregory and a series of photos of Freedom Summer. It was as comprehensive as contemporary magazine coverage could be.[56]

Los Angeles Times book editor Robert Kirsch was effusive about the *Ramparts* issue. "Lomax's careful, modulated prose is a classic of reporting and all the more impressive for its understated eloquence," he wrote. With Kunstler's and Spain's firsthand accounts, Jim Marshall's photos, and the contributions of *Black Like Me* author John Howard Griffin and *Mississippi: The Closed Society* author James Silver, the edition was vital to understanding the crisis in the South. "Considering some of the pressures which have been exerted to keep Ramparts off the newsstands," Kirsch noted, "it takes no little courage and concern to read it here in Southern California."[57]

"Sixty-nine bombings, twenty-three of them churches, have occurred against my people in the South in the past four years," Lomax said in a speech after the *Ramparts* publication. "J. Edgar Hoover hasn't found a cotton-pickin' one of them, yet he's found the Communists in the Civil Rights Movement. Bully for him!" After political failure in California and murder in Mississippi, Lomax was becoming more frustrated and more radical: "If the Negro gets his freedom through non-violence, it will be the first time in history it has happened. Everything you have gotten in America has been in blood."[58] This new language understandably led to criticism. The Reverend John Porter, leader of Chicago's newly organized Englewood chapter of the SCLC, took issue with Lomax and Malcolm X, who had made similar speeches earlier in the summer. "They're fooling the white folks," he argued. "Malcolm is fine in New York, but let him go to Mississippi," seemingly unaware that Lomax himself had recently been to that state.[59]

In December 1964, Lomax interviewed Elijah Muhammad as part of a National Educational Television documentary, *The Messenger from Violet Drive*. It was a far more complimentary view of the NOI than was *The Hate That Hate Produced* and portrayed Muhammad as a viable national civil rights leader—one who was not from the mainstream but who was culturally and nationally relevant nonetheless. Lomax was a critical voice in that narrative. "Dissension took place within the Muslim movement, and I think Malcolm was being forced out," he said in the documentary. "Malcolm had become the most articulate spokesman. After all, the

Muslims had been around since 1930; nobody heard about them until, of course, Malcolm X got out of jail."[60]

"It is my own prediction," Lomax continued, "that now that Malcolm is out of the movement, that they will return soon to the oblivion from which they came." He told a story of attending a rally at New York's Audubon Ballroom where Elijah Muhammad was to speak, along with his son, then a student in Cairo. The son appeared in a white robe, with a white formal turban. "And an old Negro from Mississippi sitting behind me said, 'My God, he looks just like the Ku Klux Klan to me,'" Lomax recalled. "The point is, no white man, or black man for that matter, draped in a white sheet, will ever sell the American Negro anything."[61]

Despite his friendship with Malcolm, Lomax remained close to Muhammad as well. "We, the American Negro, are the residual effect of five hundred years of slavery and segregation. It was inevitable, I suppose, or I know, that one day the Negro would produce a man who would come along and say, 'My god is bigger than your god, and he can slay your god. Even if he can't slay your god, he will not bow down and serve your god,'" Lomax said in the film. "You have to kind of be buggy to be black and to be sane in America. And the great thing about Elijah, about eating at Elijah's table, is that this sort of bugginess, this is what America has done to us, this is what America has made us. . . . Elijah is what America made him."[62]

Lomax was clearly what America had made him, as well. As 1964 became 1965, he continued to attack his favorite targets. In one speech, he explained that the "white, Western Christian who has not suffered, has not bled—cannot understand the problems of Africa, Asia, Latin America, or Cuba. He really believes the Communists took it. He can't understand that we let them," he said. "The white Western Christian was in Asia 100 years before Karl Marx was born. So who goofed?"[63]

Then there was also his principal punching bag from *The Negro Revolt*. In Chicago at a seminar on "Power and the American Negro," he warned the students about making the mistake of becoming wedded to one civil rights strategy, clearly referring to the NAACP. It was "like the story that's told about Roy Wilkins, who ran down the street up to a policeman and asked, 'Where's the parade? I'm leading it.'"[64]

7 *The Louis Lomax Show*

On 21 February 1965, Lomax's weekly television discussion program, *The Louis Lomax Show*, debuted in Los Angeles. It was the first hour-long syndicated talk show hosted by a Black man, another in a long line of firsts from a precedent-setting journalist, but its debut was overshadowed by the assassination, that same day, of Malcolm X while giving a speech to his Organization of Afro-American Unity in Manhattan's Audubon Ballroom. After a commotion in the crowd caused a distraction, a man rushed the stage with a sawed-off shotgun and shot Malcolm in the chest, before two men followed with pistols and shot him twenty more times. All three were members of the Nation of Islam, and all three were convicted of the crime.[1]

The assassination came as a shock but not a surprise. The last time Lomax and Malcolm had been together was at their Chicago Civic Opera House debate in May 1964, but they remained in relatively close contact through the remaining months of Malcolm's life. The rift that Lomax observed between Malcolm and the NOI had only grown in the time since his departure from the group. "Harlem was on the brink of a major crisis," Lomax observed, "for every evidence indicated the imminent outbreak of gang warfare between the Black Muslims and the followers of Malcolm X." The two groups "had been on the verge of open clashes" for months, he said. At one point, an actual confrontation occurred in front of the NOI restaurant on Lenox Avenue, the police breaking up the melee before any real violence occurred. It was a fraught period that culminated in the early morning hours of Valentine's Day, when someone firebombed Malcolm's home. His family escaped without physical harm, but the psychological toll was real. "I have reached the end of my rope!" he exclaimed in a speech at Harlem's Audubon Ballroom the following day. "My home was bombed by the Muslims!" He claimed that he knew those who had been assigned to kill him and applied to the police department for a permit to carry a gun. The following week, the assassins finally won.[2]

After word of the killing reached his adopted city, Lomax began a desperate attempt to reach Betty Shabazz, Malcolm's widow. After all attempts to revive the leader had been exhausted, Betty returned to the home of Tom Wallace, Ruby Dee's brother, a member of the Organization of Afro-American Unity, and a close friend of the family, where she was staying. When Lomax eventually got through after a series of failed calls, Betty was understandably distraught. "The niggers *did it*, Lomax," she told him. "The niggers *did it*! I didn't believe they would; but the niggers *did it*."[3]

"We'd like to see the white American public show some of the compassion for Mrs. Shabazz that they showed in donating sixty thousand dollars to Lee Harvey Oswald's widow," declared Betty Lomax. "I personally don't consider Malcolm guilty of anything wrong. But nobody, even his detractors, can equate him with Oswald. Yet Marina Oswald is cared for." She and Louis remained separated, she was no longer a part of her former husband's orbit, and her commentary carried its own weight. But the two still talked, and their theoretical positions were closely aligned. The Lomax and Shabazz families had grown close over the years. After Malcolm's death, a new group, the Committee of Concerned Mothers, chaired by Sidney Poitier's wife and aided in its organization by Betty Lomax, dedicated itself to raising money for the family of Malcolm X, even as Betty Shabazz waited for her fifth child, due in November.[4]

"Man, I'm looking for real trouble now," Lomax said in response to Malcolm's death. According to one former NOI official, Lomax "probably had closer contact with the movement than any other Negro writer," and he was well suited to evaluate the consequences of the assassination. "There will be fear and panic within the Muslim movement, I believe," said Lomax. He claimed that during Malcolm's final trip to Los Angeles, he and a friend were followed at high speeds by a black limousine and that Malcolm carried a "zip-gun ball point pen" so as to "take one with him when he went." At the Statler Hilton where he stayed on the trip, he received threatening calls. "There were mysterious men standing on the street outside the hotel, too," claimed Lomax, describing a real fear that Malcolm felt in response to a genuine threat by the NOI. At the same time, the statement provides an early indication of Lomax's bent for conspiracy thinking that would dominate much of his later life.[5]

The death of his friend on the same day as his show's debut provided an ominous start to Lomax's television career, but its precedent was inauspicious enough. The first television program hosted by an African American had debuted in July 1950, while both Lomax and Malcolm were still in prison. The host of the *Hazel Scott Show* was a singer and pianist who had performed on Broadway and in several movies. Her fifteen-minute show ran through the summer of 1950 on the DuMont Network and featured her musical performances. Despite its popularity, the show was canceled in December after Scott's testimony before the House Un-American Activities Committee. She denied charges that she was a Communist sympathizer, but the stain of the charges themselves led sponsors to abandon the show and DuMont to ultimately cancel it.[6]

More prominent was the *Nat King Cole Show*, premiering in November 1956 on NBC as a fifteen-minute, weekly musical variety show. Cole was an international jazz sensation with a multiracial following, and the television networks believed that a show he hosted could be profitable. He originally signed with CBS, but when the deal failed, he reached a new agreement with NBC. Sponsorship, however, would prove problematic. Fearful that white southern audiences would boycott their products, national sponsors were reluctant to be linked with the show, so while some corporations participated occasionally, it usually aired without sponsorship. The next year, in 1957, NBC expanded the show to thirty minutes, and Cole brought in friends from the music industry in an effort to keep it alive. Still, sponsors failed to materialize.[7]

In the inevitable postmortem for the program, Cole praised NBC for its efforts. "The network supported this show from the beginning," he told *Ebony* magazine. But advertisers simply would not get on board. "Madison Avenue is afraid of the dark," he said. "For 13 months I was the Jackie Robinson of television. I did everything I could to make the show a success. And what happened? After a trailblazing year that shattered all the old bugaboos about Negroes on TV, I found myself standing there with the bat on my shoulder. The men who dictate what Americans see and hear didn't want to play ball."[8]

This legacy did not bode well for a full-length television talk show hosted by a Black man, but Lomax was not one to be bound by history. *The Louis Lomax Show* aired at ten thirty on Sunday evenings on Channel

11, KTTV, in Los Angeles. It lasted an hour and a half and was "a kind of Johnny Carson, Les Crane–type show," the *Amsterdam News* explained to its readers. It began the same way each time with Lomax announcing, "Well, the fat's in the fire—let's stir it up!" During the second episode, on 28 February, Lomax spoke to Martin Luther King, who was in Los Angeles for Western Christian Leadership Conference business. In late March, CORE's James Farmer came to Los Angeles for a three-day speaking tour and appeared on Lomax's show. At the same time, the program included conspiracy theorists and UFO hunters as guests. Race was only one of the issues that Lomax sought to stir up.[9]

Only a few episodes of *The Louis Lomax Show* exist in archival form, but its host kept notes on all of its episodes. He devoted several programs to abortion, even more to Communism, conservatism, and the scourge of drugs. He interviewed journalists from David Frost to Hunter S. Thompson and entertainers from Artie Shaw to Elia Kazan. One episode even featured Dr. Sam Sheppard after his infamous conviction for the murder of his wife had been overturned. While much of the show was devoted to exploring race from a variety of angles, there were also bits featuring Alex the counting dog and Pepe the talking dog, just as one might expect from "a kind of Johnny Carson, Les Crane–type show" (figure 7.1).[10]

Jesse Walker of the *Amsterdam News* called it "the most talked about show in Los Angeles." It was so successful, in fact, that in April KTTV signed Lomax to a new, five-year contract at roughly twenty-five thousand dollars per year. The show would also be lengthened to two hours. Lomax was, according to the *Pittsburgh Courier*, "the first Negro in the country to be signed to an 'across-the-board' television show."[11] The show was most commonly compared to that of right-wing hate-monger Joe Pyne, not only because it was Lomax's appearance with Pyne that had first brought him to the attention of television executives, but because the two were on the same station and both discussed controversial topics. Pyne was building on the legacy of polemicists such as Father Charles Coughlin, who created the model on radio in the 1920s and 1930s. Pyne added to his screeds combative arguments with guests and then brought the model to television, creating the precedent for right-wing media of the twenty-first century. Lomax, however, was neither polemicist nor ideologue, and while the show formats may have been similar, the hosts were clearly different.[12]

Lomax saw the difference too, and in 1967 he called on the FCC to investigate television and radio talk shows. "The racial invective and misinformation going out on the airwaves from this type of show gets more

FIGURE 7.1 —
Lomax on the set
of his television
program at KTTV
in Los Angeles.
COURTESY SPECIAL
COLLECTIONS
AND UNIVERSITY
ARCHIVES OF THE
UNIVERSITY OF
NEVADA, RENO.
ITEM 82-30-6-10-3.

outrageous every day," he complained. Talk shows had "an opportunity to become an important part of community life, but we are blowing it." Lomax saw his own show as using that opportunity, but the extremists were taking over, searching for controversy to drive ratings: "It's all right to discuss issues, but the name-calling must stop and the so-called facts should be checked." Lomax, of course, also looked for controversy in pursuit of ratings, but he did attempt to check the facts. In his tirade, he referred to one talk show caller who asked a former undercover FBI agent if she had ever seen Lomax at Communist meetings. When the agent said no, the caller professed amazement. "Now there's an example of slander," said Lomax.[13]

"I spent the first month [of the program] finding myself," Lomax told the *Los Angeles Times* in April 1965. "The station wants controversy. My purpose is to try and make the most controversial issues of today informative—and at the same time entertaining." In its first six months, along with his more traditional guests, Lomax's show had featured a séance, a divining rod demonstration, and a discussion with the leader of the Eugenics Party. Lomax credited Bill Walker, the show's director, for its success. "Thanks to him we can do more interesting things and get the audience involved." Lomax also told the *Times* that he had nearly turned down the invitation to appear on Pyne's show when he heard its host agree with J. Edgar Hoover's characterization of Martin Luther King as "the most notorious liar in the country." Pyne's statement provided all the motivation he needed: "I was on the show and ready for a fight." That appearance had already led to his own show and might open future opportunities to make documentaries for the network.[14]

Lomax's rhetoric was controversial, especially to those accustomed to Pyne's views, but its power was undeniable. When "Lomax points out in parish halls that brothels were desegregated long before houses of God were opened to all," reported the *New York Times*, "his audiences have no choice but to admit the truth of the blistering charge."[15]

In April, less than two months after the show's debut, Lomax married Wanda Baker, a public schoolteacher and University of Southern California graduate student working on her doctorate in educational psychology. Less than a week before the wedding, he went to Juarez, Mexico to get an official divorce from Betty, who signed a waiver of appearance and stayed in New York.[16] Betty, meanwhile, was running the Sunday discotheque sessions at a St. Albans club known as Fuzzie's that was, according to the *Pittsburgh Courier*'s Major Robinson, "the talk of Long Island." As part of the Concerned Mothers Committee, she helped sponsor a jazz benefit concert in Westchester County to raise money for Malcolm X's family. In the absence of her former husband, she was thriving.[17]

After the wedding, Lomax was off to Boston for a speech to the local chapter of the Urban League, where he addressed an audience of more than a thousand. "The white people who serve on your Board must be prepared to make a total commitment to the cause of civil rights," he said, echoing the language of his fallen friend Malcolm. "The principal villains in the North have been the white persons who sit in executive authority on civil rights organizations and who in actual practice do little to further the cause of the colored people. The banker, businessman and community leader who is not going to practice equal opportunity and civil rights—get him off your Board." Lomax predicted, correctly, "more deaths and more bloodshed" in the civil rights movement and said that "when the demonstrations move North—and they will—we shall find out which side our liberal white friends are really on."[18]

Back in Los Angeles, Lomax was slated to be a guest speaker on 28 April at a CORE-sponsored benefit performance of two LeRoi Jones one-act plays. *The Toilet* and the Obie Award–winning *Dutchman* were directed by Burgess Meredith and performed at the Warner Playhouse on La

Cienega Boulevard. The city's major newspapers had declined to accept advertising for the productions, which led members of the cast and crew and others from local rights groups to picket the notoriously conservative *Los Angeles Times*. Lomax participated in the protest, and along with Paul Winfield and Sheree North, the male and female leads of *Dutchman*, formally requested the newspaper to run the advertisements. Their letter was also signed by a number of Hollywood luminaries, including Burt Lancaster, Bill Cosby, Sam Jaffee, and Meredith. *Times* publisher Otis Chandler released a statement claiming that his paper "refuses paid advertising for products or services which in the opinion of the newspaper are not in the public interest. The *Times* has refused and will continue to refuse paid advertising for these plays." Still, the paper reported in detail on the controversy, and its editorial section published a series of letters both praising and condemning the *Times* decision. In short, the publicity was far greater than paid print advertising could have accomplished.[19]

That month, April 1965, Lomax's "A Georgia Boy Goes Home" appeared in *Harper's*, painting a portrait of his hometown that was decidedly different from his adopted city, Los Angeles. The white population of Valdosta was still exceedingly racist, he wrote, but it was grudgingly going along with the mandates of the Civil Rights Act to avoid the kind of trouble it saw nightly on television. Valdosta was thus "an open town." Lomax could eat and talk anywhere he pleased, in stark contrast to his childhood. There had been racial tension in the first days of integrated lunch counters, he wrote, "but a well-disciplined law force invoked the law of the land. While police chiefs in other Southern towns were rousing the white rabble, the Valdosta police chief was traveling through the swamp farmlands on the town's outskirts telling white men who were most likely to get likkered up and come to town to keep calm." Meanwhile, "the Negroes were told to eat, not just demonstrate, and the whites were warned to keep the peace. They both did just that."[20]

The city had a Black middle class in virtual stasis. It was not, Lomax said, "that they don't care about the black masses. They do care; they care, at times, almost to the point of nervous breakdown." But there was a legacy to be reckoned with. "Their problem, essentially, is the same as that of the concerned white men of Valdosta: the monster created by the Southern way of life is so terrifying, and becoming so gargantuan, that nobody knows what to do or where to start doing it." So the city slowly went about its business. Restaurants were integrated; schools and churches were not. There was basic compliance with the Civil Rights Act, which took the place of any larger racial harmony. The atmosphere was peaceful and there were signs of progress, but no real chance of epiphany.[21]

His account was both right and wrong. There was never a riot in post–World War II Valdosta. Police brutality in the area did not crescendo into a galvanizing mass murder. Instead, systemic racism in law enforcement was gradual and incremental, a normalized and routinized violence that devalued Black lives and Black bodies in a way that was even more dangerous and dehumanizing. For Black Valdosta, it was death by a thousand cuts, with police murders of Black residents happening with regularity if not alacrity. Still, despite the grim reality of officially sanctioned race relations in the town, the county, and the region, pushback by the local NAACP and individual residents did happen. School desegregation lawsuits were met with massive resistance, but there were successes. Southwest Georgia became a national civil rights hotbed in the early 1960s, the Albany Movement beginning eighty-five miles to Valdosta's northwest in 1961. What Lomax's account missed about the town's "well-disciplined law force" was its willingness to attack, and sometimes kill, Black citizens, not as part of rights resistance but rather as an outgrowth of systematized police brutality, a reality that existed across the South.[22]

In other small southern towns, however, there was no peace or progress at all, and the brutality was directly related to rights resistance. It was to those cases that Lomax was particularly drawn. Founded in 1906 by the Great Southern Lumber Company, Bogalusa, Louisiana, was built on the twin pillars of labor and race tension. By the 1960s, the company's paper mills were run by the Crown-Zellerbach Company, and segregated local unions for Black and white workers in the town's factories led to a new front in the race fight. On 30 May 1964, the Original Knights of the Ku Klux Klan held their first rally in Bogalusa, and as their ranks swelled precipitously thereafter, the new membership emboldened the group to more acts of violence and intimidation. The crisis in Bogalusa began in February 1965, when members of the Deacons for Defense and Justice, based in Jonesboro, Louisiana, and several workers from CORE arrived and joined with the town's Civic and Voters' League for a series of demonstrations against segregation, racism, and the Ku Klux Klan, which by then had up to seven thousand local members. According to the *Chicago Defender*, the Klan had "long held a strangle hold on Bogalusa." Over the next several months, tensions erupted in violent confrontations and angry Klan reprisals, as the Voters' League attempted to integrate parts of the city and white residents tried to stop them.[23]

The conflict in Bogalusa, often overshadowed by the Watts riots that occurred at the same time, was significant on several fronts. Other than the New Orleans school desegregation conflict in 1960, it was the only race crisis in Louisiana to draw national attention, and it forced the state to come to terms with the Civil Rights Act of 1964. It fundamentally changed the definition of Black militancy in the South. And, like Watts—which helped develop affirmative action in Los Angeles and affected admissions practices in California state universities—Bogalusa provided legitimate legal victories for the civil rights movement. The episode was also important for Lomax, as it gave him his first sustained effort at national activism since the death of Malcolm. It offered a clear contrast to his own hometown, and he was determined to use his new media platform to help the cause.

On 13 June, Lomax's television program featured Charles Sims, leader of the Deacons for Defense and Justice, to discuss the racial strife in Bogalusa. In an interview with the *Los Angeles Times*, Sims—with Lomax at his side—discussed armed self-defense and stockpiling weapons in a state without a concealed carry law. He described coming out of the military after World War II, where he served as a sergeant. "One day in the Army I see a corporal who was a policeman in Bogalusa. He sees me in integrated places and all that. He was a die-hard. He got out of the service first. He sees me back in Bogalusa—me still in uniform," said Sims. "First thing he says, 'Remember, you're not in the Army now.' I made up my mind then not to be pushed around." He armed himself from that point on. "I would rather be caught in Bogalusa with concealed weapons than without them."[24]

Sure enough, members of the Los Angeles police intelligence unit stopped Sims's car, driven by Lomax's driver Tommy Dotray, to question the Louisiana native. They claimed afterward that they just wanted general information about his stay so that they would "be in a position to protect him." A furious Lomax said, "I raised hell with the police about this. If they were really concerned about this man's safety or mine, they could have gone forthrightly to the television station and found out whatever they wanted to know."[25] Lomax joined with several other local leaders to found the Los Angeles Committee of Concerned Californians for Bogalusa, and one of its first moves was to borrow fifteen thousand dollars for the Bogalusa Civic and Voters' League to aid CORE's Summer Project in Bogalusa, scheduled to begin in early July.[26]

The crisis in Bogalusa continued to worsen and violence ensued, as racist whites attacked protesters and they defended themselves, leading to arrests on both sides by the white police force. The Deacons were blamed for much of the violence. Lomax arrived on 11 July to take part in a CORE march led by James Farmer through the center of town. He presented the fifteen thousand dollars from the Committee of Concerned Californians for Bogalusa and spoke at that night's mass meeting, telling the crowd to great ovation that a California bonding company had promised to arrange bail for "anyone working for the freedom movement who is arrested."[27]

The crisis was such that Louisiana's governor, John McKeithen, came to Bogalusa to meet with protesters. With Lomax helping to lead the negotiations for local Black protesters (along with the Deacons' Charles Sims), they rejected the governor's call for a thirty-day moratorium, arguing that he offered nothing in return. "We had to have something to show the people," said Lomax. "He offered us nothing." He told the assembled media that Vice President Hubert Humphrey and the Justice Department's John Doar had called him to discuss the pending meeting with McKeithen. The governor, too, had received a call from Humphrey before he arrived in Bogalusa. "He did everything they told him not to do," said Lomax. Black locals demanded that schools, public facilities, restaurants, and movie theaters be desegregated, that at least ten Black clerks be hired by downtown stores and at least two Black officers join the police force, and that an official white committee be appointed to begin negotiations with them.[28]

On 15 July, Lomax led a march down to Bogalusa's City Hall, with white locals screaming epithets at protesters while police held them back. "Let the rebel voice of hate be heard," said Lomax. "Let the people of Asia and Africa know who is full of hate and who is full of love." A young white local jumped up and down and responded, "You go to hell, nigger." On 16 July, the *Bogalusa Daily News* published a front-page editorial encouraging Lomax to "get out of our community," calling him a "troublemaker" who caused more problems than he solved. He would go—back to Los Angeles if not to hell—but he was not yet done with Bogalusa. Before leaving Louisiana, Lomax predicted that the demonstrations would last "at least sixty days," ending only after the demands for integration and police force inclusion were met.[29]

When Lomax returned to Los Angeles, he hosted twelve-year-old Ben Chaney at his home. The younger brother of slain rights worker James Chaney, he was on a CORE-sponsored trip to the West Coast to raise money for rights work in Mississippi. Chaney spent his time swimming and playing with Lomax's son, Hugh, and Wanda approvingly reported that Ben even ate his vegetables while at the Lomax home.[30]

Lomax's time with Chaney demonstrated both his closeness to the Mississippi case and his instinct for public relations, but for the rest of Black Los Angeles upon his return, tensions were spiraling out of control in a Bogalusa-style conflagration writ large. On 24 July, Lomax addressed a meeting of the Negro Political Action Association of California at Los Angeles's International Hotel, where he denounced the city's mayor, Samuel Yorty, for sending "his Negroes" to meet with Black leaders rather than appearing himself. It was time for a change, Lomax argued: "After all, if courage and dedication can bring the governor of Louisiana down to Bogalusa to meet with a cook, a paper mill worker and a taxicab driver, then why can't the mayor of Los Angeles meet with Negroes and other minorities of his city?"[31]

In August 1965, months after Malcolm's death and with Bogalusa still on tenterhooks, Lomax put himself in the middle of the Watts uprising. The turmoil ostensibly began after a traffic stop on 11 August, when a police confrontation drew a crowd, the police called for backup, and violence ensued. But in reality, the uprising had been fomenting for months. Watts was a Black neighborhood with a 31 percent unemployment rate and an abusive white police force patrolling its streets. The national discussion of civil rights success in the wake of the Civil Rights Act of 1964 and the Voting Rights Act of 1965 did not reach Watts, where the problems were different, more subtle, more ingrained. The uprising continued for a week, leading to forty million dollars in property damage, more than four thousand arrests, one thousand casualties, and thirty-four deaths, many of them caused by police and National Guardsmen. Lomax publicly urged the federal government to send in mediators to facilitate talks between Black leaders and city officials as the uprising raged. "Communication has completely broken down," he said. "Negro leaders have been predicting a riot like this for three years." He compared the riots to the French Revolution: "The whites think they can just bottle people up in an area like Watts and then forget all about them. It didn't work." As the *Los Angeles Sentinel*'s A. S. "Doc" Young explained years later about Watts, "Many of the people actually involved never had a single intellectual thought about the uprising." Remembering Lomax's interviews with some of the rioters, he claimed, "Civil rights couldn't have been farther from their minds."[32]

On his television program, Lomax interviewed residents of the devastated neighborhoods of South Central Los Angeles. "The tragedy of Watts is not that the Negroes burned it down," said Lomax, "but that the white community plans to build it back just like before without assessing the real needs and without addressing themselves to their solution. Negroes in Watts have a pathology of failure—they failed in the South and failed to find the promised land in Los Angeles," largely because the infrastructure to help them succeed was not in place. The séances and UFO hunters notwithstanding, Lomax's show gave him a powerful platform that he was able to use in service of far-flung fights in Louisiana and Mississippi as well as those on his doorstep, such as the uprising in Watts—to engage with the ideology of revolt, with the art of deliberate disunity.[33]

The radical turn in the civil rights movement dramatically affected Lomax, particularly after the loss of Malcolm. In response to Watts and SNCC's new ideological shift, Lomax, while speaking at the Vernon branch of the Los Angeles City Library, circled back to one of his earlier arguments. He called Black Power "immoral and impractical," as the Black population was a substantial minority, and advised that "Negroes do not produce a bullet, a gun or a stick of explosive." Lomax encouraged his audience not to "get trapped into violence. There is nothing the Klansmen or the Birchers would rather see you do—it would give them the chance to shoot you down." Cliff Vaughs, regional chairman for southern California's branch of SNCC, was dismissive of Lomax's criticism. "For various personal reasons some Negroes are afraid to talk about anything all-black," he said. "They have too big a stake in the status quo." It was a charge to which Lomax was vulnerable, with his high-profile public status and fancy Van Nuys home. But he was also someone who spent much of his time with people on the fringes.[34]

Lomax would talk to anyone. In 1960 Otis Chandler had taken over the rock-ribbed conservative *Los Angeles Times*, the paper his family had run for generations. Chandler saw himself as a reformer, but his privilege often showed. During the Watts riots in 1965, Lomax met with Chandler in his *Times* office about the conflagration. According to one possibly apocryphal but often told story, Chandler admitted that he didn't even know where Watts was. "Over there," said Lomax, pointing out the window, "where the smoke is—that's where Watts is."[35]

Later that month, while speaking at the annual Negro Leadership Conference held at UCLA, Lomax warned against a major push to oust Los Angeles police chief William Parker. "Parker is a symptom of the problem, not the cause," he told his audience. He made clear that this was not a statement of support, and he encouraged the conference to "lay bare the issue of police brutality" before the state's special investigative committee on the riots: "I want the white community to see five or six thousand women with babies in their arms, telling of beatings in their stomachs."[36]

On his television program, Lomax interviewed Leroy Hayes, a Watts resident concerned about the state of South Central Los Angeles. Twenty million dollars had reportedly been earmarked for poverty relief in the area, but with the exception of an $800,000 grant to the Westminster Neighborhood Association and the development of the Neighborhood Adult Participation Program and the Teen Post Program, those resources had not reached those in need. "The very acute issue of unemployment of adults—the number 1 problem—still exists and virtually nothing has been done about it," Hayes told Lomax. There were no jobs available, and people were going hungry. "Undoubtedly, jobs are the thing which we need most."[37]

Lomax was always after headlines, and he was perfectly willing to take his civil rights message into spaces that were not rights-oriented or traditionally Black. On 10 December, he debated conservative pundit and *National Review* editor William F. Buckley at San Fernando State College in front of more than four thousand spectators (figure 7.2). The topic was "The Present Path of Civil Rights Is Wrong," with Buckley unsurprisingly taking the affirmative side and Lomax the negative. Buckley argued that the movement needed to be "careful that it doesn't destroy a system that has done more for achieving rights and freedom for people than any other dozen nations in the history of mankind." Lomax pointed out, however, that systems of law and justice were not synonymous. "Law without justice is tyranny," he said. "I'm as pained as Mr. Buckley that the civil rights movement is moving toward more federal intervention, but state leaders have made it clear they do not intend to give those freedoms and dignities promised in our federal documents."[38]

In his syndicated newspaper column the next week, Buckley took Lomax to task for choosing to "expatiate on the divine right of civil disobedience" without "ever mentioning the need for Negroes to obey the laws." Buckley disagreed with Martin Luther King and saw him as dangerous. In relation to Watts, he worried that insofar as Lomax and others "imply that the riots are the inevitable result of underlying injustice, they identify themselves with a dangerous determinism, of the kind that was used by some apologists to reason from the Versailles Treaty on over to the persecution of the Jews by Hitler." It was a typical Buckley argument: "However bad (a) is, (b) does not issue from it as a moral sequitur; and

FIGURE 7.2 — Lomax debating William F. Buckley. COURTESY SPECIAL
COLLECTIONS AND UNIVERSITY ARCHIVES OF THE UNIVERSITY OF
NEVADA, RENO. ITEM 82-30-6-9-2.

surely the civil rights movement will need to provide some reassurance to
the rest of the community that this much at least is understood, even if it
is not clearly understood what exactly we have to do to prevent the recur-
rence of Watts."[39]

The *National Review* was not just a white space: it was on the far right
wing. But Lomax could transfer his message to different audiences with
ease and was also never shy about criticizing the white Left. In January
1966, he spoke at the endorsing convention of the Negro Political Action
Association of California for candidates on the state Democratic Party
ticket. The association ultimately endorsed its own executive director,
William J. Williams, for secretary of state. Lomax, like others at the event,
was critical of the party and intended to make the group's presence felt
among the state's Democrats. "We were promised a long time ago that
this time around there would be a Negro on the Democratic ticket. Then
all of a sudden one day last August Watts erupted and word went out they
couldn't keep their promise for fear of a white backlash," said Lomax.

"How dare some politician look at me and say that because of Watts, I can't run because I'm colored!" He told his audience that although the fight would be difficult, it could be won. The "black bourgeoisie and their fine cars" would find out before the campaign had run its course that "they're more black than they are bourgeois."[40]

It was that willingness to provoke, whether right or left, Black or white, that made his television show—and his radio show, also begun that year—both successful and controversial. Ribbing his fellow talk-show host, KNXT's Jere Witter described Lomax's television program as visionary. Lomax, he quipped, "invites guests, and sometimes they are prominent guests, but he doesn't let them say anything. Mr. Lomax is a pioneer." The *Los Angeles Times's* Hal Humphrey was less charitable, calling the show a platform for "soapbox oratory and catcalls" by "professional rabble-rousers." Humphrey was offended that "Nazis, ex-madams, blow-hard Birchers, trained-seal Commies and various other parasites on humanity are given a platform on TV." He lumped Lomax's show in with those of Joe Pyne, Joe Dolan, and Tom Duggan and called for the FCC to step in to stop such trash from polluting the airwaves.[41]

More substantive criticism came from a letter writer to the *Chicago Defender*, who criticized Lomax for asserting on his show that "any man who has the brains and guts to get out and do it can get rich." The notion that there was equality of economic opportunity and not a massive wealth disparity in the country was not only wrong, it was damaging for the cause of civil rights. By not emphasizing economics, Lomax was creating false expectations and not properly analyzing the problems in Black America. In fact, he was not analyzing at all. He was talking without the kind of examination that the movement needed.[42]

The FCC was listening, and after reviewing a number of complaints that the show oversensationalized various issues, the regulatory agency issued a license to KTTV only after the station agreed to put in place controls over the show's content. In particular, the station would prerecord Lomax's show, along with that of Tom Duggan and Joe Pyne. Still, the talk show format had been incredibly successful for KTTV, and in January it expanded those shows, with all three getting second nights. Lomax's program would air on Thursday night in addition to his traditional Sunday slot. Controversy, it seemed, was good for ratings.[43]

The first Thursday episode aired on 27 January and featured Black activist Leonard Patterson. Patterson had been an organizer with the Young Communist League in the 1930s but later earned a dubious infamy by becoming a vigorous anti-Communist crusader who testified falsely before Congress about the Communist ties of leaders such as Ralph Bunche. He was, in other words, the perfect guest for the provocative Lomax. By March, *Newsweek* reported that Lomax's radio and television shows combined earned him more than $100,000 per year, and his success led WNEW television to pick up *The Louis Lomax Show* for broadcast in New York, though negotiations dragged on into April.[44]

In early February, his television show featured Julian Bond, who had come to Los Angeles after the Georgia legislature refused to seat him, despite his overwhelming electoral victory. Throngs of reporters were there to meet his plane, but so too was Lomax, who pulled him away, put him on a waiting helicopter, and took him to the KTTV studios to tape the show. An overflow crowd for a SNCC event in the Hotel Ambassador's Sunset Room had to wait several hours before Bond's hosts could locate and return him to his scheduled appearances. The anger of SNCC and the ensuing controversy surely pleased Lomax and boosted ratings for his 6 February episode. He was, in his provocations, reprising the role taught to him by Mike Wallace and *The Hate That Hate Produced*, telling an honest story while selling it along the way.[45]

The crisis in Watts, however, needed no selling. March 1966 was a month of further agitation, as residents threw rocks at police and continued to protest the squalid conditions in the neighborhood. Tensions in Black Los Angeles were high, as they continued to be in Louisiana. On Lomax's 11 March radio program, he decried the shooting of another Black citizen in Bogalusa, this time a military veteran, and called for a federal law against the shooting of members of the armed forces. Mervyn Dymally, a Black member of the California State Assembly, said that listeners were "nearly hysterical," calling into the program, crying, and making connections between southern racial violence and the problems facing Watts.[46]

When two people were killed in further violence in South Central Los Angeles, Lomax participated in a series of fundraising efforts for the victims' families.[47] When the California State Assembly responded to the racial violence by proposing a new law that would make it a felony to manufacture, possess, or use a Molotov cocktail, assemblyman Dymally and Lomax were outraged. Dymally viewed the move as an act of class bias; Lomax saw racial motivations. "It's white backlash," he said. "Molotov cocktails were around a long time before the riots. Why make an issue of it now?" The conservative *Times* was aghast, but the *Sentinel*'s Bill Lane supported Dymally and Lomax. The law and the *Times*'s championing of it were "much ado about nothing, and is discriminatory, un-needed, a waste of legislative time and a perfect setup to get people into jail under the flimsiest of circumstances."[48]

At the time, this was not Lomax's only legal concern. While watching Watts burn, he was named in a libel suit filed by the Bapco Financial Corporation, a group attempting to organize a new Black-owned bank. Lomax had commented on his KDAY radio show that the new bank was "a half-baked and half-cooked idea" without the proper authorization from the state banking commissioner. Lomax was a member of the advisory board of the Bank of Finance in Los Angeles, a Black-owned financial institution that would compete with the new Bapco project. Bapco argued that the commentary was intended to eliminate a competitor before it started and prejudice the state corporations commissioner from issuing the new bank its proper permit. The *Los Angeles Herald-Dispatch* was also included in the suit because its columnists called the new group "bunco," but Lomax's commentary was the principal focus of the suit, even though the state corporations commissioner granted the bank its permit. The suit ruled that the damage of Lomax's commentary had been done, leading the company's initial stock sale to fail.[49]

The controversies would continue. In April 1966, Lomax used the power that came with the popularity of his radio show on KDAY to force the cancellation of a fifteen-minute John Birch Society radio program that preceded his own, threatening to pull his show if the Birchers remained. Despite right-wing calls that Lomax "improperly contrived to force" the Birch show off the air, the station canceled the program. "The world of Louis Lomax evidently is not big enough for differing points of view if Mr. Lomax does not control the radio time himself," contended the society's John Rousselot. "Now that Mr. Lomax is in the driver's seat of the bus—and we are happy he is in the driver's seat of radio—we are surprised he will not even let us sit in the rear, but wants to kick us clear out in the street." Rousselot had been on Lomax's television show in early October 1965 and remained an acquaintance. He thus interpreted Lomax's action as "erratic."[50] And for all the faults of the Birch Society, Rousselot was right to point out Lomax's opportunism—his willingness to change if not his core beliefs, then at least his dominant message, depending on the prevailing political winds.

Of course, Lomax's principal intent was to provoke, to create his deliberate disunity. The John Birch Society was a far-right, anti-Communist organization that made even William F. Buckley cringe, a creature of the same fear-mongering that produced personalities such as Joe Pyne and Joe Dolan, but Lomax no more wanted to ban the group's voice than he did that of the *National Review*. And just as in his sparring with Buckley, the Birchers created a new opportunity for provocation, for debate, for moving the discussion into new spaces.

The *Los Angeles Times*'s Paul Coates was equally incredulous, arguing that Lomax had "tripped and fallen off his pedestal of moderation by attempting such a pressure technique." Coates claimed to abhor the Birch Society, but he believed all people should have the right to present their views, just as guests did on Lomax's show. There was, however, more than a little showmanship in Lomax's demand: later in April, he joined Rousselot for a public debate at Glendale College titled "Conservatism Versus Liberalism," which was taped and later broadcast on KTTV.[51]

In May, Lomax traveled to Washington, DC, after being invited by President Johnson to participate in a three-day conference with the theme "Where Do We Go in Race Relations?" The conference, with 2,400 participants, was mired in controversy, as a resolution introduced by CORE's national director Floyd McKissick calling on the United States to leave Vietnam and make Black equality its first priority was defeated soundly. In its place, the group passed a watered-down version asking Johnson to continue working to end the Vietnam conflict so that more federal money could be spent domestically. Lomax and his fellow delegates from Los Angeles submitted a far less controversial and unanimously accepted resolution calling for an additional White House conference where law enforcement and community leaders could deal with "the issue of lawlessness, justice, and proper law enforcement." Citing Watts, Lomax was careful to note that the delegation was "not charging police brutality. We want to make that clear. There are wrongs on both sides. We are charging a breakdown in civilization."[52]

Such diluted sentiments left Bogalusa civil rights leader Robert Hicks incredibly frustrated. "People in Bogalusa will be peeved. They spent $500 to send me to this big show, this come-on, this waste of time. I hoped I could come back and tell them some kind of action would be taken immediately," he said. "Nothing's changed in Bogalusa. We need action."[53]

Things were not much better in Chaney's Mississippi. James Meredith had long planned a march from Memphis to Jackson, but as historian Aram Goudsouzian has explained, "through most of 1965 the march remained a rumor, bigger in the minds of enemies than allies." The first real public announcement of what would become known as the "March against Fear" came from Lomax, who mentioned it during a lecture at Kentucky State University, piquing the interest of, among others, the FBI. Meredith's march also drew the attention of the Ku Klux Klan. Along his lonely trek from Memphis to Jackson, Meredith was shot, leading groups such as SNCC to come and finish the march. While many walked day and night, there was growing frustration that leaders such as Martin Luther King appeared for publicity but did not do the actual grueling work of marching. It was within that context that SNCC leader Stokely Carmichael gave an impassioned speech to an exasperated crowd of marchers. "We been saying freedom for six years and we ain't got nothing," he told them. "What we gonna start saying is Black Power." The argument was that integration and assimilation robbed African American people of the African part of their heritage and that Black values, culture, and autonomy should be fostered. SNCC broke from King's SCLC and removed its white members. In May 1967, Carmichael was replaced by H. Rap Brown, who brought an even more militant message. Brown derided white people and derided the police. He openly celebrated violence: "Black folks built America, and if America don't come around, we're going to burn America down."[54]

While he had helped spur the efforts in Mississippi, Lomax's attention was still dominated by events in Los Angeles and Louisiana. In August 1966, the Bogalusa police force filed a $290,000 slander and libel suit in Washington Parish Court against Lomax and the Johnson Publishing Company, publisher of *Jet* magazine, alleging that he described Bogalusa policemen as "adulterers and advocates of miscegenation" in *Jet*'s July 1965 issue. It was a broad interpretation of Lomax's remarks. He never said those words, at least as published in *Jet*. The magazine reported that while he was speaking at a "civil rights meeting" in Bogalusa Lomax responded to segregationist threats that they would swear out warrants on morality charges against Black residents living in common-law marriages. "If they're going to discuss the moral issue, let's all discuss it," the magazine reported Lomax as saying. "The first time they arrest anybody in our movement on such a charge as this we are going to show movies of whites [and of] some members of the Bogalusa police force going out with Negro women at night." That was enough for the Bogalusa police to file a libel suit, which was intended not to recoup financial damages but to intimidate the outside agitator from California.[55]

Back home in Los Angeles, Lomax formed his own nonprofit, Lomax Corporation, to organize charitable work under the auspices of the city's Operation Cool-It program (figure 7.3), which was funded by President Johnson's Office of Economic Opportunity and administered by the local Economic and Youth Opportunities Agency, an omnibus collection of programs designed to provide underprivileged youths opportunities during the months that school was not in session. Of the $262,000 in available grant money, Lomax Corporation received $106,000. The nonprofit was staffed with his associates and family members, including Bill Walker, the producer of his television show, Robinette Kirk, his personal secretary at Lomax Productions, and his brother-in-law, Newton Harrison. Lomax himself was paid $1,250 by the charity, while his wife worked pro bono. The group held luaus, swimming parties, and boat trips to Catalina, but the nepotism, Lomax's inflated salary, and the organization's domination of the federal grant made many suspicious, if not disgruntled. Lomax, for his part, did his best to brush off the criticism, claiming that he was approached by Vice President Hubert Humphrey's office to set up the nonprofit. "It wasn't my idea. From the time I was approached until we were operating, I had just three weeks to form a nonprofit corporation and get going. I didn't have time to advertise for help," he explained. "Until the funds actually came through, I was out $1,200 of my own money."[56]

Lomax's television show was also a source of controversy. The 31 July 1966 episode featured a Cuban refugee discussing the changes in the country before and after the revolution. "Lomax refuted all factual statements of said refugee," read one FBI account, "and whipped his huge theatre audience into uproarous [sic] applause for Castro and Communist Cuba of today." Lomax and his audience praised "Castro's benevolent treatment of negros [sic] and peasants" and castigated those who disagreed. One angry viewer wrote to KTTV, with copies sent to Hoover and Lyndon Johnson: "How long are we going to have to listen to that red nigger preach and defend communism over your station, I mean Louis Lomax." The writer found the episode disgraceful, while claiming, "I have always had a great deal of respect for the negro race." Another letter to California senator George Murphy asked for an FBI investigation. "We feel from what Lomax has said on his show that he is a danger to our security," the letter read. "I hope you can help R. Reagan to knock down the lies."[57]

FIGURE 7.3 — Lomax in a publicity photograph for Operation Cool-It.
COURTESY SPECIAL COLLECTIONS AND UNIVERSITY ARCHIVES OF THE
UNIVERSITY OF NEVADA, RENO. ITEM 82-30-8-4-17-4.

Controversy, for Lomax, was just another word for publicity. Through Bogalusa and Watts, Buckley and Rousselot, his television show was successful enough to be syndicated in New York and to be broadcast on WTTG, Channel 5, in Washington, DC. "This individual is outspoken on a wide variety of topics," went one FBI report, "and he has been critical of the President, the Director and the Bureau concerning civil rights matters." In other words, Lomax had found a formula for success.[58]

8 Thailand

On 23 October 1966, Wanda Lomax arrived at the Hollywood Receiving Hospital to receive treatment for a cut lip. She told police that her husband had struck her, but after discussing her situation with police at the Hollywood station, Wanda decided not to sign an official complaint and drove herself home.[1] An ex-con who served time for fraud, Louis Lomax had spent the summer accused of a new fraud with Operation Cool-It. Robinette Kirk, who would in relatively short order replace Wanda as Louis's wife, was serving as his assistant. Louis Lomax never admitted any spousal violence, but the recipe for that kind of behavior was certainly there.

Wanda told police that she and her husband had been having marital problems for roughly six months. She alleged that Louis pushed her against a wall mirror and punched her when she returned from a party at six thirty in the morning. In addition to the cut lip, she had chipped teeth and a lump on her right cheek. While Louis admitted to pushing Wanda, he argued that she fell after hitting the mirror. Wanda, formerly a teacher, was now a counselor in the public school system and still working on her doctoral degree at USC. Lomax's radio program on KDAY was canceled following the abuse allegations, though the station gave no official explanation, and television network KTTV remained silent about its future plans for its host. Louis Lomax was just as silent, reportedly staying in San Diego to avoid press inquiries.[2]

Once again, Lomax's behavior did not correspond to his upbringing. Whether in his serial womanizing, his car theft, his deception about his past, or his possible graft through Operation Cool-It, the interstices of Lomax's valuable contributions to the broader narrative of rights and tactics were fraught with a kind of moral corruption that did not exist, for example, in those who raised him. Potential domestic violence only added to the contradiction. There is no evidence for why this behavior manifested at this point, or whether it ever happened in previous marriages and was just never reported. In this, as in Lomax's earlier behavior, there is a behavioral question related to the environmental or inherent factors that might have driven particular elements of his personality, but as before, there is no complete or satisfactory answer. Lomax's early family life was devoid of such behavioral models, but so too were the early family lives of many con men, philanderers, and even domestic abusers. No specific event in his biography served as a catalyst for such behaviors, but history has demonstrated that such catalysts are not necessary. What is unusual about Lomax is that graft, womanizing, and domestic abuse existed alongside inspired work for civil rights and journalism that sought to translate a changing world to a series of changing audiences.

In November, Lomax gave a lecture to a group calling itself the Over 30 Singles Forum titled "The Color Spectrum: Life and Love amid Social Turmoil." A transcript of the address no longer survives, but the speech seems to be his first public admission and examination of his interracial relationship with the white Robinette Kirk. In December, Lomax officially announced his split with his wife. "Wanda and I are separated, and she's moved out of our home on Grandview in Hollywood and is now living in Baldwin Hills," he told the press.[3]

The news came as Lomax was preparing to leave for a trip to Southeast Asia arranged by the North American Newspaper Alliance, for which he was a syndicated writer. As of early 1966, Lomax had not produced any pages of "Parson Tom" for his Random House editor, Robert Loomis, but he claimed that he had no time for it. "Now I can let you in on the secret," he told Loomis. "I will be shortly headed into North Vietnam for interviews with Ho Chi Minh and others." He promised, "I will get you a few chapters in the mail shortly. Please don't give up now, as I will be a fairly valuable property once I return."[4]

The trip, which served as a welcome diversion, had been a long time coming. As early as November 1964, Lomax announced that he planned to visit China for a magazine article on the economic colonialism China was practicing in the Philippines and the South Pacific and the rising tide of nationalism it had provoked, which clearly influenced Black nationalism in the United States. Lomax assured reporters that he was not defying any travel bans: "Just as I sought and got state department permission to go into Cuba a couple of years ago, I am seeking state department permission to go into Red China."[5]

The trip fell through, and Lomax never made it to China. In September 1965, the FBI was worried that Lomax and Martin Luther King Jr. were planning a similar trip to South Vietnam. Both had been critical of American military action in the country. "We are dying in Vietnam to bring freedom there and at the same time 3,000 of our own people are in jail in Alabama for trying to vote," Lomax wrote in February 1965, anticipating many later criticisms of the conflict. "That makes us the laughingstock of the world." The bureau worked with the Los Angeles Police Department and the passport office to research possible points of departure. The State Department also chimed in, noting "no visa necessary for U.S. travel to Viet Nam for periods of seven days or less."[6]

That trip did not happen, either, but Lomax clearly wanted to go, and in June 1966, while in Switzerland for a speaking engagement, he met with North Vietnamese officials about the possibility of visiting that country. Not one to keep secrets, Lomax claimed on a television appearance after his return from Zurich that he had met with National Liberation Front and Vietminh representatives. The effort and the grandstanding seemed to pay off, and in December 1966 he announced that he had received permission from both the United States and North Vietnam to travel to Hanoi to interview Ho Chi Minh, a scoop he had worked to secure for six months. He said that he would fly to Washington for a State Department briefing, then leave for the Far East.[7]

One of Lyndon Johnson's most trusted Black advisers, the journalist Louis Martin, was in a meeting when a switchboard operator at the Democratic National Committee found him, ushered him out, and explained that he had an urgent call from Los Angeles. Lomax needed to talk with someone at the White House immediately and preferred that it be the president. He had just finagled an appointment to interview Ho Chi Minh in Hanoi, he told Martin, and would fly to Washington on the next flight out if a meeting with someone could be arranged. Martin was skeptical but nonetheless decided to help his friend, and he arranged a meeting with members of the National Security Council and the State Department.[8]

Martin was the quintessential Black foreign correspondent. Though he grew up in Savannah, Georgia, just hours from Lomax's native Valdosta, his father was from Cuba. After college at Fisk and graduate study at the University of Michigan, Martin spent two years as a freelance reporter in Havana. In 1936, he moved to Chicago to work briefly with the *Chicago Defender* before traveling to Detroit to help found the *Michigan Chronicle*. In 1940, he was one of the founders of the National Newspaper Publishers Association. Twenty years later he became an adviser to John F. Kennedy, then to Lyndon Johnson. His considered, well-planned life stood in stark contrast to Lomax's pinball-style trajectory, which had taken him from prison to journalism to radio and television and now, it seemed, to North Vietnam.[9]

During a press announcement at Los Angeles International Airport, as he waited for his flight to Washington, Lomax explained that his upcoming trip grew out of the peace conference in Geneva where he had met North Vietnamese dignitaries, and thereafter the North Vietnamese Journalistic Association had begun working on the necessary permissions for him to visit. He told the assembled reporters that he would first arrive in Cambodia, where the North Vietnamese would contact him and fly him to Hanoi. Robinette Kirk, his administrative assistant, would make arrangements for a cameraman and soundman to accompany him to Hanoi.[10]

In Washington, Lomax received his briefing. He met with several officials, including Philip B. Heyman, acting head of the Bureau of Security and Consular Affairs, and Leonard Unger, deputy assistant secretary of state for East Asian and Pacific affairs. "I wasn't given any orders, no demands were made; I'm not an agent of the State Department," Lomax said later. "Basically, they wanted to give me a handful of American position papers so I would know what I am talking about." State Department spokesman Robert J. McCloskey confirmed the briefing but was clearly ambivalent about the trip. "We validated his passport," said McCloskey. "I'll leave it at that."[11] With position papers in hand and a valid passport, Lomax left Los Angeles for Tokyo, the first stop on his trip, on 24 December. From there he went to Bangkok (figure 8.1), where he told reporters he hoped to see American prisoners of war during his time in Hanoi.[12]

The North Vietnamese also provided permission for travel to Hanoi to Harrison E. Salisbury of the *New York Times* and a handful of others. *Chicago Defender* reporter Ethel Payne was already stationed in Saigon. Known as the "First Lady of the Black Press," Payne had worked at the *Chicago Defender* for decades following World War II. Though the civil

FIGURE 8.1 — Lomax interviewing a Thai rickshaw driver while doing research in Thailand. COURTESY SPECIAL COLLECTIONS AND UNIVERSITY ARCHIVES OF THE UNIVERSITY OF NEVADA, RENO. ITEM 82-30-1-4-4-3.

rights effort had been her principal beat for much of that time, she was in Saigon for a series of reports on Black troops serving in Vietnam. That assignment would lead to later foreign reporting from various points in Africa in the late 1960s and early 1970s. Lomax did not have Payne's pedigree, but he assumed that his own work there would be a groundbreaking effort, one that would bring him additional fame and gravitas. But his flight from Phnom Penh was stalled, and Lomax temporarily returned to Bangkok. He told the media there that Salisbury was already in Hanoi, and he had the impression—accurately—that North Vietnam wanted only one American journalist in Hanoi at a time. After the delay, the Vietminh decided that they did not want Lomax after all. He never made it to Hanoi.[13]

The pseudonymous *Chicago Defender* satire column written by Ole Nosey quipped, "Ain't it interesting how Louis Lomax got the green light to go to North Viet Nam to interview Ho Chi Minh, while Dick Gregory couldn't go on a goodwill tour of duty?" Gregory had also applied for visiting privileges but was denied, leading many, including *Ramparts* magazine, a former Lomax publisher, to accuse the writer of selling out to the establishment.[14] Such was the danger in Black foreign journalism. Even when reporters did not view foreign issues through an American lens, Americans judged them based on their radical credentials. State Department approval could be a scarlet letter for Black journalists attempting to maintain authenticity or standing among radical Black thinkers.

The way to prove oneself was to produce solid journalism. Lomax's notes from the trip were clearly intended to help him write a book. "Bangkok to a Thai is like Paris to a Frenchman," read one of his entries. "Its accent is on sophistication and anything-goes spirit. The Communist Party realize this and aim for the budding intellectuals of the Colleges and Universities." His pithy commentary was accompanied by elaborate drawings, portraits of his interview subjects, hand-drawn maps, and detailed sketches of Vietcong soldiers and weapons. The notes demonstrated a real artistic ability as well as a determination to make something of the trip, whether or not he eventually made it to Hanoi.[15]

Once the North Vietnamese decisions about Salisbury and Lomax became known, the Associated Press renewed its own series of applications for entry into the country. Another group—comprising Harry Ashmore of the Center for the Study of Democratic Institutions, *Miami News* editor William C. Braggs, and Luis Quintanilla, former Mexican ambassador to the United States—sought to make the trip to invite North Vietnamese officials to Geneva for a peace negotiation. Like Lomax, they received State Department approval but were not traveling as representatives of the government.[16]

Lomax went quiet during the first week of January 1967, leading the *Los Angeles Times*'s Matt Weinstock to quip that "the indefatigable Lomax may have gone into Red China to stage an 'Operation Cool It' program for the Red Guard." When he returned to the United States in mid-January, he refused to talk to reporters about what had happened in Hanoi and whether he had even made it to the city, claiming that he was prevented from speaking by his broadcasting and newspaper contracts. The *Los Angeles Sentinel*, however, understood that he never made it to the North Vietnamese capital. "Instead, he cooled his heels in Cambodia while Salisbury—a white guy—was in Hanoi gathering all the news and making a big hero of himself."[17]

In a twist that some saw as retribution for Lomax's role in the ouster of the John Birch radio program, KTTV filled the hosting spot on *The Louis Lomax Show* with John Rousselot during Lomax's time in Asia.

FIGURE 8.2 — Lomax debating with the John Birch Society's John Rousselot. COURTESY SPECIAL COLLECTIONS AND UNIVERSITY ARCHIVES OF THE UNIVERSITY OF NEVADA, RENO. ITEM 82-30-6-9-5.

Rousselot was public relations director for the Birch Society, and the move angered the Jewish War Veterans of California, whose spokesman argued that KTTV had a "moral obligation" to provide programming in the public interest "and not for public dissemination for extremist propaganda." Despite the public outcry, it was Lomax himself who selected the Birch leader. Rousselot had first appeared on Lomax's show in early October 1965, and the two had debated publicly (figure 8.2). They were friends, and Lomax knew that Rousselot would create controversy and interest while he was away.[18]

Rousselot was a former congressman who allied himself with the Reverend Billy James Hargis, a fellow traveler in anti-Communist circles and a staunch segregationist who spent much of his airtime denouncing Martin Luther King as a Communist and integration as fundamentally unbiblical. Such attitudes were not completely anomalous within the John Birch Society membership and naturally pushed against everything that Lomax believed. Still, Lomax and Rousselot got along personally, and Lomax knew that using an outspoken representative of the society on his show would only draw interest, which served as a large part of his motivation. By keeping a handy villain at the ready, Lomax could use Birch ideas to demonstrate the problematic consequences when conservative ideology was taken to its logical conclusion.[19]

After failing to get to North Vietnam, Lomax decided to write a book about the Thailand that he experienced. He began studying the Thailand-related work of UCLA anthropologist and former CIA operative Michael Moerman, making friends with the scholar in Los Angeles to pick his brain about the region. He collected State Department fact sheets and economic projections from Thailand's National Economic Development Board.[20] Articles by experts in the field such as G. William Skinner, Maynard Parker, and George Moseley found a place alongside press releases from the Permanent Mission of Thailand to the United Nations and statements on the country's development by Senate Foreign Relations Committee chair J. William Fulbright.[21]

After collecting his notes, Lomax sent a scattershot proposal to editor Robert Loomis at Random House. "I can have the manuscript to you in sixty days, maybe sooner," he wrote. His proposal was a jumbled cache of ideas describing Thailand as a "prize takeover target" of the Communists. It was "the key to southeast Asia; if it falls, all of southeast Asia will fall with it." If it did not fall, however, "Thailand will almost certainly pull southeast Asia into modernity." Lomax compared the Thai Communist insurgency to the Maoist insurgency that had taken over China. He quoted an American diplomat to whom he spoke while in Bangkok who told him, "If Viet Nam ended tomorrow, we would simply move our men to Thailand." In truth, there was already an American military presence in the country. Lomax planned to flesh out the story through his reporting, through a history of the country and of American interest in the region, and through his own analysis of the state of the insurgency. "Thailand is the war that is," he closed, "the war that will be."[22]

Random House was interested, and Lomax began hurriedly preparing a manuscript. Even as he was turning in the final draft, he was trying to add additional sections. He proposed a final essay "in which I examine some alternatives to communism; alternatives which make sense to emerging peoples whereas our kind of democracy-capitalism does not. I contend that American liberals are attempting a new kind of colonialism."[23]

The Random House book jacket described it as "an alarming portrait of another Viet Nam in the making" and featured an author photo of

Lomax interviewing Thai Communist insurgents, as if to validate the account's legitimacy with visual evidence. Tellingly, however, the only blurb on the jacket came from Lomax himself, foreshadowing the book's lukewarm reception.[24]

Thailand: The War That Is, The War That Will Be told the story of Lomax's travels through the country, particularly in the northeast, home to the country's Communist insurgency. He interviewed a broad swath of people, from peasants to ambassadors, and concluded that the Johnson administration mired the country in another Vietnam-style defense of an authoritarian regime for the sake of Communist containment. It was a call to alarm without any real answers as to how to fix the problems. The book also lacked an expert's understanding of the region or even a full portrait of the nation's politics. Political scientist Frank Darling described the effort as "a tribute and a tragedy." It was a tribute in that "a self-made American Negro who has risen from a humble background in Georgia to the position of a prominent journalist" had bothered "to travel to Southeast Asia and from first-hand observations to discuss important regional problems." But it was a tragedy "because it is based on little more than a tourist's exposure to Thailand." It was filled with historical and political inaccuracies, Darling argued, and was built on naivete and emotion rather than a nuanced, studied effort.[25]

Lomax's reputation, of course, was built on emotional pleas and large-picture thinking rather than nuance. As he had in *The Reluctant African*, Lomax admitted that he was an educated novice. He thanked Moerman in his introduction, along with other aides, and quoted him liberally throughout the book. (Lomax dedicated *Thailand* to Robinette Kirk and thanked her children, Billy and Robin, for flying kites and playing with him in his down time. Her sisters Karen and Marsha helped him with typing and proofreading. Even before his divorce from Wanda, his relationship with his former secretary was cemented.)[26]

He began his account by describing the Communist insurgency in northeastern Thailand, its connections to North Vietnamese Communism, and the US military advisers who dotted the landscape, playing the role that such early "advisers" played in Vietnam. He also drew direct parallels with *The Reluctant African*. The political turmoil in the region "is in such stark contrast to the land's natural beauty that I felt as I did when I visited Kenya seven years ago: here is the land of God, He made a masterpiece of it; then He made man, and man made a mess."[27]

His was a decidedly American account. It was not radical in the Black nationalist sense or, for that matter, in any sense. The Communists in Lomax's account were the bad guys, tormenting those in the simple villages that bordered Laos. The Thai government, of course, was not a worthy protagonist in the tale. Bangkok imposed its will on the provinces, generating a bureaucracy that largely benefited the capital rather than the largely rural population. "Southeast Asia is a land where nobody plays by the rules, where nobody makes promises he intends to keep. It is a land of shaking ground and rattling tables."[28]

The book then moved to the rice fields and rubber farms of southern Thailand, where minority groups of Muslim Malaysians and Buddhist Chinese only complicated the potential for radicalism. "The insurgency in the south is gathering momentum," a State Department official told Lomax. "We must stop it now or it will lead to real trouble. We don't want another Viet Nam–type involvement." The narrative then shifted to Bangkok, the cultural, economic, and political hub of the country and its only real urban center, where political intrigue exacerbated every other problem in the country. "There is no constitution," wrote Lomax, "no one can vote, martial law prevails; it is a felony punishable by death for more than five people to gather and talk politics."[29]

Through this uniquely Thai turmoil, Lomax was able to draw connections back home. When Senator J. William Fulbright denounced Thailand's military dictatorship, for example, leaders in Bangkok claimed to a foreign diplomat that "it was shocking that Fulbright was so concerned about individual freedom in Thailand when the Arkansan cares so little for the rights of black people in his home state." It was a common complaint among the Communists in Russia and China, leaders in Vietnam, and many other global politicians who found themselves criticized by the United States, but it was no less effective, or less accurate, for its continued use.[30]

Another commonality was the region's belief in a religious deliverance, a messiah who would lead the people to freedom. The Thai "Pee Boon" myth, which anticipated that a miracle-working conqueror would arrive to save everyone, at first seemed to Lomax a quaint anachronism. But "all peoples have a Pee Boon," one Thai source told him. "You Americans had one in 1776. You called him—and still do—the Father of your country. Ho Chi Minh is the Pee Boon of Viet Nam; this is why you will never win there. Kenya has a Pee Boon. He led the Mau Mau and now is Prime Minister of the country. Nkrumah of Ghana called himself 'savior'—Pee

Boon. He led his nation to freedom." Lomax went on to describe his late friend Malcolm X as a version of Pee Boon for another oppressed people. Lomax had, in one way or another, been writing about Pee Boons for his entire career.[31]

Every Pee Boon, of course, needed a villain, and in Thailand that role was at least partly played by the American government. "The Johnson Administration has committed the American people to another Viet Nam–type war in Asia without seeking the advice or consent of either the people or the Congress," Lomax claimed. The US military presence in Thailand had tripled since 1964. Two-thirds of US bombing runs into North Vietnam emanated from Thailand. Yet leaders there denied that there was any viable insurgency growing in the country. "American Army officers sought a tour of duty in Thailand as an opportunity to sun themselves in the Gulf of Siam, to buy fine silks and jewelry for their wives, and to just plan relax," wrote Lomax.[32]

The face of US villainy in southeast Asia was its ambassador to Thailand, Graham Martin. "We are here to stay," he told Lomax. "Regardless of what you liberals say, *we ain't going home*!" He explained, "We are right and they are wrong. What we want for the world is good, what the Communists want for the world is bad." By that reasoning, he said, "we have the right to have our missiles pointed at Russia because they are the bad guys; they don't have the right to have their missiles pointed at us because we are the good guys." The same construct applied to Thailand. "We have the right to be in Thailand because we are good; China doesn't have the right to be in Cuba because they are bad. We offer the best hope for Southeast Asia; that is why we are here." "Suppose we have to kill Asians to do it?" asked Lomax. "Then, goddamnit," he responded, "we kill Asians!"[33]

This sort of attitude by colonizers helped explain resistance by the colonized, and both Lomax and the Thais themselves compared the politics of Thailand to those of the American civil rights movement. "The insurgency movement has an enormous following among Thai women," a rebel claimed to Lomax. "You should understand this because it is the same thing that has happened to the Negro woman in America. The Thai male has been emasculated, doomed to the rice fields. It is the Thai woman who, as a servant, has seen the better life."[34]

The comparisons worked for religion as much as they did for gender. "We Negroes of the Deep South have a saying: 'Prayer is fine in a prayer meeting, but it ain't worth a damn in a bear meeting.' Of course we are talking about our encounters with the Southern white man," Lomax wrote. "The only way we could pray our way out of the hell that was Birmingham, Alabama, was to send our prayers aloft while we sat in the streets and blocked traffic." It was when prayer migrated into action that the insurgency became effective. Buddhism was similar for the Thais, he explained: "It does not evince a social or economic commitment until earthly gripes erupt into a near riot and disturb the Establishment. Then, and only then, do the deeply religious announce that God—the Great Lord Buddha—is on their side."[35]

The situation was made all the more problematic by official American policy. Lomax closed the book with a discussion of the 1954 Southeast Asia Collective Defense Treaty and its corresponding Southeast Asia Treaty Organization (SEATO) and US manipulation of its original intent. In 1962, US secretary of state Dean Rusk and Thai foreign minister Thanat Khoman signed a bilateral action agreement that reinterpreted SEATO and justified American military maneuvers in the country, opening the door for Thailand to become another Vietnam. "America is determined to menace whatever it deems to be Communist in Southeast Asia," wrote Lomax, "and we have committed ourselves to defend any government, regardless of how corrupt and wrong it may be, that allows us to use its territory as a convenient base from which to carry on our anti-Communist activity."[36]

Lomax's critique could have lent itself to the kind of anticolonial nationalism that appealed to his friend Malcolm X. But he never pushed his narrative in that direction. He chose instead to stay in much the same lane that he occupied in his other work of foreign policy journalism, *The Reluctant African,* although the new book also reflected his own version of anti-Communism, despite his broader criticism of the official, violent American form of anti-Communist military action. The parabola of the bell curve that had risen toward radicalism during his close contact with Malcolm was again arching back toward its baseline in the years after his friend's death.

While he was in Phnom Penh waiting for his proposed trip to Hanoi, Lomax met Don O. Noel Jr., a visiting scholar in the city and, at the time, the only resident American in the Cambodian capital. Lomax was, in the words of Noel, "blissfully unaware" of the protocol of the region, the principal reason he never made it to North Vietnam. Noel, a longtime Connecticut journalist, reviewed *Thailand* for the *Hartford Times,* calling Lomax's effort "a surprisingly good book" considering that "Lomax is not an Asian specialist, nor even an American experienced in Asia." As a result,

Noel wrote, "his book is at times episodic and disjointed, and it lacks the direction of an experienced, carefully thought out philosophy of what US policy should seek in Thailand."[37]

The *Milwaukee Journal*'s Stuart Hoyt was harsher, dismissing the work as "a complaining book" written by "a 'dove' on the Vietnam war" who "went to Thailand for two and a half weeks." Frank J. Johnson, writing in the *National Review*, railed that Lomax "allows his book on Thailand to degenerate from what starts out to be a reasonably objective human-interest side of the growing guerrilla war there into a crude, factually dubious, ideological castigation of United States policy in general." The *Saturday Review* was understandably more charitable than the *National Review* but echoed the broader theme. "More often than not Lomax is apt to view Thailand and Southeast Asia in terms of black or white, neglecting the shades in between," wrote Russell H. Fifield. In addition, he noted, "errors have crept in," and while some of them were minor, "others are more serious." Lomax, for example, had completely misrepresented the Rusk-Thanat Memorandum of March 1962, inaccurately claiming that it established that the Southeast Asia Treaty Organization allowed the United States and Thailand to make bilateral agreements that would be binding to all members of the treaty organization. Such mistakes and broad-brush representations of the region without understanding its nuances gave the book its amateurish reputation among experts in the field.[38]

The problem, argued the *Los Angeles Times*'s Jack Poisie, was that the book was produced "hurriedly" and featured "gross errors and faulty conclusions." Meanwhile, in Thailand, a columnist in a leading Bangkok daily also criticized the book and concluded that "Americans are enemies of the Thai people" who were "infiltrating everywhere" for nefarious ends. The Thai people believed that the book insulted King Bhumibol Adulyadej and were incredulous at Lomax's warning that Thailand could become another Vietnam. The furor was such that American ambassador Leonard Unger issued a public statement denying any support for Lomax's views.[39]

That was the nature of Lomax's foreign policy journalism: convincing to some but not to others. The mixed reviews largely stemmed from his mistakes in interpreting volatile regions between 1960 and 1968.[40] His writing often was hyperbolic, lacked contextual accuracy, and demonstrated a novice's understanding of the regions on which he was reporting. Yet even when he got some of the facts wrong, he was consistent in arguing against colonialism and in favor of national self-determination. Though he made occasional nods to the "racial lens" of other foreign correspondents, he mostly judged movements for self-determination on the merits of the arguments made by indigenous people themselves. In so doing, he bridged early twentieth-century efforts at Black foreign policy journalism and brief paeans to Black nationalist theory, helping usher in a more modern journalistic interpretation of foreign policy, one that is often hyperbolic, sensational, and willing to jettison nuance in an effort to make a broader case. Lomax's foreign journalism was, in that sense, decidedly ahead of its time.

In early February 1967, as Louis Lomax was returning from Southeast Asia, his former wife Betty Frank Lomax came to Chicago at the invitation of the Townhall Women's Guild to give a speech, "The Afro-American Woman's Role in America," at the Wabash Avenue YMCA. Since her marriage to Louis, Betty had become a strong Black female media voice in her own right and was now a New York radio and television personality and the vice president of Media Women Inc. In the 1966 Mothers' Day issue of the magazine *Liberator*, she called for "a clear-cut definition of the Afro-American woman" and described "a certain dilemma" among Black women, who created, in the words of experts, "emasculation and the maintenance of a matriarchal household." But such conditions, she argued, were actually the result of the Black male's frustration with the Black woman's latent potential, smothered by overweening Black masculinity.[41]

Meanwhile, in Los Angeles Superior Court, Wanda was filing for divorce, based largely on the same problems with frustrated masculinity that Betty described. In her suit she charged her husband with "extreme cruelty" and claimed that he had "inflicted grievous [sic] physical and mental suffering." During the hearing in April, she repeated her earlier charges and claimed that Lomax "excluded me from his life." The divorce decree was granted, along with an undisclosed property settlement.[42]

Throughout the ordeal, Lomax kept a heavy speaking schedule, leaving him absent from his show. Again he filled the spot with John Rousselot, to the anger of many KTTV viewers.[43] The move demonstrated the malleability of Lomax's public persona and his willingness to court controversy. During that same speaking tour, for example, California governor Ronald Reagan appointed insurance salesman James E. Johnson leader of the California Department of Veterans Affairs. Though Johnson was the first African American to head a California state agency, he was a controversial choice, and Lomax denounced him publicly, recalling that while being interviewed on his television program, Johnson "defended the Birch Society and praised its aims" and claimed that the leadership of major civil rights groups were "under the influence of Communists." At the same time, Lomax maintained a close relationship with Rousselot, who was actually a leader of the Birch Society. The contradiction did not bother Lomax, as his connection with Rousselot had no policy-making consequences. Besides, he was more interested in the coverage.[44]

Not all publicity was made equal, however. In April, *Look* magazine sued Lomax for $3,500 for failing to get his promised interview with Ho Chi Minh. The magazine had given Lomax an advance on 8 June, but neither the interview nor the money ever returned to *Look*. The two parties settled out of court.[45] Chronically bad with money, Lomax wished to put Thailand behind him and bolster his public persona closer to home.

In early June, he hosted a cocktail party to demonstrate the positive aspects of living in the Crenshaw neighborhood of Los Angeles and to encourage residents to stay after an in-migration of Black and Asian families had led to an out-migration of white families worried about crime, schools, and property values. Later that month, he served as master of ceremonies for a Martin Luther King speech at a Victory Baptist Church banquet at the International Hotel. "What must the church do to serve the present age?" asked King. "Take a stand against the evils of racism, poverty, and war." He opposed riots but called on the church to "mobilize against poverty."[46]

Lomax also visited the Catholic Youth Organization's coordinator for the Imperial Courts housing project, who showed him around and explained the financial deficit her organization faced after failing to meet an economic benchmark required by the Economic and Youth Opportunities Agency, a group Lomax knew all too well from the previous summer's Operation Cool-It program. Afterward, he visited Beverly Hills philanthropist John Factor, who pledged eight thousand dollars to help the group. The good deed was also a new opportunity for publicity: when pictures were taken to show the organization receiving the check, they featured not Factor but Lomax.[47]

In early August 1967, *The Louis Lomax Show* won an Image Award from the Beverly Hills–Hollywood Branch of the NAACP. There was no doubt the show had a legitimate and immediate impact on the Black image. When KTTV's regular newscaster, Larry Burrell, was out on a Sunday night early that month, the station replaced him with Sid McCoy. It was the first time Los Angeles had seen a Black newscaster present the nightly news. The broadcast came right after Lomax's show, which, as the first such program hosted by a Black man, had opened the door for McCoy. The *Sentinel*'s Bill Lane called Lomax, who had just moved to a new Beverly Hills home and did not know about the historic event (his show had just aired but not as a live broadcast). "I'm just getting my TV antennae up," Lomax told Lane, before turning on the television and celebrating the milestone that his own program helped bring about.[48]

Another milestone came in August, when Lomax hosted a nineteen-hour "Job-a-Thon" (figure 8.3) on KTTV to bring together companies and Black, Mexican American, and Native American employment seekers. Les Crane cohosted and Jack Rourke produced the show, which was created by Lomax with the help of the California Department of Employment. The program featured civic and business leaders along with Hollywood personalities urging businesses to phone in with job openings or to create new positions for qualified applicants. The telethon, according to Lomax, "filled the communications gap in this town between the guy looking for a job and the one who has one to offer." The show "discovered" more than twenty-five thousand jobs during nineteen hours on the air. "Many people called up and said they thought the show was a phony and that the jobs really didn't exist," said Lomax. "So we told them if you really want a job and you're not equipped, here are people who will train you and hire you."[49]

On the Monday following the telethon, more than 6,100 job applicants swamped the state unemployment offices throughout Los Angeles. When the Watts branch opened at eight in the morning, more than 600 people were waiting; there were more than 700 in Compton, 550 in Inglewood. The overwhelming of state offices led to accusations and recriminations about who was to blame for the state's unpreparedness, but the applications were eventually processed, albeit slowly.[50]

Response to the telethon only redounded to Lomax's benefit. In September, word got out that he would play himself in a small role in the international movie *Wild in the Streets*. Also, late that month, Los Angeles's KCET television announced a televised debate between Lomax and SNCC leader H. Rap Brown, to be held at UCLA on 11 October. Lomax's network, KTTV, had actually turned down the offer to air the debate because of controversy surrounding Brown, leaving KCET, the city's public education channel, the only taker. The debate, however, was ultimately canceled after a letter from SNCC officials to UCLA's Associated Student Speakers Program cited "Brown's total unwillingness to debate another Black man before a white audience."[51]

That unwillingness was made all the more poignant by the riots that summer in Detroit and Newark. Lomax was on the ground for both

FIGURE 8.3 — Lomax hosting the Job-a-Thon telethon. COURTESY
SPECIAL COLLECTIONS AND UNIVERSITY ARCHIVES OF THE UNIVERSITY
OF NEVADA, RENO. ITEM 82-30-6-7-2.

conflagrations, documenting them for the National Newspaper Alliance. He found the riot in Newark particularly galling. Part of the "Long Hot Summer" of 1967, which refers to more than one hundred race riots across the nation, the Newark protest began after police beat a Black cab driver in the city. More broadly, it was a response to economic inequality, police brutality, and a lack of government services. A protest march against police brutality in July led to a full-scale uprising that lasted for most of a week, leaving twenty-six dead and hundreds wounded.[52]

In late October, Lomax traveled back to Newark and spoke at the local NAACP's Freedom Fund Dinner. Before more than five hundred people, Lomax argued that slavery had produced a mortgage on the great wealth of the United States, a debt that appeared both in racial inequality and in the radicalism of H. Rap Brown and Stokely Carmichael. He also charged the Newark police department with investigating him after his articles were published rather than looking into the impetus of his reporting. Once again, he was stoking deliberate disunity.[53]

In a November 1967 article, the *Sentinel*'s Bill Lane noted that Lomax "is always being called a 'sellout to the Negro,' 'anti-Jewish,' a 'snob who refuses to live among the people he claims to represent.' Truth is, Louis

Lomax represents one entity—Louis Lomax." Lomax agreed. "You can't please all the people all the time," he said. "My only aim is to try to keep them interested, most of the time." Some Black critics called his program "a white show," referring to the emphasis on Communism and conservatism, the talking dogs, the UFOs, and other issues not specifically focused on the Black community. But Lomax responded that whites made up the vast majority of his studio audience: "It's only when I have heavy racial topics that [Black audience members] come out." Lane asked him about the possibility of making his show "more Negro." Lomax sighed. "If I had an all-Negro or 'mostly Negro' show the public in general would not stay with me two weeks."[54]

9 Branching Out

In November 1967, Richard Zanuck announced that 20th Century Fox had hired Lomax to write an original screenplay on the life of Malcolm X, to be based on Lomax's *When the Word Is Given*. The news garnered Lomax more press attention, including an interview with the *Christian Science Monitor* about his position on Black Power. Lomax was not an advocate of Black nationalist thought, which made him an unusual choice for the Fox biopic. "Mr. Lomax regards himself as a Negro to whom certain 'black-power' leaders will still listen," the *Monitor* explained. But two and a half years after Malcolm's death, "he thinks they're wrong."[1]

The man who also wrote *The Hate That Hate Produced* told his interviewer about Black Power, "It's partly a fad, and it's partly a philosophical twitch." At the same time, he credited the movement with generating grassroots leadership: "Rather than having somebody in New York speaking at a cocktail party for the Negro, now you have ghetto people themselves doing the talking." When asked in response about "the ghetto problem," Lomax proposed a national guaranteed annual wage and massive infrastructure investment into impoverished Black neighborhoods. Even with such radical suggestions, he remained frustrated with misguided "black Jacobins" on college campuses who wanted to boycott the 1968 Olympics and create networks of Black militants to mobilize at a moment's notice. "The Negro is a total product of America—biologically, philosophically, politically," he said. "He must integrate with America. He has no choice."[2]

As Lomax began new research for the Malcolm X project in December, Jesse H. Walker, *Amsterdam News* theatrical columnist, reported that Fox was hoping that Sidney Poitier would play the lead. Before the endeavor, Lomax had first asked his friend Betty Shabazz about making a biographical film about Malcolm based on *When the Word Is Given*. She ultimately backed away from the project because she was, in the words of historian Russell Rickford, "overburdened."[3]

Columbia Pictures, meanwhile, owned the rights to Alex Haley's *The Autobiography of Malcolm X* and planned to produce a movie based on the book, with a screenplay by James Baldwin. "It looks as if there's a race on to see who can be the first to hit the screens with a film on the life of Malcolm X," wrote Walker. The FBI acquired a copy of Lomax's script and claimed that his central theme was that US intelligence played a role in Malcolm's assassination. "Los Angeles should be particularly alert that the bureau will be portrayed or mentioned in either movie," wrote J. Edgar Hoover.[4]

Lomax and Baldwin—sometimes allies, sometimes rivals—were much alike, from their positions on integration and their journalistic activism to their yearning for the spotlight. They even described the contours of the Negro revolt in much the same language. (The way Baldwin would describe the Black Power uprising in 1972 was a clear echo of Lomax's characterization of the Negro revolt ten years earlier: "It was inevitable that the fury would erupt, that a black man, openly, in the sight of all his fellows, should challenge the policeman's gun," thus "articulating the rage and repudiating the humiliation of thousands, more, millions of men.") Now, both were attempting to craft a screenplay from the life of their friend. "The idea of Hollywood doing a truthful job on Malcolm could not but seem preposterous," wrote Baldwin. "And yet—I didn't want to spend the rest of my life thinking: *It could have been done if you hadn't been chicken.*"[5]

Despite the possibility of a rival film, Fox was confident that "the only thing that would persuade us not to go ahead would be our inability to come up with a good script." Neither Fox nor Columbia expressed concern about the other's project, but privately the fight was on. In early March 1968, an arbitration committee empaneled by the title bureau of the Motion Picture Association of America gave Columbia the right to use the title "The Autobiography of Malcolm X," even though Fox had previously registered the name "Malcolm X." The bureau had no official legal authority, but it was industry custom to follow its mandates. There are a couple of possible explanations for the ruling. First, *The Autobiography of Malcolm X* was an already existing work, the adaptation of a book published three years earlier. Second, Marvin Worth, producer of Columbia's "Autobiography," submitted his treatment to Fox before sending it to Columbia, and Fox may have registered the first title before passing on the original treatment in favor of their own. Meanwhile, Malcolm's widow, Betty Shabazz, was cooperating with Baldwin on his Columbia script and had given the company exclusive rights to portray her in the film. Lomax had been there to promote Malcolm at every turn, but when in doubt, the family preferred the filmed version of Malcolm's autobiography. By mid-April, the Lomax project had died, the *Sentinel*'s Bill Lane reporting that "Lomax faded out with his Malcolm X thing."[6]

Baldwin's project ultimately died as well, leading historian Karl Evanzz to speculate that it was Hoover's FBI that killed them both. The bureau used informants to follow the progress of the films and determined that both presented the FBI in a bad light. No documents exist to prove that Hoover used his influence to end the projects, but, as Evanzz points out, "it is enough to note that two films with tremendous box office potential, given the enormous interest in Malcolm X in 1969, were never produced." Gil Noble's documentary on Malcolm, for example, was a popular feature around the nation in 1970.[7]

Undeterred, Lomax soldiered on. Though Lomax had castigated college boycotts in the *Christian Science Monitor*, when San José State sociologist Harry Edwards held his December 1967 news conference announcing his boycott of the 1968 Mexico City Olympics, Lomax was next to him. Indeed, he had arranged the event. Edwards's Olympic Project for Human Rights argued that Muhammad Ali's heavyweight championship—stripped for his refusal to participate in the Vietnam conflict—should be reinstated, that apartheid states South Africa and Rhodesia should be barred from the games, that Black coaches should be added to the American team, and that the New York Athletic Club should be desegregated. Lomax had worked with Edwards in November to craft the boycott's demands. As historian Amy Bass has explained, "Lomax counseled Edwards on how to cultivate a black image." He told Edwards to abandon his suit and tie so that he would not be seen as "another middle-class Negro with something to say about civil rights," and the two were able to present a united front at the press conference. "Thanks to Lomax," said Edwards, "slowly and quite deliberately I broke down to pseudo-revolutionary rags and began to develop that separate identity Lomax thought to be necessary in gaining critical access to and the attention of the media." As he had with Malcolm, Lomax publicly debated Edwards twice on the San José State campus, playing the foil and taking the more conservative position, but he remained a close ally.[8]

At the conclusion of the news conference, Lomax and Edwards left for New York to meet with Martin Luther King and CORE's Floyd McKissick. The two leaders "have had a great deal of experience with many types of programs aimed at getting freedom," Edwards said. "It will be foolhardy for me not to use this expertise." King and McKissick endorsed the boycott, Lomax claiming approvingly that it would cripple the US effort in Mexico City. The group demanded the resignation of International Olympic Committee president Avery Brundage, "a devout anti-Semitic and anti-Negro personality." McKissick added that an Olympic athlete "is on the field only two or three hours, then becomes a black man again and is subject to discrimination." Lomax, echoing his colleagues, argued that the stripping of Muhammad Ali's boxing championship "was a total castration of the black people in this country" and claimed to have a "long list" of Black athletes who had agreed to boycott.[9]

Edwards's contact with King had been facilitated by Lomax, and his position on the ideological fence allowed him to vacillate between the worlds of integrationism and Black Power. Theories that emphasized full Black autonomy as a goal were necessarily incongruous with integrationist thinking, but the ideological spectrum between those two poles allowed for real cooperation. Both groups, for example, sought racial justice, and both had used economic boycotts in search of it. Lomax's generic integrationist thinking and his close relationship with the Black Left allowed him to bridge some of the philosophical gaps between the two groups and unite them on issues such as the Olympic boycott. Everyone agreed, for example, on Brundage's racism, on the unfairness of Ali's punishment, and on the state of white racial hegemony in a Cold War country presenting itself as the land of the free. Lomax's advocacy, then, became the tie that bound. A skeptical A. S. "Doc" Young, *Chicago Defender* sports columnist, wondered about Lomax's role in the endeavor, asking, "Isn't the publicity angle, including controversy, the big attraction for Louis Lomax?" He argued that if Edwards, McKissick, King, and Lomax had success with "this crudity" of a boycott, "then they not only will have set back the cause of integrated sports, they also will have committed a serious crime against their race and their country."[10]

Lomax also brought Edwards onto his television show to promote the boycott. When asked by other journalists about his relationship with

King, Edwards told reporters that he was in contact with the SCLC leader through Lomax. In February 1968, two months before King's assassination, Lomax joined Edwards and King at a press conference concerning the boycott of the New York Athletic Club, part of the broader Olympic boycott movement. The club was known to make Black boxers enter through the rear of the building to compete. Lomax, Edwards, and King stayed together after the conference, planning strategy until five in the morning. After cleaning up, they finally parted, Edwards and Lomax to other meetings and King to Memphis to begin helping local garbage workers.[11]

Early March 1968 provided another turning point in Lomax's ever-revolving life. On the first day of the month, he announced that he would co-chair, with former California governor Pat Brown, a national organization to help implement the recommendations of the Kerner Report. Issued by the National Advisory Commission on Civil Disorders, the report blamed "white racism" for the Black uprisings in metropolitan areas and worried that the nation was developing two separate societies. It recommended an initiative to create two million jobs and a dramatically increased public housing program. Though less contentious than the proposed Olympic boycott, the report was still controversial. The Johnson administration, worried about public reaction to it, appointed the citizens' group with Lomax and Brown as cochairs. "We're not going to let this report become just another report," assured Lomax. He planned to call a meeting in May to discuss the Kerner Commission's findings.[12]

Two days after the announcement, on 3 March, Lomax got married again, this time to his administrative assistant, Robinette Kirk. The wedding raised eyebrows, not only because it resulted from "a courtship of more than a year," which clearly demonstrated his infidelity to Wanda, but also because Kirk was white. Married at Lomax's home in Beverly Hills, the two honeymooned in Europe and Israel as part of a planned documentary project for Metromedia, ownership group of KTTV.[13]

Two days after the wedding, on 5 March, Lomax taped the last episode of his talk show. Both the station and the host put on a brave face about the cancellation. "The audience is not holding up," explained KTTV's program director, Jim Gates. "The show has been on 3 ½ years and it has been very successful, and we're proud of it." Lomax would continue working with Metromedia to produce documentaries and other special projects. "We proved that a black man could conduct a show and it would not necessarily be a black show," said a circumspect Lomax. "I think we proved a man can be liberal without being crazy. I can honestly say now that some of my best friends are Birchers." He professed to be "happy to get off the weekly grind. It doesn't permit you to move around. You can't do anything." Besides, he would still do work for Metromedia, and he predicted that his "income will not be substantially affected."[14]

Income was always paramount for Lomax, but so too was time to do other things. That same night, 5 March, Lomax made his acting debut with a brief cameo as a police lieutenant on the pilot episode of the drama *My Friend Tony*, shown during NBC's *The Danny Thomas Hour*. The episode was a critical flop, but the *Pittsburgh Courier's* Hazel Garland was complimentary of Lomax. "The part was small," she wrote, "but Lomax had one good scene and made the most of it." (*My Friend Tony* managed a one-season run on NBC, but without Lomax.) In late May, Lomax made his big-screen debut with a small role in *Wild in the Streets*, which was produced by American International Pictures, best known for beach-party and werewolf movies.[15]

Meanwhile, King had gone to Memphis at the request of his friend James Lawson, who had taken control of a sanitation strike in the city. The efforts of the garbage workers, "almost all of whom are Negroes," reported Lomax, eventually "involved the entire black community and the issues fissioned to include the problems of the black ghetto as a whole." King had lost much of his influence in Washington because of his opposition to the Vietnam War, and he had lost much of his influence within the rights movement because of his continued insistence on nonviolence in the face of the Black Power movement's willingness to countenance armed self-defense. "Nonviolence is on trial in Memphis," King said, and though his disagreements with those who believed the days of nonviolence had passed led him to leave Tennessee, he would return in early April. "The Martin Luther King I grew up with and loved and marched with," wrote Lomax, "had no moral alternative but to return to Memphis and prove his point." It was in Memphis, while waiting for a car to take him to dinner, that he was killed, causing a massive upheaval among the Black population, leading to uprisings in more than one hundred American cities, and ushering in a new phase of Lomax's Negro revolt.[16]

Though the Black Left had always been active, King's assassination exposed African American radicalism before a mainstream white audience in an immediate way. Following the assassination, the *Boston Globe Magazine* devoted an issue to "white racism vs. Black Power" and featured an article by Lomax that evaluated the dilemma of the Black middle class, torn between wanting a better life for themselves and suffering the criticism of the militant Black Left. "While White America weighs the fine points of the Federal riot report, Black America is busy stockpiling weapons. Not merely bullets and rifles. But bazookas, machine guns and grenades. The ghettoes of virtually every major city," Lomax argued, "are being prepared for war by black militants." He quoted his new friend Harry Edwards, who discussed the immediacy of "black liberation." Lomax explained that "the architects of the current black revolution are disillusioned graduates of the nonviolent era; they are men driven to the brink of madness because their dream did not fully come true." A vicious cycle ensued, he said: "While a few gifted and trained Negroes have been ushered into the American mainstream as a result of the nonviolent civil rights struggle, literally hundreds of thousands of uneducated and poorly trained Negroes have been migrating from the Deep South to the northern and western metropolitan areas. These people, on the whole, are unemployable." Those left behind by the movement "live, and fully expect to die, on a dead-end street; their children are born on the edge of an abyss and there is nowhere to go from there but down, deep down to bottomless despair and anguish." He was describing a nonviolent civil rights movement of the 1950s and early 1960s that had served only to benefit a small Black middle class, leaving the rest of the population to fend for itself. His analysis was not new: it was, in fact, an elaboration of his 1962 argument in *The Negro Revolt*, writ large with the benefit of hindsight. But in this form, it was relatively new to the mainstream, and the emphasis Lomax placed on the immediacy of the problem was intended to provoke.[17]

He elaborated on the theme in a speech to the Progressive Californians organization in May, arguing that racial unity would allow the country to work on its crippling problem of poverty. "Those of us in the great middle class society think we have made it and the problems of the poor do not effect [*sic*] us," he told the crowd. He juxtaposed American spending in Vietnam with aid for the poor, claiming, "If the federal government would spend 15 billion dollars it would provide for every American a job."[18]

Lomax delivered the speech during the heart of the Poor People's Campaign, the summer 1968 effort led by the SCLC to call attention to the plight of the nation's indigent, which continued the work of its fallen founder. The effort included, among other things, a march on the capital, where a makeshift ramshackle neighborhood called Resurrection City had grown along the reflecting pool between the Lincoln Memorial and the Washington Monument. Lomax flew to Washington and, in denim shirt and khaki pants, led a group of the poor to a House Education and Labor Committee hearing on malnutrition. He then did an interview on television challenging South Carolina congressman Albert Watson to prove his claims that the Poor People's Campaign had been infiltrated by Communists.[19]

In early June, during an appearance on *ABC Evening News with Frank Reynolds*, Lomax charged that poor people were "caught in a vise forged by a reluctant and conservative Congress." He promised that "the leaders of the Poor People's march on Washington are now escalating their demand that something be done about hunger and poverty in this nation. It is a demand that cannot be refused." At the same time, Lomax was critical of Resurrection City, describing it as "a city of chaos" that was "completely unsafe, a jungle at night." While in the makeshift neighborhood, Lomax witnessed so-called leadership turn away a group of middle-class women who had brought donations of food and clothing to support the group. It was a "city falling apart, dangerously so."[20]

Lomax was right about Resurrection City: it was, to be sure, a city of chaos. But his criticism, coupled with his support of the Poor People's Campaign, demonstrates how far he had come ideologically since his first meeting with Malcolm and the NOI in the late 1950s. His thought underwent a philosophical bell curve, beginning at a position critical of Black nationalist thought, then moving much closer to that line as he was dragged into the gravitational pull of Malcolm's personality and the theoretical soundness of anti-integrationist rhetoric, before moving back toward his original position after Malcolm's assassination without completely abandoning the learned radicalism of his time in the NOI's orbit. And it came as he was grieving his childhood acquaintance and longtime friend Martin Luther King. He was, in fact, doing his best to continue King's work.

In June 1968, Eugene McCarthy ran a series of radio advertisements targeting Black voters before the California Democratic primary, in which his opponent was Robert Kennedy. One featured an excerpt from a King speech made earlier that year. Another featured King's grieving friend Lomax: "Hello, this is Louis Lomax. Last Saturday night on a nationally televised debate, Senator Kennedy of New York and a presidential aspirant suggested that Negroes should remain in the ghetto until they have been properly educated and job oriented. Senator Eugene McCarthy of Minnesota, also an aspirant for the presidency, said that we should break up the ghetto now, that this would be apartheid if we didn't. Kennedy says we should remain there another twenty to thirty years. I don't plan to stay there that long. That's why I'm going to vote for Eugene McCarthy."[21]

Lomax also appeared with McCarthy at his Watts district headquarters the night after race had been injected into the campaign. McCarthy, who had made several proposals to help impoverished Black California residents escape "the oppressive conditions of the ghetto and find better lives outside the inner city," was challenged in the debate by Kennedy, who asked, "You mean to say you're going to take 10,000 black people and move them into Orange County?" It was a calculated move by Kennedy to court white votes, but it was anathema to many Black residents. "Senator Kennedy may have won some votes in racist Orange County by what he said last night," Lomax explained at McCarthy's Watts offices, "but he lost mine and I suspect thousands of others" (figure 9.1).[22]

In July, prior to the 1968 Democratic National Convention, Lomax publicly called for all "concerned Americans in every American city to hold marches and rallies protesting the control of smoke-filled room politicians over the choice of the Democratic presidential nominee." At the same time, a dissident Black caucus called for a complete repeal of the draft system and guaranteed income for all citizens. Lomax was not part of that group and chose instead to make his call separately, both because he wanted to keep the spotlight on himself and because McCarthy, his candidate, did not support such radical steps.[23]

But Lomax also inserted himself into the Republican campaign. In early August, he joined James Farmer, the former leader of CORE and a Republican candidate for Congress from New York, at a "sparsely-attended press conference" at Convention Hall in Miami, the site of the Republican National Convention. Calling themselves the Citizens for Black America, the two read a prepared statement declaring that neither Richard Nixon nor Ronald Reagan was an acceptable candidate and that Black voters were "tired of choosing between the lesser of two evils." Lomax was a Democrat, but both he and Farmer claimed to represent an independent group of concerned Black citizens. "We urge that both political parties nominate candidates whom black Americans can support," read the statement, which was signed by two hundred prominent African Americans. "Our dreams since slavery indeed would come true if we could choose between Democrat and Republican presidential candidates equally pledged to racial justice." Farmer and Lomax gave their Republican support to Nelson Rockefeller, at the press conference and in an advertisement in the *Miami News*.[24]

FIGURE 9.1 — Lomax stumping for Eugene McCarthy's 1968 presidential campaign. COURTESY SPECIAL COLLECTIONS AND UNIVERSITY ARCHIVES OF THE UNIVERSITY OF NEVADA, RENO. ITEM 82-30-8-4-3-1.

William F. Buckley was incensed over the advertisement, which he saw as ignorant and racist, and he castigated his old foe, Lomax, for heading the committee. "One of the signers was Jackie Robinson," he wrote, "whose favorite sport, now that he has retired from baseball, is imputing racism to anyone he disagrees with. How it probably went was that Robinson called Lomax, in order to give the ad a West Coast feel, so as to keep it from sounding too obviously like a New York Rockefeller operation." That was obviously untrue and typical of Buckley, but it was the white conservative's bumbling attempt to throw an (unneeded) lifeline to his friend and rival.[25]

At the same time Lomax and Farmer were making their statement, SCLC leader Ralph Abernathy announced that the Poor People's Campaign would "enter the political arena" and conduct demonstrations at the 1968 Republican National Convention.[26] As Richard Nixon took the party's nomination, defeating Lomax's preferred Rockefeller, and preached the coded racial gospel of "law and order" to a largely white convention hall, Black residents in nearby Liberty City, a neighborhood with none of the splendor or money of Miami Beach, launched an uprising to protest local and national racial and economic inequalities. Three were killed and dozens injured in violence that would largely be overshadowed by the larger protests at the Democratic National Convention later that summer in Chicago. In another chilling example of "law and order," Chicago police descended on protesters, and the resulting melee led to more than five hundred casualties and a national spectacle that drew attention away from the convention itself. Amid confusion in the Democratic Party after Lyndon Johnson removed himself from the race in March, Nixon would parlay American fear and anger over the violence to carry his so-called law-and-order candidacy to victory.[27]

During the election itself, Lomax was on his honeymoon, but when he returned he went right back to work. During a speech at North Carolina A&T, he decried white religious imagery, the country's economic priorities, charges of Communism in the civil rights movement, and public calls for law and order. "Could the words 'law and order' be another middle class way of saying 'nigger'?" he asked. "Nobody said a word about law and order when we were having all those lynchings."[28] As if to drive home the point, in early January 1969, Lomax and his new wife, Robinette, joined a picket line at the Rose Bowl organized by a group calling themselves Pasadenans for Law and Order. The protesters announced that they had no intention of embarrassing the Black players of USC or Ohio State, the two teams playing in the 1969 Rose Bowl, but they believed the move was necessary to draw attention to the city's segregation in schools and discrimination in housing and employment. The Justice Department had filed suit against the city's discriminatory school practices in late November, but more needed to be done, and a national audience had to know about Pasadena's shame. The group carried American flags upside down to signal their distress to the country.[29]

With a new wife and an inherited family, and with his television program canceled, the ever-evolving Lomax began thinking about a new phase in his career. Back in November 1968, just prior to his honeymoon, he made his first appearance at Hofstra University, where he presented a lecture titled "The Negro in American History and Culture" as part of a broader national speaking tour. In the speech, he predicted dire consequences from a Nixon administration, even speculating on the use of concentration camps to hold civil rights leaders.[30]

Despite the exaggerations, the university was impressed. On 25 March 1969, Hofstra officially offered Lomax an appointment as visiting professor of humanities and social sciences for the 1969–1970 school year (figure 9.2). The university president assured him that Hofstra renewed such appointments on a yearly basis and that it "anticipate[d] your continuing association with Hofstra University for the period that you will be writing your three volume studies in Afro-American History," a proposed comprehensive account that would also be funded by a fifteen-thousand-dollar Esso Foundation grant.[31]

The appointment would provide Lomax the opportunity to put his theories into practice. At a speech at the University of Michigan, he spoke about the relationship between cloistered institutions of higher education and the Black population that existed outside of them. "The university urgently needs to reorder its priorities in the way it views its own mission," he told his audience. The academy had "allowed itself to become part of the power arm of the establishment and must bear much of the blame for the perpetuation of the myth of black inferiority." It was this deficiency that made Black studies and contributions from Black faculty so important. Hofstra would give Lomax a chance to bridge the racial divide between town and gown.[32]

So Louis and Robinette packed up and left Los Angeles for New York. He had landed his first full-time teaching position, even though he had never graduated from college and had fabricated a previous teaching job at Georgia State College in Savannah. "We consider him one of the top

FIGURE 9.2 —
Lomax in the
last year of his
life serving on
the faculty at
Hofstra University.
COURTESY SPECIAL
COLLECTIONS
AND UNIVERSITY
ARCHIVES OF THE
UNIVERSITY OF
NEVADA, RENO.
ITEM 82-30-7-3-1.

writers and academicians in the country today," said university president Clifford Lord. "We are proud to have him as a member of our faculty."[33]

It was not a smooth transition. In June, Lomax was arrested on a charge of drunk driving when police observed his car weaving across the Long Island Expressway in Roslyn Heights. He pleaded guilty and accepted a fifty-dollar fine and a sixty-day license suspension. The *Sentinel*'s Bill Lane reported that it was "the second time he and the highway had not seen things straight—nor the court," implying that Lomax had previously been charged with driving while impaired.[34]

Legal troubles, however, had never stopped him from displaying a strong public personality, and it would not do so on Long Island. At his first major college meeting, in December 1969, Lomax brought several recommendations to the Hofstra College of Liberal Arts and Sciences. He proposed a resolution that the college "express its shock and condemnation" at the violence in Vietnam, particularly the My Lai massacre, which had been made public the previous month. He also called for "a convocation of no less than one day's duration to examine the causes and nature of violence in the American personality" and suggested that a committee to be formed to set it up and to invite faculty from other colleges.[35]

While at Hofstra he continued his rigorous speaking schedule. In February 1970, in a speech titled "The Triple Revolution: Race, Space, and Nation," which was part of Fullerton Junior College's Artists Lecture Series, he described the success of the Detroit riots in forcing industry to respond with available jobs. "We could have been following Martin Luther King a dozen years around Detroit singing 'We Shall Overcome' and we never would have gotten those jobs," he argued. Though he was trying to carve out a third way, Lomax instead gave a mixed message, as he seemed to reject violence except for those times when he was rejecting nonviolence. When asked about busing, Lomax argued that segregated schools were a symptom of the disease of segregated housing but that busing was a legitimate start to correcting real problems. "One of the best things that happened to me was when my daddy bused me from Georgia to Yale," he said. Again, though he was trying to find middle ground, he ended in contradiction, as fixing symptoms only masked the root causes of racial problems. Such third-way efforts were staples of Lomax's rhetoric.[36]

In November 1969, for example, thirty-five Black students at Vassar occupied administration offices for three days. Lomax counseled college officials not to give in to Black students using extreme tactics: "You must have the guts to stand up and tell a black student no when he is wrong." He argued that universities often capitulated to Black student demands, even when they were wrong, because they were worried that not doing so would lead to a riot. The same was true with the creation of Black studies programs, he believed: "Too many times black studies programs are started at college as therapy instead of academics." Several months earlier, however, he wrote in a letter to the editor of the *New York Times*, "My faith is in today's rebellious youth. Despite their frequent tactical mistakes they are completely right about the urgent changes that are needed in American society—particularly on campus."[37]

Back on his own campus, in April 1970, Lomax made his most important contribution to Black history and literature when he discovered a document in the Long Island Historical Society Library that proved that Jupiter Hammon, the country's first Black poet, was born a Long Island slave on 17 October 1711, the property of a planter named Henry Lloyd. Hammon's poetry first appeared in print in 1761, and over the next twenty years he used his prominence to argue for the abolition of slavery. He identified himself as a slave of the Lloyd family, but scholars had been unable to find his birthdate. Lomax believed he could solve the mystery, and with the academic freedom and encouragement of a university, he began months of research in late 1969 and early 1970, aided by graduate student Lillian Koppel, in the thorny field of slave genealogy.[38] Lomax finally made his discovery at three in the morning and immediately called his friend Leroy Ramsey, a history professor at Hofstra. "Hey, Baby, wake up! It's me, Louis," he said. "Baby, I've got that thing on Jupiter. Old Jupiter was born on October 17, 1711 on the estate of Henry Lloyd of Lloyd Neck, right here on Long Island. Here it is, man, in Henry Lloyd's own big, fat handwriting."[39]

Lomax and Ramsey were working with the support of the Nassau County government to create the Black History Museum of Long Island. Their work on the early history of Long Island turned up evidence that a Black man was one of the twenty-three founders of Brooklyn, that Long Island slave owners practiced an inordinate amount of cruelty, and that Hammon was the first published Black author in colonial America, his first work composed in December 1760 and published the following year, predating that of Phillis Wheatley by seven years. (Lucy Terry Prince composed her ballad before either of these writers, but her work was not published until the nineteenth century.) Lomax would not live to see the museum's opening in September.[40]

In his "Address to the Negroes of the State of New York," Hammon said, "Yes, my dear brethren, when I think of you which very often I do, and the poor despised miserable state you are in, when I think of your ignorance and stupidity and great wickedness of the most of you, I am pained to the heart." Nearly two hundred years later, Lomax would deliver a similar message, combining legitimate concern and activism with castigation and condescension.[41]

The Hofstra that Lomax entered was, like so many campuses in 1969, seething with unrest. In May, just two months after Lomax was hired, a racist pamphlet was sent to faculty. A group of ten Black students responded by marching into the cafeteria, reading the incendiary document from the balcony, and approaching a table of white athletes. They asked one of the athletes if he was the source of the pamphlet and then, before he was able to answer, attacked him. A battle broke out in the cafeteria between white and Black students that lasted only ten minutes, but still injured several people, shattered windows, and required campus security and Nassau police to calm the tensions.[42]

In October 1969, the Organization of Black Collegians on campus accused the university president of mismanaging a program designed to increase minority recruitment.[43] The following April, students occupied the administration building to call for a stronger voice in university affairs and the removal of the school's training center for the Internal Revenue Service. (They argued that supporting a government program was tantamount to endorsing the war in Vietnam.) When threatened with a New York Supreme Court injunction, the students backed down.[44]

But they were not done. In May 1970, Hofstra president Clifford Lord sent memoranda to faculty and students lamenting American bombing in Cambodia and the violence at Kent State. Unplacated, students joined their peers from around the country in the National Strike against the Vietnam War, which protested "the present Administration's annihilation of diverse political opinions in Indochina and in the United States," among other Vietnam-related concerns. The school's Organization of Black Collegians issued a statement for the event, which read, "We the student community of Hofstra, are committed to the indefinite suspension of classes. The slaughter of our brothers and sisters in Indochina, in America's ghettos, and on campus has awakened us to the sickness and depravity which is pervasive in this society. We cannot, in good conscience, continue with 'business as usual.'" They demanded the release from jail of Black Panther Bobby Seale and the Panther 21, a group of activists accused in 1969 of planning a coordinated bombing and long-range rifle attack of two New York City police stations. The day-long strike featured speeches, seminars, "Guerilla Theater," and a concert. Lomax and other faculty enthusiastically supported the students and their causes in the protest.[45]

"We the college students of the nation," read one National Strike flyer on campus, "have been falsely accused of not supporting our fighting men in Southeast Asia. WE ARE SUPPORTING THEM!!! . . . WE WANT THEM HOME AS SOON AND AS SAFE AS POSSIBLE." Hofstra students coordinated with other institutions in the region, including Brooklyn College, Stony Brook, Rutgers, and Adelphi. They were, to some extent, successful. A group of ninety-five English majors, for example, pressed for the elimination of senior comprehensive examinations, calling them "irrelevant anachronisms." The English faculty, including Lomax, met and agreed to make the exams optional. Department chair Allan R. Davis announced the decision to a group of cheering students. "I hope I'm your friend again now," he told them.[46]

Lomax advised the students, who saw in the new professor someone who had rubbed elbows with all of the most significant protesters of the last decade. He stayed away from the public demonstrations themselves, leaving that effort to the students, but he openly supported their efforts and told them stories of his own experiences when asked. In February, he spoke at an open hearing on university governance, arguing that the traditional grading system of As, Bs, Cs, Ds, and Fs was outdated and "a terrible responsibility for a teacher." With a typical Lomax flourish, he claimed, "Hofstra should not crucify itself on the cross of academic antiquity."[47]

Classes resumed on 11 May, and with them Lomax's responsibility for grading, but the unrest was not over. In a letter to President Lord, the Organization of Black Collegians charged that he had "perpetuated the rumor that the Black students at Hofstra had conspired to disrupt the academic processes of this University" in "an attempt to establish Black people as scapegoats." The president, the group said, demonstrated "a subtle racism by appointing a Black man to the position of Assistant to the President when it was possible to do so; and after he was used to placate certain elements on and off the campus he was dismissed." The organization further accused Lord of conspiring to "prevent the incorporation of the sentiments of Black people in the upper echelons of the University Administration" in creating a committee to make an administrative appointment "although this has never been the procedure in the past." They claimed that the move represented an abdication of responsibility in hiring, so that the president would not be blamed when the committee hired yet another white administrator. Indeed, the two Black faculty on the committee, recognizing this strategy, resigned in protest.[48]

The rift illustrated the racial tension underlying the seeming unity on campus, tension that had clearly existed since the school's cafeteria incident in May 1969, soon after Lomax's hiring. Lomax was not on the committee and so could not resign, but he helped the students coordinate at every turn, giving them advice and defending them to faculty and administrators. He had been part of so many influential and important events, from his early time with Malcolm X to the publication of his books, from "The Ballot or the Bullet" to Mississippi Freedom Summer and the 1968 Olympic boycott. The list was seemingly endless, and it made him a lodestar for the frustrated student body of Hofstra.

10 Conspiracies

In August 1967, Lomax published a series of articles in Pasadena's *Independent Star News* alleging conspiracy in the Detroit riots. He argued that a Black Power group directed the riot, even organizing snipers. Operation Detroit began when a group of Black activists posing as magazine salesmen took up stations around the city, fomenting unrest by asking such questions as "Why the hell do we let Whitey, particularly the Jews, run the stores in our neighborhood?" After providing such inflammation, they knew that an arrest or some other incident could set off a riot. The charge was scandalous and reported without documentary evidence, worrying many, including the FBI, about what exactly Lomax was attempting to do. The allegations, which seemed to come out of nowhere, would be just the first of Lomax's many conspiracy theories.[1]

Lomax's suspicious nature had been born in the Jim Crow climate of southwest Georgia. It was fired in his own schemes after he left home, as he prevaricated in times of trouble during college, lied about his graduation from college altogether, and ran confidence scams in Chicago to make ends meet for his young family—activities that were fostered, at least in part, by the cloister of a different kind of segregation in the urban north. As a reporter, he had been on the front lines of some of the nation's greatest racial calamities of the twentieth century, witnessing firsthand the betrayal by the government of its own people. As a television host, he had interviewed dozens of representatives of fringe groups with their own increasingly bizarre tales of conspiracy. He had experienced the assassinations of friends and allies. In a system created to maintain power for those who already possessed it, and one that had constantly demonstrated that power to Lomax through his personal experience of Jim Crow and his own journalism, conspiracy theories were all but inevitable.

For example, in 1968, while serving as a reporter for the North American Newspaper Alliance, Lomax launched his own independent investigation of King's assassination, which was prominent enough for reporters to ask New Orleans district attorney Jim Garrison if he was following it. Garrison declined to comment.[2]

According to Percy Foreman, James Earl Ray's attorney, Lomax "checked out the phone calls at every filling station from Los Angeles to New Orleans" and provided the defense with two phone numbers that Ray used to coordinate meetings with a man who was traveling with him across the country. The information did not bear directly on the case, but it demonstrated Lomax's obsession.[3]

In the weeks immediately following the assassination, Lomax contacted Charles Stein Jr., who had joined Ray on a trip to New Orleans in December 1967. He told Stein that he believed him to be the "key" to solving the King assassination and promised, in exchange for his cooperation, that he would split any reward money they might earn. Stein was reluctant but agreed to help.[4]

In a rented white Mustang, Lomax and Stein drove from New Orleans to Houston to re-create part of the original trip and find a telephone booth that Ray had used. They arrived in Houston on 25 April, three weeks after King's death. Stein claimed that on the original journey, Ray had made at least six calls at pay telephones at various filling stations off Interstate 10. On 26 April, they arrived in San Antonio, where they rented a car and continued the search, ultimately locating a telephone at an Enco gas station on Route 90 in Uvalde, Texas, that they claimed Ray had used to call New Orleans on 16 December 1967. That effort led the FBI and local authorities to subpoena telephone records and track down phone numbers and motel registrations, which turned up no reference to Ray either by name or alias.[5]

After spending time with Stein, Lomax began claiming that Ray had received a payment from a wealthy New Orleans industrialist whom he had met at least twice near the International Trade Mart. Such broad claims led the FBI to extensively monitor Lomax's investigation, even interviewing Stein (who refused to give them information) and Stein's family, along with confidential sources in Los Angeles. It found, unsurprisingly, that

Lomax's criticism of the bureau's investigation was baseless and that he had "repeatedly proven his antagonism toward the FBI." It charged that Lomax's King conspiracy journalism was simply "a vehicle to get back in 'big time' television." (Interestingly, Stein's testimony and Lomax's investigative reports never mentioned Raoul, the mysterious mover Ray claimed had directed much of his activity, even though both Stein and Lomax maintained they had located several Ray associates whom they refused to name to authorities.)[6]

Lomax alleged in print that the FBI was hiding the fact that it held telephone records for the telephone booths at the Saint Francis Hotel on Hollywood Boulevard in Los Angeles, where he believed Ray to have stayed early in 1968. In a North American Newspaper Alliance press release in late April, he claimed that a phone booth in the hotel's lobby had the phrase "down with Mexicans, niggers and MARTIN LUTHER COON," a derogatory name for King that others contended Ray had used.[7]

Lomax had also been in contact with Edgar John Pendleton, a former resident of the Saint Francis; Marie Martin, a cocktail waitress at the hotel's Sultan Room; and Dyrell Dennis, with whom he discussed a former resident named Ray Selma, whom he presumed to be Ray, living under a pseudonym. Martin said that she had befriended James Earl Ray, even exchanging television sets with him. Ray had told her he was waiting for money from his brother in order to make another trip to New Orleans, where he would visit friends and collect the children of a woman named Rita Stein. Martin gave Ray a package of record albums and clothes to deliver to her daughter in New Orleans. Lomax paid her fifty dollars for her information.[8]

Meanwhile, the FBI noted that a woman whom Lomax identified as Jerri, a "mysterious blond," did not, as Lomax claimed, have a relationship with Ray. "Jerri" was Lomax's pseudonym for Dyrell Dennis, and the FBI said her contact with Ray "appears to have been limited to a single meeting in a bar followed by a brief visit to his room." Pendleton had a letter from Dennis asking, "Have you seen Ray? I hope he is OK." But that letter referred to Selma, who was, in fact, a Mexican American man completely independent of James Earl Ray.[9]

Lomax first reported his findings in a nationally syndicated piece published throughout the country. Jerry O'Leary, a Washington reporter who did investigative reporting on the King assassination for *Reader's Digest*, lamented that "the true facts" relating to the case, according to one FBI memo, were being skewed "out of focus by the distorted articles written by such irresponsible characters as Louis Lomax." One worried citizen sent the article to J. Edgar Hoover with the question, "Who is Louis Lomax? A Commie?"[10]

One reason for the FBI's pique was that Ray had spent time in Joliet prison in 1952 while Lomax was serving his larceny sentence. Ray worked in the diagnostic clinic and Lomax in the vocational school, however, and there was no specific evidence that the two had any meaningful contact.[11]

Regardless, the FBI saw Lomax's King assassination piece as "a vicious and unwarranted attack against the Bureau" which was "replete with mis-statements of fact and ridiculous conclusions." A lengthy FBI memo examined the article in depth and outlined each of the offending charges. Lomax argued that Hoover's dislike for King was so pronounced that few Black Americans believed the bureau was doing its best to find his assassin; that its failures in the investigation were intentional; that the wrong fingerprints for Ray were circulated the day after the shooting, preventing a potential early arrest in Atlanta; that the FBI had taken the case from local police in Memphis, keeping them from pursuing their own leads; that it had not even sought the cooperation of the Los Angeles police; that it had confiscated phone records from Los Angeles telephone booths known to be used by Ray and refused to release them; that it leaked a story suggesting a Negro was behind the murder; that powerful men were instead to blame for the killing; and that because of the bias of the FBI and Hoover, some federal responsibility should be shared with a Warren Commission–style investigation. The FBI found such charges ridiculous. The memo stated that the "total facilities" of the bureau were "fully committed to this case from the outset" and that its "record in this case is one of substantial achievement." The FBI issued only one set of Ray's fingerprints, and they were correct, the memo continued. The bureau worked closely with the Memphis police and checked the records of the Los Angeles police, never confiscated any telephone records, and had "long enjoyed the confidence of responsible Negro leaders and the responsible Negro press." The false-hoods by Lomax required vigilance, claimed the organization that built much of its civil rights investigations on its own set of falsehoods, and "vigorous investigation is continuing on a top priority basis."[12]

That the bureau would favor its own work over that of others and feel threatened by charges of conspiracy was obvious, and the bias it claimed on the part of Lomax was surely reflected in its own work. It was clear, however, that Lomax was treading out onto distant limbs, an effort re-sembling that of Garrison, the New Orleans district attorney, in its wide suppositional range. Such was the product of Lomax's conspiratorial mind combined with the real trauma of King's assassination. King was not only a powerful leader, manning the barricades against the same demons as did Lomax, but the two had known each other since they were children. "Martin and I grew up together although I am seven years his elder," wrote Lomax.[13] They had come from much the same place and were friends. An attack on one civil rights–advocating minister's kid from Georgia would necessarily be traumatic for another.

Later in May, Lomax sent a letter to the FBI's Los Angeles office, claiming that Harvey Sadler, the former sheriff of Macon County, Alabama, and an ally of George Wallace, needed more federal attention. He argued that King's assassination had been planned by "the Wallace forces" in an effort "to provoke Negroes to riot to further Wallace's political ambitions." The bureau dismissed the allegation, as it came with no demonstrable evidence and Sadler had always proven "cooperative and forthright" with the FBI's Mobile office. Although Sadler was an inveterate racist, the Mobile department of the bureau maintained, "At no time was he known to display a hostile attitude toward Negro citizens of that community."[14]

The denouement of Lomax's assassination investigation was the publication of *To Kill a Black Man*, an account of "the shocking parallel in the lives of Malcolm X and Martin Luther King, Jr." The book describes Lomax's close friendship with both leaders and the obvious similarities between the two—their religious backgrounds, their impact on society, their diminishing popularity late in life, and their assassinations by those to whom they reached out most: the separatist killed by Black men, the integrationist by white. He comes to the inevitable conclusion that "the men arrested may have pulled the trigger, but they by no means acted alone; American society was not only in concert with the assassins but there is every evidence that they were hired killers."[15]

It is the conclusion of the race theorist, not the conspiracy theorist, and the book's comparative analysis of King and Malcolm and their impact on society is in no way a work of paranoia. *To Kill a Black Man* is an intellectual biography of the two, with elements of personal memoir that are a part of all of Lomax's books. He tells the story of the rise and influence of both leaders, with particular attention to his own role in their stories. For all his obsessed investigating, talk of conspiracy is limited to the book's final chapter: Malcolm "was assassinated by hired killers" and "the American government, particularly the CIA, was deeply involved." As for King's death, James Earl Ray "carried out the will of an extremely well financed and rigidly organized group of Southern white businessmen." He even makes a nod to Jim Garrison, explaining, "After having spent several weeks investigating the murder of Martin King I know that the evidence will center around New Orleans—the focus of many investigations into the slaying of John F. Kennedy."[16]

Lomax spends much time in the book emphasizing and defending his friend Malcolm's ideology. "Integration for most of us meant nothing more than total equality of education and opportunity," he explains. But for Malcolm and those outside of the South, integration could never be the path to those goals. American racism, particularly in northern urban industrial hubs, "is designed to drive black people insane." In a Kafkaesque existence with no real chance of escape and issues fundamentally different from those talked about in civil rights reports on television, Malcolm's message was more pressing and vital to a great many. He and other Black militants realized that "the black man must manipulate the American machinery—by nonviolence or by violence—and cause it to work in his behalf." Lomax's conspiracy theories aside, his defense of the radical position so soon after King's assassination is a telling demonstration of the lasting impact of Malcolm's thought on his own ideology. "History," after all, Lomax explains in *To Kill a Black Man*, "teaches that freedom belongs to those who have the power to take it."[17]

History also taught that Lomax was, sooner or later, bound for more controversy. In May 1970, he was indicted by a federal grand jury on four counts of income tax evasion. He had failed to file returns for 1964 and 1965 and later signed fraudulent delinquent returns for those years. In 1964, he earned $36,556.81; the following year, $52,624.99. When he finally signed his delinquent return for 1964, however, he claimed only $30,152.33 of his earnings for that year. For 1965, his delinquent return claimed $31,206.32. If convicted, Lomax faced up to a year in prison and a $10,000 fine for the evasion and up to three years and a $5,000 fine for each count of fraud. His arraignment was scheduled for 8 June. For his part, Lomax claimed that he was back and forth between Los Angeles and New York during those years, delaying his returns, but that the IRS must have confused his income totals. He planned to go to Los Angeles in June, and "once I get out there, I hope we will be able to settle this quickly and quietly." It was vintage Lomax, the Brer Rabbit cunning learned from his youth. He did not deny wrongdoing but instead made vague, open-ended excuses. He was not a liar, but his problems with money had followed him through his life, just as had his cunning responses to trouble. At his Los

Angeles arraignment in June, Lomax pleaded not guilty, and his trial was set for 11 August. He was able to get the trial moved to November but did not survive to see it.[18]

Lomax spent the last months of his life tormented by current events. He was trying to write a book but would stop, leave the house, and drive to the Hofstra campus, where, his wife remembered, he would discuss "the bitter taste of the invasion of Cambodia and the Kent State–Jackson State massacres." Lomax's friend Sally Binford, an anthropologist at the University of New Mexico, was a recent acquaintance of Anthony J. Russo, who had helped Daniel Ellsberg of the RAND Corporation copy the Pentagon Papers and encouraged him to leak the documents. "He became totally disenchanted with the Vietnam War and dropped out," Binford said of Lomax. So she introduced him to Russo. The two "just got into it and talked all afternoon, all night long, all the next day, over a bottle of wine," remembered Russo, who then took Lomax to a restaurant in Malibu, where they met with Ellsberg. It was salve for Lomax's conspiratorial mind, particularly after King's assassination. He planned to speak to William Attwood, editor of *Look* magazine, about a potential exposé. "As far as I could see, this was a going relationship," said Russo, and Lomax "was ready to go." Lomax's fatal car crash occurred just days later. Without him as an intermediary between Russo and Attwood, the potential deal with *Look* fell through.[19]

On 31 July 1970, at age forty-seven, Lomax died in a one-car accident on Interstate 40, twenty-six miles east of Santa Rosa, New Mexico. He was in a rented vehicle, necessitated because three days earlier, while headed back to Long Island after a lecture tour, the car that had been left for him at the Los Angeles home of Robinette's parents broke down just beyond Victorville, California. He hitchhiked back to Victorville and had the car towed. The mechanic's diagnosis the next morning was not good, so he went to a local Avis and rented the only car available, a Ford station wagon. He made it through Arizona and into New Mexico, but on a lonely highway outside Santa Rosa, his car skidded and overturned three times before landing on the right shoulder of the road. He was ejected from the car and died at the scene. His body was taken to a Santa Rosa funeral home but was not identified until the mortician found his Hofstra ring.[20]

The police report claimed that Lomax was attempting to pass a car at high speed when he lost control. The car flipped three times. Lomax was thrown 127 feet and died at the scene at seven in the evening. At nine, the coroner held his official inquest, and twenty-six hours later, Harold Miller, vice president of university relations at Hofstra, knocked on the Lomaxes' door to tell his wife that her husband was dead.

Robinette believed that the official account of Lomax's death "made no sense whatsoever. Why did it take twenty-six hours to notify the widow? Why did the police report indicate he was speeding beyond the posted limit when, in fact, he never drove fast? Why was I told he had been carrying no identification when he did have all kinds of identification, including his press card and his Hofstra University faculty identification card, both of which would have easily led to further information?"

She was not the only one with questions or conspiracy theories. The *Sentinel*'s Bill Lane claimed that Lomax was "readying an expose piece about the gvt. . . . the same gvt. trying to prosecute him for income tax things." Tucumcari, New Mexico, near the site of Lomax's crash, was notorious. One traveler remembered that the area had "a 24-hour justice of the peace to try people on anything they could find to make money." He also noted, "It is rumored that black writer Louis Lomax's car brakes were sabotaged there." One account of the Lomax car crash had him stopping at a racist bar, where he argued with the clientele and was ultimately ambushed down the road.[21]

It seemed suspicious that the coroner's inquest in Santa Rosa had come a mere two hours after Lomax's death and that the presiding officer at that inquest, Santa Rosa magistrate Bobby Serrano, had since been suspended. Prompted by those doubts—and by the delay in contacting his wife, despite the presence of a license that clearly provided officials with his personal information—Robinette and her attorney, F. Victor Palermo, launched a months-long secret investigation into the death.[22]

In pursuit of answers, Robinette even contacted Peter Hurkos, a well-known Los Angeles psychic who had been featured on Lomax's television program and was a friend of the family. "I surprised myself by calling him," she remembered. "It was as if Louis were pushing me to call his old friend." Hurkos, who had been consulted by Los Angeles police during their investigation of actress Sharon Tate's murder, claimed to have been waiting for Robinette's call. "Louis did not die the way it was said he died," he told her. She was willing to fly back to Los Angeles to see him for answers, but he offered to fly to New York instead and meet her in Syracuse. He instructed her, "Bring me something then that Louis was wearing at the time of his death."[23]

When the two met in August, she gave him Lomax's Hofstra ring, "which, according to the officials in Santa Rosa, was all that was used to identify Louis at the time of his death." Hurkos moved the ring around in his hands before stopping, grabbing a pencil, and beginning to draw. He produced a map of the scene and a picture of the car Lomax was driving. In a state of psychic trance, he claimed that Lomax was not driving too fast and that there was "something wrong with the steering." There were people who knew where he was going. "He did not cause the accident—he was not driving fast—the car was damaged on both sides," said Hurkos. "The police said he was drinking beer. I don't see it. Outside of the car were beer cans—Louis does not drink beer—he made a phone call before he left—he signed a slip for the car and they asked where he was going—he was killed."[24]

Based on Hurkos's vision, the two hired attorney Victor Palmero to investigate what they clearly believed to be a murder. Palmero would bring in an additional attorney, his colleague George Magit, to aid in the investigation. The effort encouraged an overwhelming paranoia, a conspiracy thinking that had influenced the whole family, stemming both from Lomax's long history with racial politics and, surely, the young family's experiences as an interracial couple in the late 1960s. "During all of our searching I was aware that my telephones were tapped and that my attorney's phones were tapped," remembered Robinette. As she understood it, all involved in the case had their phones tapped, forcing them to use public phone booths to communicate.

Yet their investigation turned up no politically motivated assassination. Instead, they discovered a "defective design of the front end mechanism, including the lower control arm," of the Ford station wagon that Lomax was driving. "Ford has been aware of this deadly defect for years," claimed Robinette. "The Department of Transportation has known about it for some time also. In other words, we, the public, have been driving these loaded guns with hair triggers for years."[25]

Lomax's body was flown to Los Angeles, where his funeral took place on 5 August at the Church of Christian Fellowship.[26] James Jones, a close friend of Lomax and pastor of Westminster Presbyterian, performed the service. Rather than a formal eulogy, he introduced a taped sermon Lomax had given at Westminster several years before.

To Jones, Lomax was "a modern Odysseus on an odyssey, Iliad and exodus in the 20th century. An odyssey in that his life was a series of travels, an Iliad in that his life was a long series of woes, an exodus in that his life was a going out from the land of misunderstanding into the land of reconciliation." His life was not a classical tragedy, Jones said, but instead had been filled with "a series of woes that befalls any Prophet, but especially woes to a Black Prophet and proclaimer in the complexity of a sophisticated politics and a whimsical Madison Avenue oriented society with a Dow-Jones average syndrome."[27]

Sales of *The Negro Revolt* and *Thailand* spiked following his death. The Los Angeles City Council stood in a moment of silence to honor Lomax, recognizing his influence on the city. Telegrams of condolence poured in from around the country. Robert E. Johnson, editor of *Jet*, and Lerone Bennett Jr., historian and editor of *Ebony*, expressed their sympathies. The Urban League's Whitney Young called Lomax "a great voice for the civil rights movement." William G. Nunn, white superintendent of the school system in Lomax's hometown, also lamented the passing. "Valdosta," he wrote, "has lost a very famous son."[28]

Hofstra held a memorial service for its fallen faculty member, featuring Manhattan borough president Percy Sutton along with a variety of faculty and students. Jim Cleaver, editor of the *Los Angeles Sentinel*, presided over the service, which included readings from Lomax's books. The university president and the dean of the College of Liberal Arts and Sciences spoke, the latter claiming, "I know of no other faculty member who became so involved and accomplished so much in the space of one short year."[29]

Cleaver offered one of the most moving eulogies to Lomax in his newspaper. "There was nothing un-positive about Louis Lomax," he wrote. "He feared little or nothing in terms of making his criticisms and whatever repercussions came from his writings were either accepted with grace or shrugged off." He "took black people to task as easily as he took white people to task," wrote Cleaver, even as "the tongues of his detractors wagged as major changes in his personal life took place." Perhaps even more importantly, Cleaver cast doubts about the police account of his death, saying that any report that Lomax "was killed in an automobile accident is incidental to the real facts." A Black man attempting to make changes within the system had to work twice as hard and twice as fast as a white man. "He cannot fail to file his income tax on time and he must not make a mistake of any kind. These are unforgivable sins. His private life must be completely above board and even his choice of religion is open to criticism from the public," Cleaver wrote. "He may not marry outside his race lest he be ostracized by both blacks and whites and he dare not speak out against the inequities within the system. These are fatal errors that he must avoid at all costs." Cleaver stopped before calling for conspiracy, but the allusion was there. Lomax surely would have been pleased.[30]

Robinette asked Lomax's friend Leroy Ramsey to contact the historian John Hope Franklin to tell him of Lomax's death. Franklin was stunned and distraught. "When he called the 'movement' a 'revolt' nearly ten years ago, most people regarded that as a literary excess. The fact that it has indeed become a revolt merely reveals the insights of Louis Lomax."[31]

At the end of October, having concluded their investigation, Robinette and her attorney announced that they would file a lawsuit in the near future.[32] The next month they brought a $110 million suit against Ford, Avis, and Drahos Transportation Inc., the Avis affiliate that rented Lomax the car he was driving at the time of his death. The car, claimed the suit, was "unsafe because of defects in the manufacture, design, assembly, maintenance, inspection and repair" and was "carelessly maintained, inspected and repaired." The suit also stated that the crash was the result of a mechanical defect in the lower control arm of the steering mechanism and charged the defendants with breach of implied warranty, breach of express warranty, negligence, and wrongful death. It asked $10 million in actual and $100 million in punitive damages. Explaining the large figures, Palermo insisted that Ford "and all the other companies who would take advantage of an unsuspecting public must be made examples of."[33]

It was true that Ford had recently recalled about eighty-five thousand police cars after the National Highway Safety Bureau found cracks in some of those control arms, but the NHSB claimed to have discovered no such failures in private vehicles. Consumer advocate Ralph Nader, however, had argued otherwise and had demanded a larger recall spreading to civilian vehicles.[34]

Ford, for its part, had more lawyers, with more experience, than did Robinette. In its demurrer to her suit, Ford challenged the notion of intent and therefore the claim for punitive damages. Without intent, the company maintained, the suit was valid only to cover Lomax's clothes, destroyed in the accident, and "since the value of that clothing could not possibly equal the $5,000.00 jurisdictional level of the Superior Court," the entire case was invalid. It was unsurprising when the court ruled in Ford's favor. Robinette's attempt at a wrongful death claim failed.[35]

That is not to say, however, that his death was not wrongful. The influence of Lomax was palpable. His writings were included, for example, in the collected materials of radical Washington, DC, civil rights activist Julius Hobson, alongside works of Eldridge Cleaver, W. E. B. Du Bois, Alex Haley, Dick Gregory, Kwame Nkrumah, Elijah Muhammed, and H. Rap

Brown. Famed journalist and political adviser Louis Martin wrote that Lomax "was one of the few black newsmen I have ever met who lived up to the image of the daring, hard-driving reporter that is often portrayed in the American theater and works of fiction." He hoped that one of Lomax's colleagues would write the story of his life: "I would like to know how this short, bespectacled, bundle of restless human energy, who was born in Valdosta, Ga., where blacks used to fear a white man's frown, developed the self-confidence and intelligence that enabled him to try almost anything and laugh even when he failed."[36]

Perhaps the most fitting eulogy for Lomax, one that corresponded with his own experience, was a coda that he wrote for his friends Malcolm X and Martin Luther King:

> And so the formula, the recipe, for killing black men emerges. Imbue them with the American dream; then deny them the fulfillment of that dream. Tantalize them with the faith that things can be changed through application of the Christian gospel; fill them with guilt if they deviate from this gospel and then violently refuse to respond to their attempts at nonviolent protest. Finally, push the black man to the point where he must violate his own ethical code in order to achieve that which he deems to be good, worthy, and just.
>
> Stir all this well; administer liberal doses in church, in school, at work, in all of the public media, in every aspect of the black man's daily life. Repeat as often as needed.
>
> Death will follow.[37]

Notes

ABBREVIATIONS

ADW — *Atlanta Daily World*

BAA — *Baltimore Afro-American*

BG — *Boston Globe*

CD — *Chicago Defender*

CT — *Chicago Tribune*

FBI File No. 62-102926 — Louis Lomax, FBI Central Headquarters File, 62-102926, FOIA, Federal Bureau of Investigation

FBI File No. 100-399321 — Malcolm Little (Malcolm X), FBI Central Headquarters File, 100-399321, FOIA, Federal Bureau of Investigation

Illinois v. Lomax — *Illinois v. Louis Lomax*, case no. 49CR-2439, 49CR-2440, 49CR-2441, Files of the Criminal Court of Cook County, Office of the Clerk of Court, Chicago

King Assassination Documents — King Assassination Documents—FBI Central Headquarters File, Assassination Archives and Research Center, Washington DC

LAS — *Los Angeles Sentinel*

LAT — *Los Angeles Times*

Lomax File — Louis Emanuel Lomax student file, Registrar's Office, Paine College, Augusta, GA

Lomax Papers — Louis E. Lomax Papers, 82-30, Special Collections, University of Nevada, Reno

NYAN — *New York Amsterdam News*

NYHT — *New York Herald Tribune*

NYT — *New York Times*

PC — *Pittsburgh Courier*

WP — *Washington Post*

1 *LAS*, 29 August 1963, A9, C3.
2 *LAS*, 29 August 1963, A9, C3.
3 Undated interview, box 1, series 1, subseries 3, folder 2, Lomax Papers.

1. FROM PRIVILEGE TO PRISON

1 Macedonia First Baptist Church now rests at 715 J. L. Lomax Drive. Twelfth Census of the United States, 1900, Population Schedule, Valdosta District, Lowndes, Georgia, Sheet No. 53A; *Valdosta Daily Times*, 6 November 1933, 5; Thirteenth Census of the United States, 1910, Population Schedule, Valdosta District, Lowndes, Georgia, Sheet No. 8B; Fourteenth Census of the United States, 1920, Population Schedule, Valdosta, Lowndes, Georgia, Sheet No. 11A.

2 Vieth, "Kinderlou." For more on the historical development of Valdosta and Lowndes County, see Schmier, *Valdosta*; Shelton, *Pines*.

3 Boyd, *Blind Obedience*, 97–108 (quote from 105).

4 It would later be known as Georgia Baptist College. Beset by financial woes, it closed in 1956. Fourteenth Census of the United States, 1920, Population Schedule, Valdosta, Lowndes, Georgia, Sheet No. 11A; Manis, *Macon*, 51, 80.

5 Emanuel Curtis Smith and Sarah Louise Lomax, Marriage License, Bibb County, Georgia, 464, retrieved from Ancestry.com; Emanuel Curtis Smith, Registration Card, World War II, Serial No. 464, Order No. 10144, Local Board for the County of Wilcox, Abbeville, Georgia, retrieved from Ancestry.com. The FBI wrongly placed Emanuel Smith's birthplace in Sandersville, Georgia, in Washington County. While it was an understandable mistake given the number of small towns in central Georgia and poor record keeping by white officials, it is notable that Sandersville was in fact the birthplace of Elijah Poole, later known as the Honorable Elijah Muhammad, who also played a considerable role in Lomax's life. "Louis Emanuel Lomax: Internal Security—Cuba," 4 October 1963, FBI File No. 62-102926.

6 Later in the 1920s, Lomax's father married teenager Louisa Watkins, eleven years his junior, and had two children with her. He then moved to neighboring Dodge County, where he lived until his death on 1 January 1963. *BAA*, 19 August 1961, 19; Emanuel Curtis Smith, Registration Card; Emanuel C. Smith, Georgia Death Index, 1919–1998, Certificate No. 00473, Office of Vital Records; Fifteenth Census of the United States, 1930, Population Schedule, Militia District 1254, Dodge, Georgia, Sheet No. 10A; Sixteenth Census of the United States, 1940, Population Schedule, Mitchell, Dodge, Georgia, Sheet No. 8A; Manuel Smith, US Social Security Applications and Claims Index, Social Security Administration; Sarah Smith, Georgia Death Index, 1919–1998, Certificate No. 2320106, Office of Vital Records.

7 Myers, "Killing." See also Buckner, *Mary Turner*.

8 *R. L. Polk & Co.'s Valdosta City Directory, 1923*, 156; *R. L. Polk & Co.'s Valdosta City Directory, 1925*, 115.

9 Louis Lomax, "American Negro's New Comedy Act," 42.

10 *Houston Informer*, 23 April 1932, 3; *Boston Chronicle*, 31 December 1932, 1; *Indianapolis Recorder*, 9 July 1932, 2; *Lynchings*, 2; Norman Thomas, *Human Exploitation*, xiv–xv; Wolters, *Negroes*, 98–113, 196–203; Frederickson, *Dixiecrat Revolt*, 13; Warren, *Herbert Hoover*, 241–242.

11 Louis Lomax, "Georgia Boy," 152–153.

12 Quote from Lomax's acceptance speech for the Anisfield-Wolf prize, reprinted in *NYAN*, 20 May 1961, 13.

13 Louis Lomax, *Negro Revolt*, 65; Richard King, *Civil Rights*, 46–47.

14 Headstones in Sunset Hill Cemetery, Valdosta, Georgia.

15 James L. Lomax would outlive his nephew. He died on 19 July 1976. Fourteenth Census of the United States, 1920, Population Schedule, Valdosta, Lowndes, Georgia, Sheet No. 11A; James Leonidas Lomax, Registration Card, World War I, Serial No. 34, Local Board for Lowndes County, Valdosta, Georgia, retrieved from Ancestry.com; Sixteenth Census of the United States, 1940, Population Schedule, Valdosta, Lowndes, Georgia, Sheet No. 39A; Moore, *From Whence We Came*, 182–185.

16 "About the author" (draft), n.d., box 1, series 1, subseries 1, folder 2, Lomax Papers.

17 Sitkoff, *New Deal*, 49; Kirby, *Black Americans*, 97; Lerner and Kerber, *Majority*, 68–69; Godshalk, *Veiled Visions*, 233; Ferguson, *Black Politics*, 19–24, 29–43, 49–51.

18 Louis Lomax, *Negro Revolt*, 39.

19 "Author information—Lomax," box 1, series 1, subseries 1, folder 1, Lomax Papers.

20 Kenneth Clark described Lomax, along with such contemporaries as James Baldwin, Richard Wright, and Lorraine Hansberry, as writers who, "though they leave the ghetto physically, they do not do so psychologically." *LAS*, 1 July 1965, A9; Clark, *Dark Ghetto*, 195.

21 Knight was born in Valdosta in 1932, making her younger than both Davis and Lomax. She received a track scholarship to attend Albany State, where she majored in elementary education, before heading to graduate school in California. She became superintendent of the Lynwood Unified School District in Southern California. *LAS*, 27 September 1984, A13; Louis Lomax, *Negro Revolt*, 47. For more on Davis, see Davis and Dee, *With Ossie and Ruby*.

22 Louis Lomax, "American Negro's New Comedy Act," 41–42.

23 Louis Lomax, *Negro Revolt*, 29.

24 "Author information—Lomax," Evan Thomas to Richard H. Sanger, 23 September 1960, box 1, series 1, subseries 1, folder 1, Lomax Papers; *ADW*, 8 January 1943, 5; Ritchie, *American Journalists*, 313–314.

25 *CD*, 15 June 1963, 12; Marable, *Malcolm X*, 160; "Louis Lomax Named Visiting Professor at Hofstra," *News from Hofstra*, 16 April 1969, box 12, series 7, folder 24, Lomax Papers.

26 The claim, like many Lomax made about his life, seems suspect. In 1938, Georgia State College played football games at home against Edward Waters, Claflin, Allen, and Paine. The only loss was to Edward Waters on 22 October. The team won the rest of its contests, including its Thanksgiving finale with Paine, and neither the university press nor Savannah's local Black newspaper reported any trouble with any of the teams during their stays on campus. The team's only other loss of the season was to Benedict on the road. The *Savannah Tribune* mentioned nothing about any trouble with any of the visiting teams. The paper did report that the Allen game had "the fans' enthusiasm to a boiling point" and that "a large crowd of Allen supporters is planning to come to Savannah" for the game. But that was the closest thing to any hint of potential trouble relating to a football game that season. (Georgia State's original campus newspaper was the *Georgia Herald*, published in this early incarnation once monthly.) *Georgia Herald*, February 1938, 6, November 1938, 1–6, *The Hubertonian*, 1939, 39, Gordon Library; *Savannah Tribune*, 20 October 1938, 7, 27 October 1938, 7, 3 November 1938, 7, 10 November 1938, 7 (quote), 17 November 1938, 7, 1 December 1938, 7; J. L. Lomax to W. L. Graham, 8 November 1939, Lomax transcript, Georgia State College, Lomax File. The historical record of the school's athletics is similarly silent on any potential football controversy in Lomax's one academic year in Savannah. Elmore, *Athletic Saga*, 6.

27 In his application, Lomax described himself as a Baptist and expressed his desire to be a pastor. He claimed membership at Macedonia First Baptist Church in Valdosta and listed the church's pastor, the Reverend M. N. Lyde, as a reference, along with Dr. L. W. Williams. He identified his address dually as 632 River Street and 808 S. Toombs Street, which was the home of his uncle and aunt. He gave his own name as Louis Emanuel Curtis Lomax and listed William Joseph Hunter and Leslie Dawson as relatives who attended Paine. J. L. Lomax to W. L. Graham, 8 November 1939, W. L. Graham to J. L. Lomax, 10 November 1939, application for admission, Lomax File; *Valdosta Daily Times*, 3 February 2015, 1. For more on Paine, see Clary, *Paine College*.

28 Transcript, schedule cards, 23 January 1940, 7 May 1942, 14 January 1943, Lomax File; Louis Lomax, "Georgia Boy," 152.

29 Louis Lomax, "Georgia Boy," 153.

30 Schedule cards, 7 May 1942, 14 January 1943, Lomax File.

31 Louis Lomax to Edmund Clarke Peters, n.d., schedule card, 14 January 1943, Lomax File; "Student Roster, Session 1942–1943, College Division, Senior Class," *Paine College Bulletin, Register for 1942–1943*, 61; "Degrees and Diplomas, College Division, Bachelor of Arts Degree, Session 1942–1943," *Paine College Bulletin, Register for 1943–1944*, 58, Collins-Callaway Library, Paine College.

32 Howard does not make such enrollment information available to researchers, but it seems that his successful time as a student there was also a fabrication. Edmund Clarke Peters to Louis Lomax, 1 February 1944, Lomax File; Howard University Archives, correspondence with the author.

33 American's commencement programs for the 1940s do not include Lomax, nor does the student newspaper include any mention of him between 1942 and 1944. When later student newspapers mentioned his speaking appearances at the university in the late 1960s, there was no mention of him as a former student, graduate, or alumnus of American. That was because he was at the school only briefly and never earned a degree. Correspondence with the registrar, American University, Washington, DC, in possession of the author. For an example of these absences, see "30th Commencement Program, American University, Spring 1944," Digital Research Archive, American University, https://dra.american.edu/islandora/object/auislandora%3A12836, accessed 10 May 2018; *American University Eagle*, 4 October 1963, 5, 11 February 1969, 2, 14 March 1969, 3, 15 April 1969, 1, 31 October 1969, 3, 14 November 1969, 5.

34 Louis E. Lomax to Edmund Clarke Peters, 22 March 1946, Edmund Clarke Peters to Louis Lomax, 26 March 1946, Lomax File; "About Bethlehem," Bethlehem Baptist Church, http://bethlehembaptistdc.org/index.php/about-us/, accessed 21 May 2018.

35 *CD*, 30 June 1945, 11; L. B. Nichols to M. A. Jones, 2 February 1956, FBI File No. 62-102926.

36 *CD*, 8 September 1945, 13.

37 *CD*, 30 June 1945, 15.

38 The show ran at 10:00 p.m. *CD*, 29 September 1945, 11, 20 October 1945, 13.

39 *The Hubertonian*, 1947, *Georgia State College Bulletin*, 1946–1947, 14–18, *Georgia State College Bulletin*, 1948–1849, 10–15, *The Tiger*, 1949, Gordon Library. He appears in no registration materials and has no folder in Yale's records of students who received a degree and those who did not. All of the possible folders that would demonstrate his registration at Yale were searched diligently by Nancy Lyon, archivist and head of collections management for the Manuscripts and Archives Division of the Yale University Library. Correspondence with the author. In November 1948, the Black press placed a Louis Lomax as pastor of the Stratford Baptist Church in Connecticut, which would match the period when he claimed to have been a student in New Haven, but there is no proof that the subject of that particular article is the same Louis Lomax and no other corroboration of his time there. *NYAN*, 20 November 1948, 1; *BAA*, 27 November 1948, A1; *PC*, 20 November 1948, 1.

40 *CD*, 15 June 1963, 12; "Author Louis Lomax Dies in Auto Crash," box 17, series 8, folder 4, Lomax Papers. Lomax was a young stringer and thus did not appear in any bylines. When combined with a lack of archival records for the newspaper, his claim about writing for the *Chicago Herald-American* cannot be specifically corroborated. In the small sample of coverage in the paper devoted to Black citizens, there does seem to be the imprint of a Black writer, a lack of condescension in coverage that normally appears in this period from white writers. Such is not the same as corroboration, and Lomax was known to lie about his past, but he was in Chicago at the time, and journalism was the one field where he had been able

to hold a job. For an example of coverage that indicates race-sympathetic author-ship, see "Negro Youth Wins Two Honor Titles," *Chicago Herald-American*, 3 April 1948, 4.

41 FBIHQ Investigative and Administrative Files, File No. 26-15499, NARA-26-HQ-134264, FOIA; "Witness Memorandum to Clerk," *Illinois v. Lomax*.

42 FBIHQ Investigative and Administrative Files, File No. 26-15499; FBI, Chicago (94-627), to FBI director, 7 February 1956, L. B. Nichols to M. A. Jones, 2 February 1956, FBI File No. 62-102926.

43 According to documents in a case filed against Lomax in Cook County, his wife made $154 per month. Although the case mentions the University of Chicago, that institution has no record of Dolores or her husband either working or matriculating there. She instead worked at Chicago State University. "Official Shorthand Reporter's Copy, Proceedings before Judge William J. Lindsay, January 18, 1950," *Illinois v. Lomax*; Special Collections Research Center, University of Chicago, correspondence with the author.

44 "Motion to Expunge and Vacate an Order Entered of Record in Cause 49-2441," "Count 1, Grand Jury Indictment," *Illinois v. Lomax*.

45 Louis E. Lomax (otherwise called Robert J. Frost), General No. 49-2439, *Illinois v. Lomax*. See also "Criminal Subpoena for Joseph Cheramonte, Gary Indiana," 18 January 1950, *Illinois v. Lomax*. The rest of the subpoenas exist in the same criminal file in the Office of the Cook County Clerk of Court.

46 Copy of indictment and affidavit, "Memorandum of Orders," Hermann Post, "Memorandum to Judge Lindsay in re The Lomax Case," "Motion to Expunge and Vacate an Order Entered of Record in Cause 49-2441," Louis E. Lomax to Sidney R. Olsen, 2 November 1952, *Illinois v. Lomax*.

47 "Affidavit of Hermann F. Post in re Louis E. Lomax's 'Motion for an Order of Restraint' in the Federal District Court of Chicago," *Illinois v. Lomax*.

48 Louis E. Lomax to Joseph Graber, Cook County Criminal Court, 14 November 1952, *Illinois v. Lomax*.

49 At the same time, the report noted that Lomax waived his right to a trial by jury, instead choosing to go before a judge, but then closed by stating, "This cause is submitted to the Court for trial and the intervention of a jury." Such discrepancies seemed minor, as the first two were generally understood assumptions by law enforcement officials and the third was a typographical error, but Lomax argued that changes in the actual record portended larger falsifications, that "a defendant is entitled to a true record of his cause." "A Motion to Correct the Record of Causes 49-2339–2440–2441 in the Criminal Court of Cook County Illinois," *Illinois v. Lomax*.

50 "A Motion to Correct the Record of Causes 49-2339–2440–2441 in the Criminal Court of Cook County Illinois," "Motion to Have the Official Shorthand Reporter of the Criminal Court of Cook County to Produce a Just and Accurate Record," "Count 1, Grand Jury Indictment," *Illinois v. Lomax*.

51 See, for example, Lawson, "Joliet Prison Photographs."

52 Lomax even included an affidavit from his wife, Dolores, claiming that the court had given her similar difficulties in trying to get his records. In his case for only a one-year minimum sentence, he argued "that the aggregate charges against the Petitioner involve less than $1500, (fifteen hundred dollars) and that no bodily threat or injury were complained of" and that Lomax had "no previous criminal record." "Motion for an Order of Restraint Against the Criminal Court of Cook County Illinois, the Clerk of the Criminal Court of Cook County Illinois, and the Office of the Shorthand Reporter of the Criminal Court of Cook County Illinois," *Illinois v. Lomax*. Lomax's application for bond and Dolores N. Lomax's affidavit on her husband's behalf appear as Exhibit B and Exhibit D, respectively, in his motion for order of restraint. While he was in prison, Lomax carried on a correspondence with attorney Curtis A. Huff, general counsel for First Federal Savings and Loan Association of Chicago, one of the largest savings and loan associations in the nation. *Stewart v. Huff*, 14 Ill. App.3d 782 (Ill. App. Ct. 1973); FBI, Chicago (94-627), to FBI director, 7 February 1956, FBI File No. 62-102926.

53 FBI, Chicago (94-627), to FBI director, 7 February 1956, FBI File No. 62-102926.

54 Marable, *Malcolm X*, 161; FBI, Chicago (94-627), to FBI director, 7 February 1956, Hostetter to FBI, Chicago, 6 February 1956, FBI File No. 62-102926; Sixteenth Census of the United States, 1940, Population Schedule, Chicago, Ward 19, Cook County, Illinois, Sheet No. 2B.

55 FBI, Chicago (94-627), to FBI director, 7 February 1956, FBI File No. 62-102926.

56 In May 1956, for example, he represented the organization in a speech to the American Economic League banquet in Chicago. *CD*, 16 May 1956, 2; Marable, *Malcolm X*, 161; FBI, Chicago (94-627), to FBI director, 7 February 1956, FBI File No. 62-102926.

57 LAS, 16 November 1967, A1. Lomax always claimed to have been in Little Rock covering Central High School's desegregation, but if he was, none of his coverage of the event remains, which tends to argue for his absence, as Lomax's hunger for publicity would surely have left him highlighting that coverage later in his life. He did write about the Arkansas governor in later years. See Louis Lomax, "Integration"; Louis Lomax, "Two Millionaires."

2. THE HATE THAT HATE PRODUCED

1 *BAA*, 3 February 1945, 9, 17 February 1945, 5, 6, 24 February 1945, 13, 2 June 1945, 13, 30 June 1945, 20, 28 July 1945, 20, 18 August 1945, 20, 25 August 1945, 20; *Breedlove v. Suttles*, 302 US 277 (1937). See also Novotny, *This Georgia Rising*. For more on the development of the *BAA*, see Farrar, *Baltimore Afro-American*. For more on Murphy's willingness to take risks in hiring, see chapter 7 of Aiello, *Grapevine*.

2 *Shelley v. Kraemer*, 334 US 1 (1948); *McLaurin v. Oklahoma State Regents*, 339 US 637 (1950); *Sweatt v. Painter*, 339 US 629 (1950). For more on the Montgomery Bus Boycott, see Robinson, *Montgomery Bus Boycott*. For more on the death of Emmett Till, see Tyson, *Blood of Emmett Till*.

3 Beito and Beito, *Black Maverick*; *LAT*, 28 August 2009, A25; J. Edgar Hoover to Communications Section, 3 February 1956, J. Edgar Hoover to T. R. M. Howard, 16 January 1956, T. R. M. Howard to J. Edgar Hoover, 19 January 1956, T. R. M. Howard to J. Edgar Hoover, 20 January 1956, "The Dr. TRM Howard Controversy," FBI File No. 62-102926. Hoover also contacted Thurgood Marshall about the dispute, Marshall assuring him that Howard was not a part of the NAACP and did not represent the organization in any way. J. Edgar Hoover to Thurgood Marshall, 30 September 1955, Thurgood Marshall to J. Edgar Hoover, 24 January 1956, FBI File No. 62-102926.

4 Louis E. Lomax to J. Edgar Hoover, 30 January 1956, FBI File No. 62-102926.

5 There is no evidence that the conversation between Rabb and Lomax actually took place, and Lomax demonstrated no sense of intimidation that could theoretically have resulted from such a meeting. L. B. Nichols to Mr. Tolson, 8 February 1956, FBI File No. 62-102926; "FBI and J. Edgar Hoover," box 45, series II, Eisenhower Administration, 1953–1958, Rabb Papers, Dwight D. Eisenhower Library; Maxwell Rabb to Andrew Goodpaster, n.d., box 37, series II, Eisenhower Administration, 1953–1958, Rabb Papers.

6 L. B. Nichols to Mr. Tolson, 9 February 1956, FBI File No. 62-102926.

7 L. B. Nichols to M. A. Jones, 8 February 1956, FBI File No. 62-102926. In preparation for the meeting, the bureau created a document that contained no specifics on the Howard feud or the Till case but instead outlined the bureau's constitutional role in local criminal cases. "Federal jurisdiction in the civil rights field is not broad," the document explained. Statutes relating to federal jurisdiction were few and were "very restrictive in nature," but when such jurisdiction warranted, "the FBI gives the highest priority to civil rights investigations." "Civil Rights Material for Contemplated Interview with Louis E. Lomax: Civil Rights Investigations," 6 February 1956, FBI File No. 62-102926.

8 J. Edgar Hoover to Louis E. Lomax, 7 February 1956, L. B. Nichols to Louis E. Lomax, 10 February 1956, Louis E. Lomax to Louis Nichols, 13 February 1956, Louis B. Nichols to Louis E. Lomax, 14 February 1956, Hostetter to director, 12 March 1956, FBI File No. 62-102926.

9 *BAA*, 24 March 1956, 1, 2, 19 May 1956, 1, 3, 28 July 1956, 5, 11 August 1956, 20, 18 August 1956, 6, 7, 13, 25 August 1956, 1 (quote), 6; *CD*, 25 April 1956, 4, 9 August 1956, 7; *1956 Democratic Party Platform*.

10 Meanwhile, a grade school in Clay, Kentucky, underwent a similar crisis after two Black students decided to attend. Again the National Guard had to protect the students. *BAA*, 15 September 1956, 1, 22 September 1956, 1, 6, 7, 13 October 1956, 20; Trowbridge and LeMay, *Sturgis*.

11 Louis Lomax, "American Negro's New Comedy Act," 43.

12 Louis Lomax, "Lord Help Me," 117; *BAA*, 21 September 1957, 5.

13 The conflict in Clinton would last through the spring semester in 1957, but Lomax was there only in September. *BAA*, 15 September 1956, 12; Adamson, "Few Black Voices."

14 *BAA*, 8 December 1956, 1, 2, 14, 22 December 1956, 1, 2, 29 December 1956, 1, 2, 13, 23 March 1957, 1, 2, 6 April 1957, 1, 2, 4 May 1957, 1, 2, 8 June 1957, 1, 2.

15 *BAA*, 27 April 1957, 13. A draft of Lomax's novel, "The Wheel and the Cistern," survives in his archival papers (box 2, series 1, subseries 6, folder 23, Lomax Papers). It is a biographical account of Charles Haddon, who deals with race and racism in late 1920s Richmond, Virginia.

16 Louis Lomax, "Inter-Racial Marriage," 6, 13; *BAA*, 23 November 1957, 11.

17 *BAA*, 23 November 1957, 5.

18 After *Those Who Have Made Good*, he produced a new show the following year, *All Men Are Created Equal*, on wNEW, before ultimately returning to wNYC at the conclusion of World War II. "Radio Reviews"; *NYAN*, 14 June 1941, 2; *PM*, 25 August 1941, 20; *New York Age*, 17 October 1942, 5; Morrison, "Success"; George, *Black Radio*, 61–62; "Radio Producer Clifford Burdette," lot 13074, no. 85 [P&P], Library of Congress Prints and Photographs Division. Burdette's interview, "Cullen on Those Who Have Made Good," wNYC, 22 June 1941, is available at Amistad Research Center.

19 Louis Lomax, *To Kill a Black Man*, 49–50; *BAA*, 19 October 1957, 3, 2 November 1957, 1, 9 November 1957, 1, 2, 20, 16 November 1957, 1, 2, 7, 23 November 1957, 3, 5, 17, 19, 30 November 1957, 1, 2, 14 December 1957, 3, 9, 21 December 1957, 1, 2, 15, 20, 28 December 1957, 1, 2, 8, 4 January 1958, 1, 2, 11 January 1958, 8, 18 January 1958, 3, 7, 19, 25 January 1958, 1, 2, 15, 22 March 1958, 1, 2, 29 March 1958, 1, 2, 9, 5 April 1958, 1, 2, 5, 12 April 1958, 2, 5, 19 April 1958, 1, 2, 5, 3 May 1958, 1, 2, 10 May 1958, 1, 2, 24 May 1958, 2, 19, 21 June 1958, 1, 3, 28 June 1958, 1, 2, 12 July 1958, 1, 2, 19 July 1958, 1, 2, 9, 26 July 1958, 1, 2, 2 August 1958, 1, 2, 9 August 1958, 3, 16 August 1958, 1, 2, 6 September 1958, 19, 13 September 1958, 3, 27 September 1958, 1, 2, 4 October 1958, 3, 18 October 1958, 1, 2, 5, 15 November 1958, 9, 29 November 1958, 1, 2, 20, 6 December 1958, 1, 2, 13 December 1958, 1, 2; Martin King, *Autobiography*, 117–120; Pearson, *When Harlem Nearly Killed King*. See also Hamilton, *Adam Clayton Powell, Jr.*

20 *NYAN*, 17 June 1961, 24, 2 August 1961, 22.

21 *BAA*, 19 July 1958, A8.

22 *LAS*, 16 November 1967, A1; Louis Lomax, *To Kill a Black Man*, 52–53. Malcolm X, of course, had close relationships with other leaders outside the Nation of Islam. The aforementioned Lincoln was a confidant that he and Lomax shared. Alex Haley would also become dramatically important to Malcolm later in his life. He also had alliances with such leaders as E. U. Essien-Udom, Haywood Burns, and Elombe Brath. But the latter were ideological fellow travelers: Essien-Udom and Brath were Garveyite Pan-Africanists, Burns a Black Power nationalist. Burns's book on the NOI appeared in 1963. Haley's *Autobiography of Malcolm X* appeared the following year. Beginning in 1959, none of these relationships had the public benefit for Malcolm X that his relationship with Lomax did. And none saw the bell-curve shaping of their own ideological positions in response to that relationship. See Burns, *Voices*; Essien-Udom, *Black Nationalism*; Lincoln, *Black Muslims*; Haley, *Autobiography*; Brath, *Selected Writings*.

23 The father of Malcolm X was also a Baptist minister. Goldman, *Death*, 62; Haley, *Autobiography*, 271; Louis Lomax, *To Kill a Black Man*, 54–55.

24 Goldman, *Death*, 62; Haley, *Autobiography*, 271; "Mike Wallace's 'Newsbeat' Uncovers Major Anti-White Crusade," box 4, series 2, subseries 1, folder 1, Lomax Papers.

25 Lomax claimed that Malcolm was unsure that the program would ever make it to television. "You know the Devil will not let you put that strong teaching on the air," Malcolm told him, referring to the white power structure. *LAT*, 23 April 1965, C18; Louis Lomax, *To Kill a Black Man*, 60; "Tonight at 8:00 p.m. a 'Must See,'" "Mike Wallace's 'Newsbeat' Uncovers Major Anti-White Crusade," box 4, series 2, subseries 1, folder 1, Lomax Papers; transcript and binder of miscellaneous material, box 12, Wallace Papers, Syracuse University Libraries; *The Hate That Hate Produced*, Administrative File, box 9, Wallace Papers, Bentley Historical Library, University of Michigan.

26 Evanzz, *Judas Factor*, 76–77; "Report of [Redacted], 67C, 17 November 1959," NY 105-8999, FBI File No. 100-399321; *NYHT*, 12 July 1959, D6; Gibson, "Nation Women's Engagement," 4–5.

27 DeCaro, *On the Side*, 134; Abernethy, *Iconography*, 44–45.

28 "The Hate That Hate Produced: A Television Documentary, 23 July 1959, transcript," box 2, series 1, subseries 5, folder 17, Lomax Papers.

29 "The Hate That Hate Produced: A Television Documentary, 23 July 1959, transcript."

30 "The Hate That Hate Produced: A Television Documentary, 23 July 1959, transcript."

31 "The Hate That Hate Produced, WNTA-TV, New York, 22 July 1959," box 4, series 2, subseries 1, folder 1, Lomax Papers; *NYAN*, 28 November 1959, 15; Marable, *Malcolm X*, 161; DeCaro, *On the Side*, 135; Wagner and Hebel, *Pictorial Cultures*, 205.

32 Although the NOI became extremely vigilant about the kinds of exposure it received, the year after the documentary appeared, Lincoln gained access to the group for his doctoral dissertation, later published in 1961 as *The Black Muslims in America*. The sociological study was the academic version of *The Hate That Hate Produced*, and its comprehensive analysis has made it far more important to our body of knowledge about the NOI. Louis Lomax, *To Kill a Black Man*, 62–63; Evanzz, *Judas Factor*, 93; Goldman, *Death*, 61; Marable, *Malcolm X*, 162–163; Hussein, "Born of Our Necessities," 111; Abernethy, *Iconography*, 26.

33 Abernethy, *Iconography*, 44–45; "'Black Supremacy' Cult"; DeCaro, *On the Side*, 134; *Detroit Free Press*, 14 August 1959, 1-1, 15 August 1959, 2-1; "Media Scrapbook: The Hate That Hate Produced," box 4, series 2, subseries 1, folder 1, Lomax Papers. Despite the controversy that surrounded the series, everyone involved benefited. Wallace received an offer to cover the 1960 presidential campaign, which he ultimately parlayed into anchoring the CBS morning news by 1963. From there, he joined the team of *60 Minutes*. Marable, *Malcolm X*, 161–162.

34 For more on the Nation of Islam and its place in the history of the African American relationship with Islam, see Lee, *Nation*; Curtis, *Black Muslim Religion*; Gib-

son, *History*; Curtis, *Islam in Black America*; Turner, *Islam in the African American Experience*; Rashid, *Black Muslims*). For more on Black radicalism and the Black Power movement, see, among others, Van Deburg, *New Day*; McCartney, *Black Power Ideologies*; Ogbar, *Black Power*; Joseph, *Waiting 'til the Midnight Hour*; Andrews, *Back to Black*.

35 Arnold, *In Retrospect*, 62–63; Abernethy, *Iconography*, 59. Historian Peter Goldman argued that Malcolm liked Lomax "for his energy and his endless line of black gossip." Goldman, *Death*, 62.

36 Osha, *Best of Enemies*, 102–103. For more on Lomax's relationship with *Harper's*, see Gregory, *Southern Diaspora*, 191–192.

37 Louis Lomax, "Negro Revolt against 'the Negro Leaders,'" 268–269; Schmidt, "Conceptions," 654–655; Schmidt, "Divided by Law," 133–134.

38 Louis Lomax, "Negro Revolt against 'the Negro Leaders,'" 280. In one UANM speech featured in *The Hate That Hate Produced*, John Davis said, "Awwww—them phony liberals. I've told you like it is. Then you got the NAACP—the National Association for the Advancement of <u>Some</u> Colored Folk. And you got Uncle Tom Roy Wilkins. Am I right or wrong?" "The Hate That Hate Produced: A Television Documentary, 23 July 1959, transcript," box 2, series 1, subseries 5, folder 17, Lomax Papers.

39 Louis Lomax, "The Negro Revolt against 'the Negro Leaders'"; *BG*, 20 May 1960, 19; *NYHT*, 20 May 1960, 11.

40 *PC*, 11 June 1960, 13.

41 Martin Luther King Jr. to Marie F. Rodell, 30 November 1960, box 61, King Papers, Gotlieb Archival Research Center, Boston University; *NYAN*, 10 January–16 January 2008, 6, 34.

42 *BAA*, 18 June 1960, 4.

43 *CD*, 6 July 1960, 11. For more on the Huntley incident, see Bodroghkozy, *Equal Time*, 68–75.

3. THE RELUCTANT AFRICAN

1 Horne, *Mau Mau*, 1–2 (Bunche quote); Louis Lomax, *Reluctant African*, 73–74.

2 Fanon, *Wretched*. The historiography here is vast. For coverage of the Black Power movement and its philosophical perspective, see Ogbar, *Black Power*; Joseph, *Waiting 'til the Midnight Hour*; Jeffries, *Huey P. Newton*; McCartney, *Black Power Ideologies*. For coverage of the evolution of African American foreign policy thinking in the twentieth century, see Galliccho, *African American Encounter*; Makalani, *In the Cause*; Bush, *End*; Brent Edwards, *Practice*; West, Martin, and Wilkins, *From Toussaint*.

3 Broussard, *African American Foreign Correspondents*, 15–16. See also Rhodes, *Mary Ann Shadd Cary*; Levine, *Lives of Frederick Douglass*; Franklin, *George Washington Williams*; Lewis, *W. E. B. Du Bois*; Kirschke, "Du Bois."

4 Washburn, "George Padmore." See also Hooker, *Black Revolutionary*.

5 Louis E. Lomax to John Fischer, 16 May 1960, Louis E. Lomax, "Africa South: The World's Newest Dilemma," box 1, series 1, subseries 1, folder 1, Lomax Papers.

6 Louis Lomax, "Africa South."

7 See Liebenow, *Liberia*; Asserate, *King*; Grilli, "Nkrumah's Ghana."

8 Louis Lomax, "Africa South."

9 Louis E. Lomax to John Fischer, 16 May 1960, Evan Thomas to Louis E. Lomax, 23 May 1960, box 1, series 1, subseries 1, folder 1, Lomax Papers.

10 Evan Thomas to Louis E. Lomax, 23 May 1960, preliminary contract, 31 May 1960, box 1, series 1, subseries 1, folder 1, Lomax Papers.

11 Nothing but the book itself survives as a documentary record of this journey to Africa. Louis E. Lomax to Evan Thomas, 24 August 1960, box 1, series 1, subseries 1, folder 1, Lomax Papers.

12 See Louis Lomax, *Reluctant African*.

13 Louis Lomax, *Reluctant African*, 15, 44–45, 47.

14 Louis Lomax, *Reluctant African*, 64–69, 99–110.

15 Louis Lomax, *Reluctant African*, 113–114.

16 Louis Lomax, *Reluctant African*, 114–117.

17 The book was initially priced at $2.50, though it increased to $2.95 before publication. Bradley believed that the draft needed chapter breaks, and he did not like the title, as the manuscript demonstrated Lomax "to be anything but 'reluctant.'" He also thought that after Lomax's journey to Nairobi, "the manuscript begins to fall down and get confused." With changes, however, it could be a beneficial title for the press. Preliminary manufacturing estimate, 1 September 1960, D. F. Bradley to Evan Thomas, 6 September 1960, Manufacturing Department Memorandum, Evan Thomas, memo to RIF, SH, VO, FL, FW, DFB, and LH, 21 September 1960, box 1, series 1, subseries 1, folder 1, Lomax Papers.

18 Royalties would be 10 percent on the first 5,000 copies, 12.5 percent up to 7,500, and 15 percent on everything after that. Evan Thomas to Canfield, MacGregor, Harwood, and Pace, 7, 8 September 1960, "The Reluctant African—Lomax," box 1, series 1, subseries 1, folder 1, Lomax Papers.

19 Evan Thomas to Harriet Pilpel, 8 September 1960, Evan Thomas to Richard H. Sanger, 8 September 1960, Richard H. Sanger to Evan Thomas, 12 September 1960, Evan Thomas to Richard H. Sanger, 15 September 1960, box 1, series 1, subseries 1, folder 1, Lomax Papers. "Lomax was introduced to me by John Fischer, the editor of Harper's Magazine," he wrote to one such acquaintance, Roy Herbert, managing editor of *Reader's Digest*. "Fischer vouches for his reliability one hundred percent." They also sent the book to the Reverend James H. Robinson, leader of Operation Crossroads Africa, who sent along his endorsement. Evan Thomas to Roy Herbert, 18 October 1960, Genevieve Young to James H. Robinson, 22 September 1960, Genevieve Young to Louis E. Lomax, 30 September 1960, Evan Thomas to James H. Robinson, 11 October 1960, James H. Robinson to Genevieve Young, 14 October 1960, box 1, series 1, subseries 1, folder 1, Lomax Papers.

20 David Silver to Evan Thomas, 27 September 1960, box 1, series 1, subseries 1, folder 1, Lomax Papers.

21 Nicol, *Good-Looking Corpse*; Modisane, *Blame Me.*

22 Louis Lomax, *Reluctant African*, 13–15.

23 David Silver to Evan Thomas, 11 October 1960, Evan Thomas memorandum to SH, FW, n.d., box 1, series 1, subseries 1, folder 1, Lomax Papers.

24 Robert Coughlan to Evan Thomas, 19 October 1960, box 1, series 1, subseries 1, folder 1, Lomax Papers.

25 Louis Lomax, *Reluctant African*, 1, 10.

26 Murray, "Study," 82, 92; Simmons, *African American Press,* 117–118; Aptheker, *Documentary History*, 98; Prattis, "Role," 274.

27 Evan Thomas to Robert Coughlan, 25 October 1960, box 1, series 1, subseries 1, folder 1, Lomax Papers.

28 Evan Thomas to Martin Luther King Jr., 25 October 1960, Evan Thomas to Fitzhenry, Lindley, Wagner, Harris, Lomax, Rodell, Giacomini, Collett, 16 November 1960, Stuart Cloete to Evan Thomas, 19 November 1960, Evan Thomas to Fitzhenry, Lindley, Wagner, Harris, Lomax, Rodell, Giacomini, Collett, 28 November 1960, box 1, series 1, subseries 1, folder 1, Lomax Papers.

29 By the end of November, the book had earned Lomax royalties of $1,850.29, which minus his $1,500 advance left the author with $350.29. Genevieve Young to Louis Lomax, 29 November 1960, "Later re Lomax," n.d., box 1, series 1, subseries 1, folder 1, Lomax Papers; *NYHT*, 3 November 1960, 25, 15 November 1960, 25; *BAA*, 5 November 1960, 5.

30 Evan Thomas to Marie Rodell, 16 December 1960, box 1, series 1, subseries 1, folder 1, Lomax Papers.

31 *NYHT*, 20 November 1960, D32.

32 *NYHT*, 22 November 1960, 27.

33 *BAA*, 20 January 1962, A2.

34 Publicity for the award was handled by Commco Public Relations, a firm led by M. B. and Robert Zerwick and hired by *Saturday Review*. *NYT*, 12 May 1961, 26; *NYAN*, 13 May 1961, 20; Gene Young to Mrs. Lindley, 20 April 1961, William D. Patterson to Cass Canfield, 19 July 1961, William D. Patterson to Cass Canfield, 26 June 1961, box 1, series 1, subseries 1, folder 2, Lomax Papers.

35 Lillian Smith to Rochelle Girson, n.d., Smith Letters, Hargrett Rare Book and Manuscript Library, University of Georgia.

36 *NYAN*, 20 May 1961, 13.

37 *NYHT*, 3 November 1960, 25, 15 November 1960, 25, 17 November 1960, 18, 18 November 1960, 38; *WP*, 11 February 1961, A15; *BAA*, 5 November 1960, 5, 17 December 1960, 5.

38 When VSC rejected the press's offer, it suggested Southern Stationery and Printing Company on Valdosta's North Ashley Street as a possible vendor. Genevieve Young, who handled such orders for the press, heard from Southern Stationery that it had ordered copies that never arrived. But she knew better. "This may just

have been said to pacify Lomax's relatives," she told the Harper office, "and may not be true since I remember some store down there refused to carry it." Genevieve Young to Louis Lomax, 2 February 1961, Gene Young to Mrs. Lindley, 20 April 1961, box 1, series 1, subseries 1, folder 2, Lomax Papers.

39 Genevieve Young to Louis Lomax, 2 February 1961, "Dolores Gentile to Book Order Department, Harper & Brothers, 18 January 1961," Alma Whittaker to Genevieve Young, 19 February 1961, Genevieve Young to Louis Lomax, 1 March 1961, Genevieve Young to Louis Lomax, 17 April 1961, Genevieve Young to Louis Lomax, 29 March 1961, box 1, series 1, subseries 1, folder 2, Lomax Papers.

4. THE NEGRO REVOLT

1 His first effort for *Frontiers of Faith*, "The Bitter Cup," appeared on 12 February. Another, "Three Gentlemen from Africa," appeared on 5 March. *NYAN*, 4 February 1961, 13; *NYHT*, 5 March 1961, G8; "The Bitter Cup" / by Louis E. Lomax, 12 February 1961, box 325, folder 6, National Broadcasting Company Records, Wisconsin Historical Society Archives; "Three Gentlemen from Africa" / by Louis E. Lomax, 5 March 1961, box 325, folder 7, National Broadcasting Company Records.

2 Genevieve Young to Marie Rodell, 5 May 1961, box 1, series 1, subseries 1, folder 2, Lomax Papers.

3 The two would ultimately debate twice more, in April and May 1964. *NYAN*, 11 March 1961, 17; *PC*, 29 April 1961, A2; Smallwood, "Intellectual Creativity," 258–259.

4 "The Negro today must speak with conviction," he wrote in the article. "He must find no merit in threats, but he must realize that should the American Negro come to full stature without suffering, he will be the first man in human history to do it." Marable, *Malcolm X*, 188; Louis Lomax, "Act," 17, 30.

5 Louis Lomax, "American Negro's New Comedy Act," 41, 46; Boskin, *Sambo*, 219–222.

6 *NYAN*, 17 June 1961, 13. For more on Wilson, a white columnist for a Black newspaper for much of the 1960s, see Priestley, *By Gertrude Wilson*.

7 Louis Lomax to Gene Young, n.d., box 1, series 1, subseries 1, folder 2, Lomax Papers.

8 See Schmidt, *Sit-Ins*; Morgan and Davies, eds., *From Sit-Ins to SNCC*; Murphree, *Selling*; Carson, *In Struggle*.

9 See Chafe, *Civilities*.

10 See Brown-Nagin, *Courage*; Houston, *Nashville Way*; Lovett, *Civil Rights Movement*.

11 See Arsenault, *Freedom Riders*; Catsam, *Freedom's Main Line*.

12 Genevieve Young to Louis Lomax, 6 July 1961, box 1, series 1, subseries 1, folder 2, Lomax Papers.

13 Harper gave Lomax a $1,750 advance against royalties of 10 percent to five thousand copies, 12.5 percent to ten thousand, and 15 percent thereafter. Genevieve

Young to Canfield, Bradbury, Thomas, Harwood, and Pace, 17 July 1961, Genevieve Young to Marie Rodell, 25 July 1961, box 1, series 1, subseries 1, folder 2, Lomax Papers. In September, with the press expecting a draft of the manuscript in roughly six weeks, Young wrote to Thurgood Marshall and asked if the eminent lawyer would read what Lomax submitted, as "your opinion of the book would mean a great deal to us." At the same time, she prodded Lomax to submit his manuscript draft as soon as possible. Genevieve Young to Thurgood Marshall, 22 September 1961, Gene Young to Louis Lomax, 26 September 1961, box 1, series 1, subseries 1, folder 2, Lomax Papers.

14 Evan Thomas to Robert F. Kennedy, 10 October 1961, Genevieve Young to Andrew Hatcher, 10 October 1961, box 1, series 1, subseries 1, folder 2, Lomax Papers.

15 Louis Lomax to Lorraine Hansberry, 26 June 1961, box 65, folder 3, Correspondence—Civil Rights Movement, Congress of Racial Equality 1961–1964, Hansberry Papers, Schomburg Center for Research in Black Culture.

16 *NYAN*, 17 June 1961, 24, 2 August 1961, 22; *NYT*, 10 September 1961, xx2.

17 "About the Author" (draft), n.d., box 1, series 1, subseries 1, folder 2, Lomax Papers; *NYHT*, 2 July 1961, F28; *NYAN*, 8 July 1961, 1, 17, 15 July 1961, 16.

18 *NYAN*, 29 July 1961, 19, 23 September 1961, 1; *NYHT*, 21 August 1961, 11; *PC*, 23 September 1961, 1; *CD*, 25 September 1961, 15; Arsenault, *Freedom Riders*, 436–437. The program is available online: "Walk in My Shoes—feat. Dick Gregory's First TV Appearance (1961)," https://www.youtube.com/watch?v=082Z9w1BequU, accessed 26 August 2018.

19 "Walk in My Shoes." For archival holdings of the 16 mm film released by ABC after the airing, see "Walk in My Shoes, Parts 1 and 2," 1963, 16 mm 51913, Holland and Terrell Libraries, Washington State University, Pullman; "Walk in My Shoes, Parts 1 and 2," 1963, 16 mm film E185.W29, McKeldin Library Media, University of Maryland, College Park.

20 "Walk in My Shoes."

21 Curtin, *Redeeming the Wasteland*, 169–175 (quote from 174).

22 *NYAN*, 29 July 1961, 19, 23 September 1961, 1; *NYHT*, 21 August 1961, 11; *PC*, 23 September 1961, 1; *CD*, 25 September 1961, 15; *NYT*, 15 September 1961, 67; *WP*, 21 September 1961, B19.

23 *NYAN*, 23 September 1961, 1; *PC*, 23 September 1961, 1; *CD*, 25 September 1961, 15; *LAS*, 28 September 1961, A7.

24 *NYAN*, 23 September 1961, 19; *NYHT*, 20 August 1961, G30; "Dr. Frederic Wertham and Louis Lomax reel tape, ¼," 7½ ips, ID#: wallace_m_136, Oversize 4, Wallace Papers, Syracuse University Archives.

25 *WP*, 29 October 1961, A1 (quote); *BAA*, 4 November 1961, 11, 11 November 1961, 8; *NYAN*, 4 November 1961, 1; *PC*, 4 November 1961, A5. Not only was Lomax spending time with Africans, he was still writing about Africa policy, even though he had moved on to this new domestic argumentation. See Louis Lomax, "Prelude."

26 *NYAN*, 14 October 1961, 15, 11 November 1961, 14; *BAA*, 18 November 1961, 7.

27 *ADW*, 12 November 1961, 1, 14 January 1962, 4. See also Fleming, *Yes We Did?*, 50–51.

28 During the previous month Lomax had changed agents, leaving Marie Rodell for Jane Kronholtz just before he submitted the final manuscript. *PC*, 18 November 1961, A21; Jane Kronholtz to Jean Young, 6 October 1961, Jane Kronholtz to Genevieve Young, 21 November 1961, Genevieve Young to Jane Kronholtz, 30 November 1961, Gene Young to Louis Lomax, 8 December 1961, box 1, series 1, subseries 1, folder 2, Lomax Papers.

29 Genevieve Young to Louis Lomax, 18 December 1961, box 1, series 1, subseries 1, folder 2, Lomax Papers.

30 Young was so concerned about Terry's project that she sent a copy of *The Negro Revolt* to James H. Robinson of Operation Crossroads Africa for his review. She had done so for *The Reluctant African* as well, but this time she sent Robinson an incomplete draft with only fourteen of the scheduled eighteen chapters. "I must apologize for the fact that it is somewhat untidy," she told the minister. "Your copy of the manuscript has not been copy-edited. Spellings, small grammatical changes and minor revisions are now being made on the master copy." She sent the same partial manuscript and apologetic introductory letter to Thurgood Marshall. Gene Young to Louis Lomax, 26 September 1961, Genevieve Young to Louis Lomax, 9 January 1961, box 1, series 1, subseries 1, folder 2, Lomax Papers; Genevieve Young to James H. Robinson, 1 February 1962, Genevieve Young to Thurgood Marshall, 13 February 1962, box 1, series 1, subseries 1, folder 3, Lomax Papers. Terry would publish one book during his lifetime, *Bloods: An Oral History of the Vietnam War by Black Veterans*. It appeared in 1984, a generation after the publishing contest with Lomax, and has become a seminal account of Black participation in Vietnam. There has yet to be a book-length history of Terry or of Luce, both important intellectual and journalistic figures of the American twentieth century who deserve biographical treatment. For more on Terry, see Terry Papers, Schomburg Center for Research in Black Culture.

31 The stress of hurriedly completing the manuscript took a toll, as it led Lomax to sever his short relationship with agent Jane Kronholtz. He asked Harper to take over prepublication magazine sales and foreign rights negotiations, though Kronholtz claimed she was entitled to a share of money from certain foreign publishers with whom she had begun negotiations before the break. She retired from the business in February 1963. Genevieve Young to Nancy Wechsler, 26 February 1962, Genevieve Young to Thurgood Marshall, 26 February 1962, "GY to LH, 27 February 62," Louis Lomax to Gene Young, 12 May 1962, box 1, series 1, subseries 1, folder 3, Lomax Papers. Gene Young to Frances Zajic, 26 February 1963, box 1, series 1, subseries 1, folder 4, Lomax Papers.

32 Nancy F. Wechsler to Gene Young, 5 March 1962, box 1, series 1, subseries 1, folder 3, Lomax Papers.

33 Louis Lomax, *Negro Revolt*, 84–97, 107–109. James H. Robinson had no such reservations. For him, *The Negro Revolt* was "one of the most dramatic and most

significant books on the whole problem of the American Negro in the United States" and was "brilliantly and carefully done." His view that Lomax had been careful contrasted with the concerns of the press's lawyers and foreshadowed the mixed reaction the book would receive. James H. Robinson to Genevieve Young, 21 March 1962, box 1, series 1, subseries 1, folder 3, Lomax Papers. In late March, to gauge such reactions and to solicit positive reviews, Harper sent bound galleys to journalist and author Norman Cousins, anthropologist Ashley Montagu, southern novelist Lillian Smith, *Black Like Me* author John Howard Griffin, historians Oscar Handlin and John Hope Franklin, and novelist Pearl Buck. Franklin, who was then teaching at Brooklyn College, pointed out several factual errors, while Montagu saw the book as "one of the most enlightening and moving contributions to our understanding of the new Negro I have read." Griffin was equally impressed. "We need this book, and I cannot imagine its being done better by anyone," he responded. "We say, about a great many books, that everyone should read them; but I have never felt this quite so strongly about other works as I do about this one." Genevieve Young to Norman Cousins, 28 March 1962, Genevieve Young to Ashley Montagu, 28 March 1962, Genevieve Young to Lillian Smith, 28 March 1962, Genevieve Young to Mrs. R. J. Walsh, 28 March 1962, Genevieve Young to John Howard Griffin, 28 March 1962, Genevieve Young to Oscar Handlin, 28 March 1962, Genevieve Young to John Hope Franklin, 28 March 1962, John Hope Franklin to Genevieve Young, 5 April 1962, Gene Young, office memo, 17 April 1962, John Howard Griffin to Genevieve Young, 18 April 1962, box 1, series 1, subseries 1, folder 3, Lomax Papers.

34 PC, 25 November 1961, A17; Louis Lomax, *Negro Revolt*, 180; Meltsner, *Making*, 99.

35 Forman, *Blacks*, 43–44. See also Heller and Pinkney, "Attitudes."

36 The plot of the proposed novel involves the Johnson family, who have come to New York as part of the Great Migration to live in a predominantly white community. Beginning in 1930 with ten-year-old Reginald Johnson walking to his predominantly white school, the book would track the life of Reginald and his sister Pamela over the next thirty-five years as the neighborhood develops into a Black enclave. Their counter in the tale is the LaHood family, second-generation Italian Americans whose parents experience problems with bigotry after arriving from overseas. The families are bound by the relationship between their children, as Reggie is involved in a fight after racial taunts finally get the best of him and young Frank Johnson comes to his aid. Over time, the neighborhood grows Black through further migration, and an older Reggie barely escapes with his life after "two Negroes shoot it out in the streets." The neighborhood has reached what Lomax calls the "Tip Point, the ratio of Negroes that can be allowed into a community before bad things happen." He adds, "The white liberals were wrong. Crime, community disorganization and property defilement did come in the wake of Negroes." Reggie later marries a wealthy Black woman and moves to Westchester County, while Pamela remains in St. Albans and becomes a schoolteacher. "Through her eyes," explains Lomax, "we see what happens to the

school system when Negroes become the majority and we also see the change in other community institutions." She becomes an alcoholic, hooks up with a pimp, and ultimately dies during a botched abortion. Meanwhile, the head of the La-Hood family "is killed during a holdup of his liquor store. The killers are Negroes." Ultimately, Reggie comes back to St. Albans, successfully operates a pharmacy, and becomes a civic leader dedicated to fixing the social and economic problems that have come to the region. "The future of St. Albans is uncertain. But, as William James said, all futures are that way." "St. Albans by Louis Lomax," box 1, series 1, subseries 1, folder 3, Lomax Papers.

37 In her extended response, Young mapped out a book decidedly different from the one Lomax proposed, while remaining encouraging about the project itself. "You may disagree with my suggestions in part or as a whole, but at least this should give you a working start towards your own ideas for a new outline for the book." In other words, the project was not going to work in its current form. Genevieve Young to Louis Lomax, 30 April 1962, box 1, series 1, subseries 1, folder 3, Lomax Papers.

38 Genevieve Young to Louis Lomax, 8 May 1962, "Request for Payment, 8 May 1962," Gene Young to Bradbury and Harwood, 4 May 1962, box 1, series 1, subseries 1, folder 3, Lomax Papers.

39 *BAA*, 2 June 1962, 5. At the state dinner, Lomax spoke to Robert Kennedy about writing his biography. The attorney general agreed to cooperate, telling Lomax that there were two biographies in the works and a later book promised to John Seigenthaler but that Kennedy was unenthusiastic about the two in progress. Again Lomax's ambition pushed beyond his capability to fulfill it. "Louis just won't let go of this," wrote Young, trying to convince herself of the Kennedy project's merit, "and it's probable that some other publisher will do it if we don't. (And if we publish it I can at least make sure it's a responsible job.) I don't know how to behave—I've been discouraging Louis but he just won't be." She tried to convince him to consider writing a children's book about Kennedy. "This seems the only way out." Evan Thomas suggested a short book on Kennedy as "a fighter for civil rights" but shared Young's skepticism. The erratic nature of Lomax's varied interests, however, would ultimately halt the potential project. "GY to EWT, 25 May 1962," box 1, series 1, subseries 1, folder 3, Lomax Papers.

40 Lomax also secured the services of a new agent that month, switching his representation to Malcolm Reiss at the Paul Reynolds agency. The press set the book's price at $4.50. Before it appeared in late May 1962, Harper sent a copy to Eleanor Roosevelt. "GY to EWT, 25 May 1962," "GY to Helen Bailey, IF, FL, FW, Joe Vesely, and Joe Madewell, 24 May 1962," Eleanor Roosevelt to Genevieve Young, 25 May 1962, box 1, series 1, subseries 1, folder 3, Lomax Papers; *NYAN*, 26 May 1962, 17, 18; *NYT*, 27 May 1962, X12; *CD*, 23 August 1962, 10.

41 Cass Canfield to Martin Luther King Jr., 16 August 1962, Papers of Martin Luther King Jr., King Library and Archives. The letter also appears as "Harper & Row, Publishers to Martin Luther King, 16 August 1962," box 1, series 1, subseries 1, folder 3, Lomax Papers.

42 Louis Lomax, *Negro Revolt*, 11 (quote), 93 (quote), 164–177.

43 Louis Lomax, *Negro Revolt*, 38–39.

44 Louis Lomax, *Negro Revolt*, 42–45 (quote from 43); Malcolm X, "Race Problem."

45 Louis Lomax, *Negro Revolt*, 52–53.

46 Louis Lomax, *Negro Revolt*, 112–115 (quote from 113).

47 Louis Lomax, *Negro Revolt*, 76–79.

48 Louis Lomax, *Negro Revolt*, 164–177 (quote), 219 (quote).

49 "New Lomax quotes from reviews," box 1, series 1, subseries 1, folder 3, Lomax Papers.

50 *NYT*, 1 March 1964, SM23.

51 The *Los Angeles Sentinel* emphasized Lomax's quoting of Jackie Robinson, a member of the NAACP board, about the need for the organization to be more militant. Robinson, who had been critical of Lomax's earlier efforts, seemed to be on board with the author's new thesis. The book was also recommended by the American Library Association. *LAS*, 12 July 1962, A22; *NYHT*, 24 June 1962, E4, 5 August 1962, E11; *NYT*, 13 February 2011, A30; Dunbar, *Black Expatriates*.

52 *NYAN*, 7 July 1962, 11.

53 Fischer, "What the Negro Needs"; *NYAN*, 14 July 1962, 11.

54 On 3 July, he appeared on NBC's *The Tonight Show* and later that week on the Patty Cavin radio program on Washington's WRC radio. These were followed by a radio interview with Barry Farber on New York's WINS and one with Lee Graham on WNYC. *NYAN*, 30 June 1962, 17, 7 July 1962, 3; *WP*, 1 July 1962, G5; *NYHT*, 3 July 1962, 13, 27 July 1962, 13.

55 *NYT*, 17 July 1962, 57, 5 August 1962, 96; *NYHT*, 27 July 1962, 13; *ADW*, 29 July 1962, 8, 2 August 1962, 3; *CD*, 4 August 1962, 2; *PC*, 11 August 1962, 18.

56 *NYT*, 8 August 1962, 45, 12 August 1962, X12; *NYHT*, 15 August 1962, 17; *NYAN*, 18 August 1962, 17.

5. AMBITIONS

1 "GY to WIB, CC, RCH, and DP, 26 July 1962," preliminary manufacturing estimate, 26 July 1962, Genevieve Young to Louis Lomax, 6 August 1962, box 1, series 1, subseries 1, folder 3, Lomax Papers.

2 "Gene Young to RCH, 21 August 1962," Malcolm Reiss to Genevieve Young, 7 August 1962, box 1, series 1, subseries 1, folder 3, Lomax Papers.

3 Edward L. Burlingame to Virginia Olson, 24 August 1962, "Notice of Reprint Contract, 27 August 1962," Genevieve Young to Oliver Swan, 2 August 1962, Oliver G. Swan to Genevieve Young, 24 August 1962, box 1, series 1, subseries 1, folder 3, Lomax Papers.

4 Genevieve Young to Louis Lomax, 28 August 1962, box 1, series 1, subseries 1, folder 3, Lomax Papers.

5 "GY to WIB, 30 August 1962," box 1, series 1, subseries 1, folder 3, Lomax Papers; Gabbard, *Better Git It*, 140; Santoro, *Myself*, 252; Mingus and Goodman, *Mingus*, 159–163.

6 Gabbard, *Better Git It*, 140–142; Porter, *What Is This Thing*, 138–139.

7 By the end of October, it had sold more than 7,500 copies. Genevieve Young to Louis Lomax, 30 August 1962, Genevieve Young to Louis Lomax, 30 October 1962, Genevieve Young to Louis Lomax, 6 August 1962, box 1, series 1, subseries 1, folder 3, Lomax Papers.

8 Carson, "SNCC and the Albany Movement"; Branch, *Parting the Waters*, 524–561.

9 *NYHT*, 6 August 1962, 15, 19 August 1962, 1; *NYT*, 19 August 1962, 74; *CD*, 20 August 1962, 8; *NYAN*, 18 August 1962, 38, 1 September 1962, 10.

10 That same month, August 1962, Grant Reynolds, legal adviser to the chair of the Republican National Committee, made a speech in Chicago denouncing President Kennedy and arguing that he and his brother Robert were engaged in an "intellectual snow job" and using mouthpieces such as journalists Carl Rowan and Lomax to defend their positions. But Lomax's work with Malcolm and his efforts in Englewood disproved such claims, to say nothing of the journalist's own participation in politics. *NYAN*, 15 September 1962, 10; *CD*, 1 February 1968, 8.

11 He was also an officer with the Alban Manor Neighborhood Association in Jamaica, working closely with the Borough President's Committee on Urban Renewal and Neighborhood Conservation to help create the Jamaica Coordinating Committee for Urban Renewal and Neighborhood Conservation. *NYT*, 28 June 1962, 35; *NYAN*, 7 July 1962, 10, 21.

12 When the Liberal Party held its state convention in September, Lomax was also voted secretary of the party's platform committee. *NYAN*, 18 August 1962, 21, 27 October 1962, 1; *NYT*, 6 September 1962, 20; *NYHT*, 4 November 1962, 11.

13 *NYHT*, 4 November 1962, 19; *NYT*, 5 November 1962, 24, 7 November 1962, 19, 8 November 1962, 25.

14 *NYAN*, 15 September 1962, 17, 39; *NYT*, 25 September 1962, 75.

15 *WP*, 19 September 1962, D30; *CD*, 25 September 1962, 13; Shaw, *Hollywood's Cold War*, 180.

16 When the drive culminated on 13 October, Lomax spoke at the concluding rally along with Ossie Davis, Ruby Dee, and others, making a final appeal for citizens to register on the last possible day to make them eligible for the November elections. *NYAN*, 22 September 1962, 8, 29 September 1962, 39, 6 October 1962, 46, 13 April 1962, 8; *BAA*, 29 September 1962, 15.

17 *LAT*, 25 January 1963, C9; "Announce Filming," 58; *NYAN*, 26 January 1963, 14; *CD*, 2 February 1963, 10; Crump, *Burn, Killer*.

18 "GY to FW, 23 January 1963," box 1, series 1, subseries 1, folder 4, Lomax Papers; *CD*, 28 January 1963, 13; *WP*, 1 February 1963, 22; *NYAN*, 26 January 1963, 15, 17, 2 February 1963, 12, 39, 9 February 1963, 16, 16 February 1963, 1, 9 March 1963, 17; *BG*, 13 March 1963, 18.

19 "GY to WIB, 26 February 1963," box 1, series 1, subseries 1, folder 4, Lomax Papers.

20 Unknown to JF, 28 November 1962, box 1, series 1, subseries 1, folder 3, Lomax Papers.

21 Just before that withdrawal, on 23 November 1962, the New York City marshal served Harper a levy after Leslie H. Cramer, a journalist headquartered in Addis Ababa, Ethiopia, won a judgment against Lomax for $602.03 plus 6 percent interest. No records survive of the levy because of the strange pseudo-independence of New York City marshals, but it was essentially a small claims debt from Lomax's time overseas. Genevieve Young to Louis Lomax, 10 December 1962, Louis F. Haynie to Gene Young, 10 December 1962, Genevieve Young to Louis Lomax, 17 December 1962, box 1, series 1, subseries 1, folder 3, Lomax Papers; "In the Matter of the Guardianship and Tutorship of Almaz Fufa, A Minor," Civil Case 132/56, High Court, Addis Ababa, Civil Division No. 1, *Journal of Ethiopian Law* 5 (No. 1, 1968): 79–82; "1974–1975," SAD.873/15/12–16, Lush Papers, Sudan Archive.

22 *BAA*, 23 March 1963, 1; *CD*, 23 March 1963, 8; *NYAN*, 23 March 1963, 11.

23 *LAS*, 28 March 1963, A5, 4 April 1963, C2; *WP*, 31 March 1997, B4. According to Lomax, a woman at the party asked Malcolm why he began his statements with "The Honorable Elijah Muhammad teaches . . ." Malcolm responded with a comparison to ventriloquist Edgar Bergen and his dummy, Charlie McCarthy, with himself as the dummy. "Mr. Muhammad is everything, and I am nothing." Lomax, *When the Word*, 80–81.

24 Louis Lomax, *To Kill a Black Man*, 93–94; DeCaro, *On the Side*, 159–161; Hartnell, "Between Exodus," 214; Curtis, "Islamism," 693. The visit was not Malcolm's first to Los Angeles. The previous year, the Los Angeles Police Department shot seven members of the Nation of Islam, paralyzing one and killing another. Malcolm made the trip to investigate the murder, and biographers have credited his frustration with the broader faith's inaction as an early cause of Malcolm's disillusionment with Muhammad and his eventual split from the organization. See Knight, "Justifiable Homicide"; Taylor, "Black Radicalism," 312; Perry, *Malcolm*, 191–194; "Los Angeles Shooting Incident," NY 105-8999, FBI File No. 100-399321.

25 Haley, "Interview," 220–221. Haley remembered that Malcolm "felt that his greatest safety lay in really trusting only a few people—and those few only to certain degrees. The late author Louis Lomax and I used to laugh about how we didn't discover until much later that once Malcolm had visited and given each of us interviews in different rooms in the same hotel, with never a mention to either about the other, although he knew well that Lomax and I were good friends." Gallen, *Malcolm X*, 247.

26 *CD*, 15 June 1963, 12, 22 June 1963, 5, 27 June 1963, 3, 29 June 1963, 6, 6 July 1963, 7.

27 *NYT*, 5 June 1963, 59, 7 June 1963, 15; *CD*, 13 June 1963, 9; *In the Matter of Louis M. Broido et al., Petitioners, v. State Commission for Human Rights, Respondent*, 40 Misc.2d 419 (1963).

28 Myrna Goodman to Harper & Row, 8 March 1963, Jean LaCouture to Harper & Row, 18 June 1963, box 1, series 1, subseries 1, folder 4, Lomax Papers; *LAS*, 16 May 1963, C9; *NYAN*, 1 June 1963, 15.

29 Charles P. Howard began his career as a Des Moines attorney. His three sons worked for the *Observer*, too, and in its first year, 1939, the family expanded the

enterprise to include two additional publications, the *Waterloo Observer* and the *Tri-City Observer*. Howard used his paper to fight for civil and human rights, becoming more and more involved in progressive politics. His attendance at the World Peace Conference in Poland in 1950 led to his being disbarred the following year, because the gathering was sponsored by Communists. With no law practice, Howard began focusing all of his attention on journalism, reporting often from Africa on anticolonial fights before becoming a United Nations correspondent. He died in 1969. *ADW*, 6 August 1939, 1, 16 October 1939, 6, 22 January 1940, 3, 25 July 1940, 6, 31 May 1941, 4, 18 July 1941, 6. See also Garfinkel, *When Negroes*; Pfeffer, *A. Philip Randolph*; Lucander, *Winning the War*.

30 *NYT*, 7 July 1963, 22; *CT*, 26 July 1963, 3; *NYAN*, 10 August 1963, 9; *BG*, 25 August 1963, 35.

31 Muhammad was also vigorously opposed to Communism, arguing that its refusal to recognize God was an abomination. When Malcolm and Castro met at the United Nations in 1960, Muhammad was outraged. However, he also saw Communism as a tool that existed "to destroy the whites" and thus never launched a public assault against it. Clegg, *Life*, 156.

32 *LAT*, 14 August 1963, 6. For more on the Nation of Islam and efforts overseas, see Ambar, *Malcolm X*.

33 Press accounts, UPI-173, UPI-51, confidential report, 27 September 1963, FBI File No. 62-102926; "U.S. Denies Hampering Writer's Visa," 21; US Department of State, "On the Record," Mary Ferrell Foundation.

34 Lomax's planned article about the Cuba trip for *Harper's* never appeared. The archive does not indicate why, but it is likely either that the public grievance with the State Department about a trip to a Communist country put the magazine in an uncomfortable position or that Lomax chose not to write the piece or wrote something too scathing about the federal government to be publishable in a mainstream magazine.

35 Jones, *March*; Euchner, *Nobody*; Patrick Bass, *Like a Mighty Stream*.

36 Lomax had actually written approvingly of Taconic in *The Negro Revolt*, describing its 1961 effort to underwrite a voting rights drive. The group ultimately provided a quarter million dollars to a consortium of groups that included the National Urban League, CORE, the SCLC, SNCC, and "after considerable delay" the NAACP. He gave particular attention to attorney Lloyd Garrison, "the man who functioned as catalyst for all who are involved in the pincers movement." Lomax was worried, however, that "foundation officials refused to say just where their money comes from." Louis Lomax, *Negro Revolt*, 219, 234; *LAT*, 20 August 1963, 1; *WP*, 20 August 1963, A4; Student Nonviolent Coordinating Committee, 1960–1961, 1965, box 142, folder 1413, series 1: Grants, Taconic Foundation Records, Rockefeller Archive Center; NAACP Legal Defense and Educational Fund: General, 1961–1966, box 81, folder 816, series 1: Grants, Taconic Foundation Records; Congress of Racial Equality (CORE): Special Purpose Fund, 1963, 1966–1967, box 33, folder 341, series 1: Grants, Taconic Foundation Records;

Southern Regional Council: General Program, 1958–1964, box 139, folder 1372, series 1: Grants, Taconic Foundation Records; Southern Regional Council: Voter Education Project, 1963–1964, box 141, folder 1397, series 1: Grants, Taconic Foundation Records.

37 While in the region, Lomax also committed to return in late September for an Oakland conference on the Mind of the Ghetto, where he would appear along with Baldwin, Muhammad Ali, Malcolm X, Sidney Poitier, Mahalia Jackson, and others. *LAS*, 29 August 1963, A9, C3.

38 Roy Wilkins celebrated the March on Washington as an unqualified success. "Louis Lomax joined Senator Stennis of Mississippi in criticizing the March. But despite Lomax and Stennis, it was the greatest day!" Goldman, *Death*, 104–105; *NYAN*, 7 September 1963, 10; Marable, *Malcolm X*, 255–258.

39 For more on the March on Washington, see Jones, *March*.

40 *NYAN*, 7 September 1963, 33.

41 William Bundy, "Leading Negroes Flay Kennedy; Condemn Both Major Parties," *The Militant* (New York), 30 September 1962, 1, 2; Exhibit 1342 in United States, Warren Commission, *Investigation of the Assassination*, 22:565–566; *NYT*, 17 September 1963, 26, 21 September 1963, 8; *CD*, 24 September 1963, A9; *BAA*, 28 September 1963, 8.

42 "The Black Revolution—What Next?" flyer, 1963, box 3, folder 8 (political and protest flyers), Wells Papers, Amistad Research Center; *NYT*, 20 September 1963, 21.

43 *NYT*, 22 September 1963, 1, 72; *CD*, 2 October 1963, 5; *PC*, 5 October 1963, 11; *BAA*, 5 October 1963, 14; Weems, *Desegregating the Dollar*, 67.

44 *PC*, 5 October 1963, 11; *CD*, 7 October 1963, 4.

45 Malcolm made no attempt to avoid Lomax but did not endorse the boycott effort. *PC*, 26 October 1963, 17.

46 *CD*, 9 November 1963, 1, 14 November 1963, 16; *NYAN*, 9 November 1963, 24; *BAA*, 16 November 1963, 1, 23 November 1963, 11.

47 There were local efforts at Christmas boycotts, but they too were unable to meet the mark they set for themselves. The Jackson, Mississippi, boycott prompted the mayor and other officials to create incentives for downtown shopping, which at least demonstrated an acknowledgment of the protest, but those incentives also largely ended it. There was limited success in Danville, Virginia; Cambridge, Maryland; and Birmingham itself. *WP*, 2 January 1964, A6; Marable, *Malcolm X*, 163.

6. WHEN THE WORD IS GIVEN

1 Louis Lomax, *When the Word*, 10.

2 Louis Lomax, *When the Word*, 81.

3 Louis Lomax, *When the Word*, 31, 91.

4 Louis Lomax, *When the Word*, 92.

5 The book also caused raised tensions within the organization's leadership because Malcolm X appeared on the cover and Elijah Muhammad did not. *CD*, 1 August 1963, 13; Evanzz, *Judas Factor*, 197–201, 207; Leclerc, "Malcolm X," 17.

6 Marable, *Malcolm X*, 163.

7 Louis Lomax, *When the Word*. The National Memorial African Bookstore held a party on 2 November for the book's debut, featuring Lomax, Baldwin, and Killens, among others. "Fresh African coffee from the Gold Coast will be served," read a bookstore advertisement for the event. "So take a tip and be present at the party's sip . . . it will be worth your trip." *NYAN*, 2 November 1963, 15.

8 Louis Lomax, *When the Word*, 41, 60.

9 *CT*, 10 November 1963, J3.

10 Goldman, *Death*, 111; Louis Lomax, *When the Word*, 179; Breitman, *Last Year*, 18–19.

11 *CD*, 16 November 1963, 19; *CT*, 8 December 1963, 12; *ADW*, 9 January 1964, 4, 18 December 1963, 1. For more on Robeson, see Boyle and Bunie, *Paul Robeson*; Goodman, *Paul Robeson*; Swindall, *Paul Robeson*.

12 *NYAN*, 18 January 1964, 9.

13 Baldwin, *No Name*, 11 (quote), 50–52 (quote), 60 (quote), 92–98, 118 (quote).

14 Brathwaite devoted the rest of his life to African nationalist causes. He hosted *Afrikaleidoscope* on New York's WBAI radio for more than three decades, participated in several African anticolonial efforts, and wrote extensively. He died in 2014. Brath, *Color Us Cullud!*; "Who Is Elombe Brath?," the Elombe Brath Foundation, https://www.elombebrathfoundation.org/legacy, accessed 1 September 2018.

15 Brath, *Color Us Cullud!*

16 *NYAN*, 18 January 1964, 23; *CD*, 11 April 1964, 7.

17 "Louis E. Lomax Addresses Freedom Stay-Out Rally in Boston," "Freedom Stay Out Day in the Boston Public Schools, Press Releases and Statements of Support," box 3, Ryan Papers, Northeastern University; *BG*, 9 February 1964, 16, 11 February 1964, 6.

18 *BG*, 11 February 1964, 1, 24 February 1964, 1, 2, 25 February 1964, 1, 4; "Stay Out for Freedom; Freedom Stay-Out: What Happened This Afternoon," 26 February 1964, WGBH Media Library and Archives, accessed August 28, 2018, http://openvault.wgbh.org/catalog/A_9CC67C044F5D49C189D5B656DE950F98; Theoharis, "I'd Rather Go."

19 Just as with the Howard-Till affair, Lomax's Pomona speech earned him the attention of the FBI. SAC, Los Angeles, to director, FBI, 29 February 1964, FBI File No. 62-102926; *LAT*, 29 February 1964, 3; Perlstein, *Before the Storm*, 295.

20 *LAT*, 29 February 1964, 3.

21 Louis Lomax, "Negro View," 38; Gaillard, *Cradle*, 212; Leuchtenburg, *White House*, 180–181. See also Louis Lomax, "Kennedys."

22 His new agent for the project was Malcolm Reiss. Malcolm Reiss to Jean Young, 28 January 1964, "GY to EWT, 31 January 1964," Genevieve Young to Malcolm

Reiss, 4 February 1964, box 1, series 1, subseries 1, folder 4, Lomax Papers; Louis Lomax to Bob Loomis, n.d., box 2, series 1, subseries 4, folder 1, Lomax Papers.

23 Genevieve Young to Louis Lomax, 18 March 1964, box 1, series 1, subseries 1, folder 4, Lomax Papers.

24 Gene Young to Frances Zajic, 13 April 1964, "Genevieve Young to Louis Lomax, 21 April 1964, Louis Lomax to Genevieve Young, 25 April 1964, box 1, series 1, subseries 1, folder 4, Lomax Papers.

25 Genevieve Young to Louis Lomax, 8 July 1964, box 1, series 1, subseries 1, folder 4, Lomax Papers.

26 Harold T. Anderson to Mrs. Walter Coe, 11 August 1964, Gene Young to Harold Anderson, 24 August 1964, box 1, series 1, subseries 1, folder 4, Lomax Papers.

27 Valera, "Politics," 22–25; Tirella, *Tomorrow-Land*, 76–82; *BAA*, 14 March 1964, 13.

28 Evanzz, *Judas Factor*, 209–210, 229–230; Marable, *Black Leadership*, 172.

29 *BG*, 24 March 1964, 8, 27; Evanzz, *Judas Factor*, 213; "Muslim Mosque, Incorporated," Memorandum, 30 April 1964, FBI File No. 100-399321.

30 *BAA*, 4 April 1964, 1.

31 "Appearance of Malcolm X with Louis Lomax at a CORE Sponsored Meeting on April 3, 1964 at Cleveland," 7 April 1964, FBI File No. 100-399321; Abdullah, "Malcolm X," 215; *BAA*, 18 April 1964, 3; Marable, *Malcolm X*, 303; Malcolm X, "Ballot."

32 Swiderski, "Approaches," 147, 235; *Cleveland Call and Post*, 11 April 1961, 1; *Cleveland Plain Dealer*, 5 April 1964, 1.

33 Days after the event, the two continued their publicity tour, Lomax interviewing Malcolm for local radio where he expanded on his "Ballot or the Bullet" speech. *NYAN*, 11 April 1964, 1; "Malcolm X on Civil Rights," 133, Lincoln Collection, Woodruff Library. Available online at http://digitalcommons.auctr.edu/celcav/133/.

34 *NYAN*, 11 April 1964, 25; *CD*, 16 April 1964, 5.

35 *CT*, 10 May 1964, F10, 17 May 1964, F10, 22 May 1964, B9; Evanzz, *Judas Factor*, 207; Goldman, *Death*, 193.

36 Marable, *Malcolm X*, 332; Evanzz, *Judas Factor*, 239–240; *NYT*, 24 May 1964, 61.

37 Gallen, *Malcolm X*, 215.

38 *NYT*, 15 June 1964, 1; Felber, "Harlem," 217.

39 Silberman, *Crisis*, 217; Nemiroff, *Lorraine Hansberry*, 237; Cruse, *Crisis*, 206; *Village Voice*, 9 July 1964, 1.

40 For a broader description and critique of the position of the representatives of the Association of Artists for Freedom, particularly in relation to the Town Hall debate and the rejection of white liberalism, see Cruse, *Crisis*, 193–224.

41 Felber, "'Harlem"; Sales, *From Civil Rights*, 97–132.

42 "Go Shine Shoes"; UPI-133, FBI File No. 62-102926; *NYT*, 1 July 1964, 22; *CD*, 2 July 1964, 3; *BAA*, 11 July 1964, 18; *PC*, 11 July 1964, 4.

43 See Watson, *Freedom Summer*.

44 See Cagin and Dray, *We Are Not Afraid*; Huie, *Three Lives*.

45 *BAA*, 4 July 1964, 11.

46 *CD*, 25 July 1964, 8.

47 *LAT*, 15 July 1964, 12; *LAS*, 16 July 1964, A1; Theoharis, "'Alabama,'" 46–48; Self, *American Babylon*, 167–168, 263–264; Felker-Kantor, "Fighting the Segregation Amendment," 73–74.

48 *LAS*, 20 August 1964, B12, 27 August 1964, D3.

49 *LAT*, 23 August 1964, B12; *LAS*, 27 August 1964, A7, 3 September 1964, A2.

50 *LAT*, 30 August 1964, C14; *LAS*, 27 August 1964, A11, D11, 3 September 1964, A1; *CD*, 3 September 1964, 2.

51 *LAS*, 16 November 1967, A1; Press, *Toxic Talk*, 9–10; Halper, *Icons*, 182–189.

52 *LAS*, 24 September 1964, B3, 1 October 1964, D1, 22 October 1964, D1.

53 *LAS*, 24 September 1964, C2, C4, 1 October 1964, A5, C2, C6, 8 October 1964, C2, 15 October 1964, A3, 5 November 1964, C2, C6; Felker-Kantor, "Fighting the Segregation Amendment," 77.

54 *LAS*, 1 October 1964, D1.

55 *LAT*, 5 November 1964, 22; Felker-Kantor, "Fighting the Segregation Amendment," 83–84.

56 Lomax did not cite his sources of information for his account. Louis Lomax, "Road." See the full edition of the magazine for the other accounts.

57 *NYT*, 26 October 1964, 20; *WP*, 3 November 1964, A5; *BAA*, 7 November 1964, 12; *LAT*, 4 December 1964, D10.

58 [Redacted] to J. Edgar Hoover, 16 October 1964, UPI-39B, FBI File No. 62-102926.

59 *CD*, 12 September 1964, 5.

60 *Messenger from Violet Drive*; *NYAN*, 28 November 1964, 17, 5 December 1964, 19; *CD*, 7 December 1964, 20; *NYT*, 7 December 1964, 71; *WP*, 7 December 1964, B9.

61 *Messenger from Violet Drive.*

62 This is not to say that Lomax had lost his taste for the poison pen. "Elijah Muhammad has really come up with nothing new," he said. "You take the first five books of the Old Testament and everywhere it says, 'Jew,' you write, 'Negro,' you get Elijah Muhammad." *Messenger from Violet Drive.*

63 *CD*, 10 February 1965, 1; *WP*, 10 February 1965, A3.

64 *CD*, 28 January 1965, 12.

7. THE LOUIS LOMAX SHOW

1 *NYT*, 22 February 1965, 1, 11 March 1966, 1.

2 Louis Lomax, *To Kill a Black Man* 198–200, 228–229, 247–248.

3 *LAT*, 21 February 1965, A5, A12; *LAS*, 16 November 1967, A1; Rickford, *Betty Shabazz*, 232–233.

4 *NYAN*, 6 March 1965, 2; Rickford, *Betty Shabazz*, 264.

5 *LAS*, 25 February 1965, A1; Barnette and Linn, "Black Muslims," 26.

6 Bogle, *Primetime Blues*, 15–18.

7 Bogle, *Primetime Blues*, 57–59; Bronstein, "Televising the South," 31–35; "Host with the Most"; *CD*, 22 February 1958, 10. See also Dates and Barlow, *Split Image*.

8 Cole, "Why I Quit My TV Show."

9 When Thomas Kilgore, leader of the western branch of King's SCLC, hosted a special event for King, Lomax was among the attendees. *NYAN*, 27 February 1965, 14; *LAT*, 27 February 1965, B2, 4 January 1967, A6; *LAS*, 4 March 1965, C13, 8 April 1965, A1.

10 *Louis Lomax Show* topic and comment forms, box 12, series 6, folder 11, Lomax Papers. For extant episodes available in the archive, see "The Louis Lomax show. [1967, unidentified issue, no. 1390] / KTTV, Los Angeles," Inventory no. T42193; "The Louis Lomax show. [1967, unidentified issue, no. 1452] / KTTV," Inventory no. T42191, University of California, Southern Regional Library Facility, UCLA Film and Television Archive, Los Angeles.

11 Mildred Mosier was the associate producer of *The Louis Lomax Show*. She would later leave the business to become the administrator of the Contemporary Crafts Gallery in Los Angeles after finding herself under a glass ceiling in the television business. *NYAN*, 20 March 1965, 16; *LAS*, 8 April 1965, D1, 26 September 1974, A2; *PC*, 17 April 1965, 16.

12 See, for example, *LAT*, 3 March 1967, D17, 12 March 1967, A55, 21 July 1967, D1; Didion and Dunne, "Hate Hour." For more on Coughlin's legacy, see Casey and Rowe, "'Driving Out the Money Changers'; Carpenter, "Father Charles E. Coughlin"; Kay, Ziegelmueller, and Minch, "From Coughlin." For more on Pyne, see chapter 6.

13 *LAT*, 3 October 1967, C12.

14 *LAT*, 23 April 1965, C18.

15 *NYT*, 2 May 1965, SM48.

16 The divorce was amicable, as the couple had been legally separated since February 1964. The wedding ceremony was a hasty one, taking place after the church's usual service. It was Baker's second marriage, Lomax's fourth. No invitations were sent for the event. Baker's six-year-old son served as ring bearer, and there was a coffee reception after the ceremony. Reporters snapped photographs of the new couple. *LAS*, 8 April 1965, D1, 15 April 1965, A1, A8, C2; *CD*, 13 April 1965, 3; *PC*, 17 April 1965, 16.

17 By the end of 1966, she was seen wearing, according to the *Amsterdam News*, "a natural coif and African-inspired garb" at a party for Livingston Wingate. *PC*, 1 May 1965, 13; *BAA*, 21 August 1965, 17; *NYAN*, 3 December 1966, 12.

18 *BAA*, 17 April 1965, 11.

19 *LAS*, 22 April 1965, B5; *LAT*, 15 May 1965, 22, 22 May 1965, B4.

20 *LAS*, 22 April 1965, D1; Louis Lomax, "Georgia Boy," 155.

21 Louis Lomax, "Georgia Boy," 158. See also Vandiver, "Harper's," 320–322.

22 See Aiello, "Not Too Far Removed."

23 Fairclough, *Race*, 344–363; *NYT*, 14 July 1965, 1; *CD*, 12 August 1965, 10; Wendt, "'Urge People'"; Strain, "'We Walked." For more on the early, racially problematic development of Bogalusa, see Wyche, "Paternalism"; Norwood, "Bogalusa."

24 *LAT*, 12 June 1965, A12, 14 June 1965, 25. See also Hill, *Deacons* 150–154; Cobb, *This Nonviolent Stuff'll Get You Killed*.

25 The following week, to supposedly less controversy and harassment, Lomax's show featured Fannie Lou Hamer, leader of the Mississippi Freedom Democratic Party. *LAT*, 16 June 1965, 12, 19 June 1965, B2.

26 *LAS*, 1 July 1965, A1.

27 *LAT*, 11 July 1965, D1, 13 July 1965, 1; *CD*, 13 July 1965, 5.

28 Despite the public animosity between McKeithen and Lomax, the governor was impressed with his rival, and the two would later meet in private. Still, that respect did not advance negotiations. *NYT*, 14 July 1965, 1; *LAT*, 15 July 1965, A1, A2; *CD*, 15 July 1965, 8; Fairclough, *Race*, 369–370.

29 *NYT*, 15 July 1965, 12; *Bogalusa Daily News*, 16 July 1965, 1; *LAT*, 16 July 1965, 1, 8, 17 July 1965, 11; *CT*, 17 July 1965, 13.

30 *LAS*, 15 July 1965, A9.

31 That night, he hosted a fundraising event at his home for Bogalusa, where about five hundred people crammed into the mountain home, as drivers shuttled guests up the narrow path to the event. He spoke at another rally for Bogalusa at Wilshire Christian Church on 4 August. *LAT*, 25 July 1965, 8; *LAS*, 29 July 1965, A10, C2, 31 July 1965, 19.

32 *NYT*, 15 August 1965, 81; *LAS*, 5 June 1980, A7. For more on the uprising, see Horne, *Fire*.

33 The show had always been broadcast in black and white, but KTTV announced its plan to convert the stage where it was filmed to color and to broadcast its first color show in October. *LAT*, 17 September 1965, D16; *LAS*, 2 September 1965, A1, D1, 18 November 1965, A7; *NYT*, 20 March 1966, 1.

34 At the same time, Lomax was also dismissing the white liberal elite. "America is still a white man's country," he wrote in an August 1965 essay for *Ebony*. "White men, and they alone, make the decisions that actually affect our lives. True, non-whites have some influence, but it is secondary at best." He argued that "white liberal money and bodies have moved in and taken over every national civil rights organization with the exceptions of . . . CORE, and the Student Non-Violent Coordinating Committee," two of the groups advocating the Black Power positions he had also criticized. *LAS*, 14 July 1966, A1, 28 July 1966, C15; Louis Lomax, "White Liberal," 60, 66; Walmsley, "Tell It Like It Isn't," 304–305.

35 Louise Sweeney, "Otis Chandler: Hemingway Could Have Invented Him," *Christian Science Monitor*, 5 February 1980, B1; Adam Bernstein, "Otis Chandler: Publisher Established Los Angeles Times as Respected Voice," *WP*, 28 February 2006, B7.

36 In September, Lomax made the first in a series of lectures about the Watts uprising at Woodland Hills Methodist Church, sponsored by the denomination's Lay Academy. The title of his speech, "Watts New, White Pussycat?," was used in literature designed to smear the series by whites supportive of the Los Angeles Police Department. The Nation of Islam's John Shabazz was supposed to be the second speaker but was forced to cancel after threats of violence. *LAT*, 29 August 1965, B1, 24 September 1965, SF8, 27 September 1965, SF8; *LAS*, 2 September 1965, A1, D1.

37 *LAS*, 18 November 1965, A7.

38 Days later on 13 December, the duo debated again at UCLA. *LAT*, 5 December 1965, SF-A2, 11 December 1965, 13, 12 December 1965, WS12. See Bogus, *Buckley*; Felzenberg, *Man and His Presidents*.

39 In early February Lomax and Buckley debated again, this time on television. Jackie Robinson, who often had a contentious relationship with Lomax, thought Buckley "got soundly whupped. I do not mean whipped. I do not mean beaten. I do not mean defeated. I mean that Louis Lomax, God bless him, gave Bill Buckley a good, old-fashioned, merciless, woodshed whuppin.'" The debate was largely a retread of the pair's previous two efforts, but it turned Robinson, at least temporarily, into a fan of Lomax. "May Bill Buckley rest in peace," wrote Robinson, "and may Louis Lomax live forever." *LAT*, 22 December 1965, B6; *NYAN*, 12 February 1966, 13; *CD*, 19 February 1966, 10. Sometime in September, Lomax's assistant called Buckley and asked if he would debate civil rights at the University of Moscow. Buckley refused, wondering why he would debate American civil rights "before a group of political slaves" and was met with incredulity from his assistant. Buckley later talked to Lomax himself and offered some alternative topics relating to political freedom, but either Lomax or officials in Moscow vetoed the idea. *LAT*, 14 October 1966, A6.

40 On 21 January, Lomax began his two-hour radio program, *The World of Louis Lomax*, which aired Monday through Saturday beginning at noon on Los Angeles's KDAY. Albert Lanphear, vice president of the station's parent company, announced the new signing and explained that the show would feature interviews, discussion, and listener phone calls. Advertisements trumpeted special guests such as James Farmer, Martin Luther King, Wayne Morse, and Robert Weaver. *LAT*, 16 January 1966, B1, 17 January 1966, 3, 21 January 1966, 26, 30 January 1966, 38; *LAS*, 27 January 1966, B7, 3 February 1966, B3; *NYAN*, 29 January 1966, 20.

41 *LAT*, 19 July 1965, C23, 20 July 1965, C12.

42 *CD*, 31 July 1965, 11.

43 *NYAN*, 8 January 1966, 2; *LAT*, 21 January 1966, C12.

44 As a supplement to his lucrative income, and despite his own lack of a college degree, in the spring 1966 semester, Lomax taught a course on race relations at Valley State College in Northridge. *NYAN*, 12 March 1966, 13, 18, 2 April 1966, 18; *LAT*, 23 December 1965, SF2, 27 January 1966, C12. For more on Patterson, see Miller, *Born along the Color Line*, 286; Pederson, *Communist Party*, 6, 86.

45 It was also in late February that the Center for the Study of Democratic Institutions released a series of tape-recorded discussions about national racial problems. One of those tapes, "Have Slums, Will Travel," featured Lomax analyzing the center's national education plan through a racial lens. *LAS*, 3 February 1966, A1, 10 February 1966, D2, 24 February 1966, C11; *LAT*, 3 February 1966, 3, 5 February 1966, B3; Louis Lomax, "Have Slums, Will Travel."

46 *LAT*, 17 March 1966, 3.

47 The victims were Lawrence Gomez and Joe Crawford. *LAT*, 18 March 1966, 3, 31 March 1966, A1; *NYT*, 20 March 1966, 1; *LAS*, 24 March 1966, A1. The donation

checks were presented on Lomax's television show on April 21 and 24. *LAS*, 21 April 1966, D3.

48 *LAT*, 20 March 1966, B1; *LAS*, 31 March 1966, B6.

49 *LAS*, 24 March 1966, A1.

50 On May 23, Lomax won one of the city's Unity Awards, sponsored by the Hollywood Unity Awards Committee and the Cordova Club of Los Angeles, given annually to film, television, and radio personalities who made "meritorious contributions to the betterment of human relations" in the previous year. Higgins, "Talking About"; *LAT*, 21 April 1966, 3, 4 May 1966, 2, 2 June 1966, D16; *LAS*, 19 May 1966, B10. See also Mulloy, *World*.

51 At the same time the radio changes were taking place, KTTV hired left-wing comedian Mort Sahl for a Friday night show, who raged not only against the political right but also against his former Hollywood friends like Paul Newman and Steve Allen brushing him off. "They've all moved in with the Establishment," he said. "I called Bill Cosby to come on my KTTV show a couple of weeks ago and he said he didn't do local TV now, but if he did he'd go on the Lomax show. I thought that was pretty funny." *LAT*, 25 April 1966, 3, 26 April 1966, C14, 28 April 1966, SG2, 1 June 1966, C14.

52 *LAT*, 27 May 1966, D14; *CT*, 3 June 1966, A1.

53 *WP*, 3 June 1966, A6.

54 Goudsouzian, *Down to the Crossroads*, 14. See also Carmichael and Thelwell, *Ready for Revolution*; H. Brown, *Die, Nigger*.

55 *CT*, 14 August 1966, A6; *Jennings Daily News*, 16 August 1966, 8; "Let Whites Give Something," 7.

56 *LAT*, 19 September 1966, A1, 30 September 1966, B8.

57 [Redacted] to J. Edgar Hoover, 1 August 1966, [redacted] to KTTV Television, August 1966, 28 July 1966, [redacted] to George Murphy, 11 August 1966, FBI File No. 62-102926.

58 J. Edgar Hoover to [redacted], 5 August 1966, FBI File No. 62-102926.

8. THAILAND

1 Wanda was thirty-four, and Louis was forty-four. They lived at 8310 Grandview Drive. *LAT*, 24 October 1966.

2 *LAS*, 27 October 1966, A1.

3 *LAT*, 3 November 1966, WS6, 10 November 1966, OC4, 13 November 1966, B6; *LAS*, 22 December 1966, A1.

4 Louis Lomax to Bob Loomis, 28 June 1966, box 2, series 1, subseries 4, folder 1, Lomax Papers.

5 *CD*, 25 November 1964, 3; *LAS*, 3 December 1964, C14.

6 Lomax wound up spending much of that month in England and Denmark, speaking at a conference in Copenhagen. SAC, Los Angeles, to director, FBI, 20 October 1965, FBI File No. 62-102926; Eldridge, *Chronicles*, 60 (quote); "Cable Re

Martin Luther King Louis Lomax Possible Travel Plans to Vietnam," 29 September 1965, 1993.07.26.19:07:02:340310, box 51, folder 16, Kennedy Assassination Records Collection, National Archives and Records Administration.

7 SAC, Los Angeles, to director, FBI, 26 July 1966, "Confidential Security Matter—O," US Department of Justice, 28 July 1966, FBI File No. 62-102926; *CT*, 23 December 1966, 17; *NYT*, 23 December 1966, 10.

8 *CD*, 22 August 1970, 3.

9 For more on Martin, see Poinsett, *Walking with Presidents*.

10 *LAT*, 23 December 1966, 1; *Louisiana Weekly*, 7 January 1967, 1.

11 Lomax said that his trip would be funded by KTTV, the North American Newspaper Alliance, Metromedia, and *Look* magazine, but that was not necessarily true. He made the trip under the auspices of the Vietnam Journalists Association and the Vietnam Peace Committee. *BG*, 24 December 1966, 10; *WP*, 24 December 1966, A5; *BAA*, 31 December 1966, 1; *NYAN*, 31 December 1966, 3; *LAS*, 29 December 1966, A1; *LAT*, 24 December 1966, 5.

12 Lomax was incredibly complimentary of his time in Phnom Penh. He met with officials from North Vietnam and the National Liberation Front as well as Australian officials acting as representatives of the United States in Cambodia. His hosts took him to a large town hall meeting, where, among other things, an indignant citizen rose to denounce obscenity in Cambodian magazines. Cambodian Premier Prince Norodom Sihanouk responded by asking the man how many children he had. "Seven," he responded. "Then what have you to protest against love?" asked the prince. The biggest news Lomax took from his brief stay in Phnom Penh was Sihanouk's announcement that Cambodia had made a mutual assistance agreement with the National Liberation Front if and when they eventually won the war. While not technically violating the country's neutrality in the conflict, the move clearly gave Cambodia a rooting interest in the outcome. Vietnam Peace Committee to Louis Lomax, 21 December 1966, Vietnam Journalists Association to Louis Lomax, 24 December 1966, box 2, series 1, subseries 4, folder 1, Lomax Papers; *LAT*, 25 December 1966, 3, 26 December 1966, 14, 28 December 1966, 2, 30 December 1966, 1, 31 December 1966, 4; *BG*, 30 December 1966, 4; *WP*, 30 December 1966, A6, 1 January 1967, A6.

13 In early January, he reported from Bangkok that Cambodia had concluded a secret mutual assistance treaty with the Vietcong, prompting Cambodia's Information Ministry of the Royal Government to denounce "the mendacious character of his statement" and to stress that Lomax's "statements were inspired by his vengeance on Cambodia for refusing to allow him to stay in Cambodia for a few days so that he could [travel] to Hanoi afterward." *NYT*, 25 December 1966, 6E; *BG*, 29 December 1966, 1; *CD*, 27 December 1966, 6; Louis Lomax to Robinette Kirk, 27 December 1966, Louis Lomax to Robinette Kirk, 1 January 1967, Louis Lomax to Robinette Kirk, 5 January 1967, box 2, series 1, subseries 4, folder 1; "Radio Cambodia: Statement by Louis Lomax on Viet Cong Denied, 4 February 1967," box 2, series 1, subseries 4, folder 11, Lomax Papers. For more on Payne, see James Morris, *Eye on the Struggle*.

14 *CD*, 27 December 1966, 12; *LAS*, 19 January 1967, A3.

15 "Field Notes, undated," box 2, series 1, subseries 4, folder 3, Lomax Papers.

16 *CT*, 5 January 1967, 7; *NYT*, 8 January 1967, 22.

17 *LAT*, 19 September 1966, A1, 30 September 1966, B8, 11 January 1967, A6; *CD*, 16 January 1967, 2; *LAS*, 19 January 1967, A3.

18 *Indiana Jewish Post*, 20 January 1967, 5; *LAS*, 12 January 1967, A2; *LAT*, 2 October 1965, B3.

19 For more on Hargis's use of anti-Communism as a cudgel for segregationism, see Aiello, "Jim Crow Ordained."

20 Moerman, *Western Culture*; Moerman, "Minority and Its Government"; "Fact Sheet: Notes on Thai-US Relations," "History of Bangkok," "Quarterly Economic Survey, July-September 1966," "Press Kit: Thailand; for the Official Visit of the President of the United States of America, October 28–30, 1966," "Summary of Current Economic Position and Prospects of Thailand," National Economic Development Board, Office of the Prime Minister, Bangkok, Thailand (October 1966), box 2, series 1, subseries 4, folder 5, Lomax Papers.

21 George Moseley, "The Chinese in North Thailand," unpublished manuscript, box 2, series 1, subseries 4, folder 9; Parker, "Americans in Thailand"; G. William Skinner, "The Thailand Chinese: Assimilation in a Changing Society," third lecture in a series organized by the Thailand Council of the Asia Society (March 1963), box 2, series 1, subseries 4, folder 7; "Press Release No. 6," 18 April 1967, "Press Release No. 9," 4 May 1967, "Press Release No 10," 5 May 1967, Permanent Mission of Thailand to the United Nations, box 2, series 1, subseries 4, folder 6; "Statement by Senator J. W. Fulbright, Chairman, Committee on Foreign Relations, United States Senate, 3 October 1966," box 2, series 1, subseries 4, folder 11, Lomax Papers.

22 Louis Lomax to Bob Loomis, n.d., "Theme: Thailand," box 2, series 1, subseries 4, folder 1, Lomax Papers. To help develop his ideas, in May 1967 he presented a paper with that title at a foreign policy roundtable conference on US involvement in Thailand at Washington University in St. Louis. "Foreign Policy Roundtable Conference on United States Involvement in Thailand, Washington University, May 5–6, 1967," box 2, series 1, subseries 4, folder 11, Lomax Papers.

23 Louis Lomax to Bob Loomis, n.d., box 1, series 1, subseries 4, folder 23, Lomax Papers.

24 *Thailand: The War That Is, The War That Will Be*, book jacket proof, box 1, series 1, subseries 4, folder 23, Lomax Papers.

25 Louis Lomax, *Thailand*; Darling, Review of *Thailand*; Handley, *King Never Smiles*, 185–186. See also "Louis Lomax Discusses the Book *Thailand*."

26 Louis Lomax, *Thailand*, x.

27 Louis Lomax, *Thailand*, 31.

28 Louis Lomax, *Thailand*, 32.

29 Louis Lomax, *Thailand*, 47, 64.

30 Louis Lomax, *Thailand*, 53.

31 Louis Lomax, *Thailand*, 72–75.

32 Louis Lomax, *Thailand*, 79.

33 Louis Lomax, *Thailand*, 91–92.

34 Louis Lomax, *Thailand*, 105.

35 Louis Lomax, *Thailand*, 133.

36 Louis Lomax, *Thailand*, 154.

37 Don O. Noel Jr., "US Writer Sees Perils in Our Thailand Policy," *Hartford Times*, 11 November 1967, box 1, series 1, subseries 4, folder 24, Lomax Papers.

38 Stuart E. Hoyt, "Clouds in Thailand Trouble a Visitor," *Milwaukee Journal*, 26 November 1967, Frank J. Johnson, "Will the Real Red China Please Stand Up?," *National Review*, 13 February 1968, 148, Russell H. Fifield, "Rivalries Revived," *Saturday Review*, 17 February 1968, box 1, series 1, subseries 4, folder 24, Lomax Papers. See also Jackson and Mungkandi, *United States–Thailand Relations*.

39 In a more favorable review, the *Chicago Tribune*'s Robert Cromie agreed with Lomax's thesis that "if Viet Nam ended tomorrow we would simply move our troops to Thailand." His depiction of American takeover in Thailand and the anger of its people was convincing to Cromie, if not to the Thai king. *LAT*, 29 December 1967, 5; *NYT*, 5 February 1968, 2; *CT*, 16 May 1968, 2; Streckfuss, "Kings," 467.

40 As one last example of that inconsistency, in early 1968, Lomax teamed with noted cartoonist Don Sherwood for a reporter-themed comic strip titled *Deadline*. Sherwood had risen to fame creating the *Dan Flagg* comic about the trials and tribulations of US Marines, which earned him an invitation from Lyndon Johnson to visit the White House at the height of the Vietnam War. He was therefore an unlikely collaborator with Lomax, who had made much of his opposition to American imperialism and certainly did not celebrate American Marines and their efforts in Vietnam. "Deadline," box 4, series 2, subseries 3, folders 7–8, Lomax Papers.

41 In July, Betty Frank Lomax was quoted in *Ebony* challenging the dominant paternalistic opinion that it was matriarchal control that led to a higher-than-average Black divorce rate. "No man is dominated by his woman," she argued, "unless it appeals to his neurotic needs." *CD*, 4 February 1967, 16, 7 February 1967, 8; *NYAN*, 29 July 1967, 11; Betty Frank Lomax, "Afro-American Woman." The *Liberator* would remain a vehicle for Black radical thought throughout the 1960s. See Tinson, *Radical Intellect*.

42 *LAT*, 8 February 1967, 2, 22 April 1967, A12; *LAS*, 9 February 1967, A1; *WP*, 22 April 1967, 10.

43 In April, KTTV won a local Emmy Award for airing Lomax's debate with John Rousselot. *LAS*, 9 February 1967, B8, B12, 16 February 1967, D2; *LAT*, 12 February 1967, SF-A12, Q6, WS8, 19 February 1967, SG-A6, 23 February 1967, WS3, 5 March 1967, WS10, 6 March 1967, C18, 16 March 1967, B5, 20 April 1967, C14.

44 *LAS*, 16 March 1967, A2.

45 *LAT*, 29 April 1967, B8; *NYAN*, 6 May 1967, 2; *LAS*, 4 May 1967, D7.

46 Late in the month, Lomax served as toastmaster for a Beverly Hilton testimonial dinner for H. Hartford Brookins, pastor of the First AME Church of Los Angeles and chair of the United Civil Rights Council. He also hosted Brookins on his

television program, where the minister told the audience about a group of Watts children in need. *LAT*, 8 June 1967, E1, 26 June 1967, A2; *LAS*, 29 June 1967, D4, 6 July 1967, C8.

47 *LAS*, 29 June 1967, B9.

48 *LAS*, 27 July 1967, B7, C5, 3 August 1967, B8, 10 August 1967, B10; *LAT*, 7 August 1967, D29.

49 *LAT*, 12 August 1967, B2, 25 August 1967, 101, 27 August 1967, B1; *LAS*, 24 August 1967, A6, C9, D4.

50 Television success could also have negative consequences. Later that month, on 20 September, an Ontario, California, schoolteacher was indicted by a federal grand jury after publicly destroying his draft card on a 19 February episode of the Lomax television show. Lincoln Adams Robbins could have received a maximum sentence of five years in federal prison or a fine of ten thousand dollars. He was convicted in October 1968. *LAT*, 29 August 1967, 3, 22 September 1967, B2, 29 September 1967, 2, 9 October 1968, 2; *BAA*, 30 September 1967, 16; *LAS*, 31 August 1967, B11.

51 *LAS*, 28 September 1967, B6; *LAT*, 29 September 1967, D18, 3 October 1967, C12, 10 October 1967, SF9, 11 October 1967, 2.

52 *Detroit News*, 30 July 1967, 1, 8 August 1967, 1; *LAS*, 21 May 1970, A1; James Boggs and Ward, *Pages*, 29; Joseph, "Black Power Movement," 1013–1014; Fine, *Violence*, 360–361; Grace Boggs, Glover, and Kurashige, *Next American Revolution*, 23.

53 Lomax was a speaker and entertainer, but he was still a reporter at heart. After California Governor Ronald Reagan fired two members of his staff in August without explanation, Lomax reported that a Reagan adviser had told him "that homosexualism was involved." While he was back east for his New Jersey speech, he "directly confronted one of the Nation's leading conservatives, a man high in the Reagan-for-President drive, with the information I had obtained. He not only confirmed the story but commented, 'thank God the truth is now known.'" Reagan denied that the employees were released because of their sexual orientation, leading many to question either his honesty or his administration's competence to vet employees. *NYAN*, 28 October 1967, 36; *BAA*, 11 November 1967, 15; *WP*, 4 November 1967, B11.

54 *LAS*, 16 November 1967, A1.

9. BRANCHING OUT

1 "20th Inks Lomax for Malcolm X Script," *Hollywood Reporter*, 29 November 1967, 1; "Life of Malcolm X Used as Basis for Film Script," Kimmis Hendrick, "Lomax Sizes Up 'Black Power,'" *Christian Science Monitor*, 28 November 1967, box 4, series 2, subseries 2, folder 6, Lomax Papers; Sieving, *Soul Searching*, 62.

2 Hendrick, "Lomax Sizes Up 'Black Power.'"

3 In January 1968, Lomax sold to 20th Century Fox the rights to his own role in Malcolm X's story, receiving $2,500 for the company's "right to portray you in our motion picture," with the promise of an additional $22,500 if he actually

was portrayed. *CD*, 16 December 1967, 25; *NYAN*, 2 December 1967, 20, 23 December 1967, 20; Rickford, *Betty Shabazz,* 272; 20th Century Fox Film Corporation to Ella Collins, 29 January 1968, box 4, series 2, subseries 2, folder 5, Lomax Papers.

4 Baldwin, Alex Haley, and Elia Kazan had originally agreed to make the *Autobiography* into a play. That project never happened, and producer Marvin Worth bought the rights to the book and planned to produce it for Columbia. Baldwin, *No Name*, 91; "Malcolm X to Be Subject of Two Films," box 4, series 2, subseries 2, folder 6, Lomax Papers; [redacted] to W. C. Sullivan, 26 March 1968, FBI File No. 100-399321; *NYAN*, 10 February 1968, 22; Evanzz, *Judas Factor,* 318; *LAT*, 6 January 1968, B1; *LAS*, 18 January 1968, D2. J. Edgar Hoover was interested in both scripts, ordering the bureau's Los Angeles office to obtain advance copies to discover whether they were critical of the FBI. Both Baldwin and Lomax had suggested that the bureau played a role in Malcolm's murder. Evanzz, "Black Hollywood," 19; Albany Special Agent in Charge to J. Edgar Hoover, 5 August 1968, COINTELPRO-Black Extremism, FBI Central Headquarters File No. 100-448006, Assassination Archives and Research Center, Washington, DC; *ADW*, 18 November 1979, 10; *BAA*, 24 November 1979, 11.

5 Baldwin, *No Name*, 99, 165.

6 Malcolm X's family lived largely off royalties from the *Autobiography*, though there were other sources of income. Historian Russell Rickford explains that Lomax speculated that Malcolm "had become a political and financial beneficiary of Algeria's and Ghana's revolutionary leaders, and that this 'Ben Bella–Nkrumah axis' had funneled him cash to sustain his family and spotlight American imperialism." There was no evidence of such payment, but significantly, Lomax, a chronic exaggerator, was not alone in such speculation. *NYT*, 8 March 1968, 49; *LAS*, 18 April 1968, B11; Rickford, *Betty Shabazz*, 285.

7 In May 1972, Warner Bros. released a documentary on the slain leader produced by Marvin Worth and Arnold Perl and authorized by Betty Shabazz. It included, among many others, comments by Malcolm's friend and rival, Lomax. Evanzz, "Black Hollywood," 19; *ADW*, 11 May 1972, 7; *LAS*, 25 May 1972, B1; *BG*, 25 May 1972, 77; *BAA*, 20 May 1972, 11; *NYAN*, 27 May 1972, D1; *CD*, 17 May 1972, 12.

8 Amy Bass, *Not the Triumph*, 143–144; Cromartie, "Harry Edwards," 1432; Damion Thomas, *Globetrotting*, 142; Hano, "Black Rebel."

9 *LAT*, 14 December 1967, C1 (quote); *CT*, 15 December 1967, C2; *NYT*, 15 December 1967, 69; *NYAN*, 23 December 1967, 1, 44.

10 *CD*, 20 December 1967, 27, 2 January 1968, 24. See also Harry Edwards, *Struggle.*

11 *NYAN*, 30 December 1967, 28, 9 January 1971, 28; *LAS*, 11 January 1968, A11.

12 *LAS*, 7 March 1968, A1.

13 Of course, no trip of Lomax's was just for pleasure. He was also working, and upon his return he published "Memo from Amman." *LAS*, 7 March 1968, A1; *NYAN*, 16 March 1968, 3.

14 The cancellation did not stop the local Emmys from granting the *Lomax Show* another award. *LAS*, 7 March 1968, A1, 28 March 1968, D6.

15 *BG*, 5 March 1968, 29; *PC*, 16 March 1968, 13; *NYT*, 30 May 1968, 21.

16 Louis Lomax, *To Kill a Black Man*, 189–197 (quotes from 192, 195). See also Pepper, *Act of State*; Sides, *Hellhound*.

17 He even titled his article "The Black Middle Class and the Fire This Time," directly engaging his friend and rival James Baldwin and his book *The Fire Next Time* to make the case that the revolutionary spirit among the Black working class had arrived.

18 *LAS*, 16 May 1968, C3.

19 *CD*, 23 May 1968, 11. See McKnight, *Last Crusade*; Wright, "Civil Rights"; Mantler, *Power*.

20 *PC*, 15 June 1968, 10; *CD*, 1 July 1968, 17.

21 "McCarthy Ad Spots with Dr. Martin Luther King, Louis Lomax," June 1968, box 60-GU 226, folder 4, Contributors 1968 Campaign Calif. (K–O), 1968, McCarthy Historical Project, University of Minnesota Libraries.

22 Ron Karenga, Black nationalist founder of US Organization, also publicly endorsed McCarthy. But Kennedy was not without Black support. When he was assassinated after his primary victory, Rosey Grier of the Los Angeles Rams and decathlete Rafer Johnson were by his side, as they had been throughout Kennedy's California swing. *LAT*, 3 June 1968, 1; *LAS*, 9 June 1968, A1; *NYT*, 4 June 1968, 1. For more on Karenga, see Scott Brown, *Fighting for US*.

23 *CD*, 2 July 1968, 7. For more on the Democratic National Convention, see Schultz, *No One Was Killed*; Kusch, *Battleground Chicago*; Mailer, *Miami*.

24 *BG*, 6 August 1968, 1; *LAT*, 6 August 1968, C1. Lomax and Farmer's ad, which appeared on Sunday, 4 August, was one of many favoring Rockefeller, Nixon, and Ronald Reagan that ran in the paper during the week of the convention. See *Miami News*, 3–7 August 1968. For examples of Rockefeller ads and the paper's coverage of Black reaction to the convention, see 5 August 1968, 36A, 6 August 1968, 1A, 36A, 8 August 1968, 1A.

25 *BG*, 10 September 1968, 13.

26 *LAT*, 6 August 1968, C1.

27 See Mailer, *Miami*; Kusch, *Battleground Chicago*; Tscheschlok, "Long Time Coming."

28 *CD*, 30 November 1968, 8.

29 *LAS*, 2 January 1969, A1.

30 It was a lecture that he gave at many universities. At Portland State University, for example, he gave an address in December 1967 called "The Negro and Social Change in America," which was substantially the same. Just after his Hofstra address, in December 1968, he returned to Portland State and gave "An Address to Faculty and Students on the Historical Roots of Black Power," which would presage the kind of work he would do at Hofstra. *CT*, 23 November 1968, B19; Louis E. Lomax, "The Negro and Social Change in America," 7 December 1967, No. 42,

Louis E. Lomax, "An Address to Faculty and Students on the Historical Roots of Black Power," 2 December 1968, No. 65, Oregon Public Speakers Collection, Portland State University Library. Both Oregon talks are available online. See https://pdxscholar.library.pdx.edu/orspeakers/42/ for "The Negro and Social Change in America" and https://pdxscholar.library.pdx.edu/orspeakers/65/ for "An Address to Faculty and Students on the Historical Roots of Black Power."

31 He was hired at a salary of twenty-two thousand dollars, with three thousand dollars in fringe benefits. The university also offered Lomax a temporary one-week appointment as visiting professor in Afro-American literature so that he could participate in a workshop in June 1969. "Author Louis Lomax Killed"; Clifford Lord to Louis Lomax, 25 March 1969, box 12, series 7, folder 24, Lomax Papers.

32 "News . . . From the University of Michigan," press releases, 6 May 1969 (12), 7 May 1969 (14), box 79, News and Information Services, Bentley Historical Library, University of Michigan.

33 *LAS*, 17 April 1969, B6. Lomax received honorary doctorates from Allen University in Columbia, South Carolina, and Virginia Union University in Richmond in 1963 and 1964, respectively. *NYAN*, 26 April 1969, 31; "Louis Lomax Named Visiting Professor at Hofstra," *News from Hofstra*, 16 April 1969, box 12, series 7, folder 24, Lomax Papers.

34 His trial was scheduled for 18 September but was ultimately delayed until December. *NYAN*, 14 June 1969, 5, 27 December 1969, 29.

35 "Louis Lomax to All HCLAS Faculty, 5 December 1969," "Minutes of the Second Regular Meeting of the Hofstra College of Liberal Arts and Sciences, 5 December 1969," box 12, series 7, folder 25, Lomax Papers.

36 *LAT*, 21 September 1969, OC5, 23 October 1969, H12, 17 February 1970, OC-C1, 23 February 1970, D10.

37 "35 Negro Girls Seize Part of a Building at Vassar and Sit In," *NYT*, 31 October 1969, box 14, series 8, folder 38, Lomax Papers; *NYT*, 1 August 1970, 23.

38 *CD*, 14 April 1970, 6; *NYAN*, 2 May 1970, 30; *BAA*, 18 April 1970, 3.

39 Leroy L. Ramsey, "Remembering Louis Lomax," *Newsday*, box 17, series 8, folder 4, Lomax Papers.

40 Of course, Lucy Terry Prince was actually writing poetry in the 1740s, though it would not be published until 1855, but at the time the Hammon news was a startling revelation. *NYT*, 21 September 1970, 51. See also Hammon, *Collected Works*.

41 *NYT*, 21 September 1970, 51.

42 "All Quiet at Hofstra after Brief Fracas," "Blacks, Whites in Hofstra Melee," box 12, series 7, folder 26, Lomax Papers.

43 The New Opportunities at Hofstra (NOAH) program was designed to waive the stringent admission requirements for certain students for the sake of diversity. The group argued that NOAH lacked financial transparency and accountability, which could lead to mismanagement of a program that the OBC felt was ignored anyway. That same semester, Lomax alleged that Planned Parenthood was aggressively recruiting Black students for clinical tests and that two Black students in

4 Los Angeles 44-1574, 24 April 1968, Section 41, King Assassination Documents.

5 Stein ultimately resented his contact with Lomax, telling the FBI he felt that Lomax had "'used' him for publicity purposes" and feared that the publicity endangered his life, that "whoever shot KING might take a shot at him." A. Rosen to Mr. DeLoach, 2 May 1968, Section 28, King Assassination Documents; redacted, "James Earl Ray, Top Ten Fugitive; Dr. Martin Luther King, Jr. (Deceased)— Victim," 17 May 1968, 44-38861, Section 50, King Assassination Documents; Joe C. Hester, "James Earl Ray; Dr. Martin Luther King, Jr.—Victim," 5 June 1968, 44-1987, 44-38861, Section 52, King Assassination Documents; Frank, *American Death*, 183.

6 Stein was not compensated by Lomax, though he said that someone had promised him two hundred thousand dollars for his investigative help. "An Analysis of the Assassination Investigation of the Department of Justice and the Federal Bureau of Investigation," in US Congress, House, Select Committee on Assassinations, *Appendix*, 180–181, 187; "An Analysis of James Earl Ray's Trip to New Orleans, December 15–21, 1967," in US Congress, House, Select Committee on Assassinations, *Appendix*, 273; "An Analysis of the Performance of the Department of Justice and the Federal Bureau of Investigation," in US Congress, House, Select Committee on Assassinations, *Appendix*, 56–58, 70; A. Rosen to Mr. DeLoach, 2 May 1968, Section 28, King Assassination Documents; Frank, *American Death*, 183, 187.

7 Lomax's role in propagating conspiratorial assassination theories led the House Select Committee on Assassinations, established in 1976, to study the deaths of the Kennedys and King and to request all information collected on Lomax by the FBI and other organizations. A. Rosen to Mr. DeLoach, 2 May 1968, FBI Los Angeles to FBI Washington, MURKIN, 30 April 1968, Section 28, SAC, Kansas City, to Director, FBI, 8 May 1968, Section 33, King Assassination Documents; Administration Folder K1, National Archives and Records Administration.

8 Martin claimed that she believed the check Lomax gave her to be worthless. FBI Los Angeles to FBI Washington, MURKIN, 6 May 1968, Section 30, Los Angeles 44-1574, 6 May 1968, Section 41, King Assassination Documents; FBI Los Angeles to FBI Washington, MURKIN, 1 May 1968, Section 38, King Assassination Documents; A. Rosen to Mr. DeLoach, 15 May 1968, Section 40, King Assassination Documents.

9 Lomax and Stein had also traveled to the Vegas Club, a Hollywood Boulevard strip joint, searching for a Greek belly dancer named Helena or a white blonde named Jerri (Dyrell Dennis). The club's owner, Harry Streen, directed them elsewhere. Significantly, though, the FBI arrived at the Vegas to ask Streen similar questions later that day. Lomax's investigation was keeping up with that of his federal counterparts. A. Rosen to Mr. DeLoach, 7 May 1968, Section 32, King Assassination Documents; FBI Memphis to director, 20 May 1968, Section 44, King Assassination Documents; Los Angeles 44-1574, 6 May 1968, 24 April 1968, Section 41, King Assassination Documents.

10 The *Los Angeles Herald Examiner* titled the syndicated piece "King Killer Aided by Hoover's Hate!" The *St. Petersburg Times* ran it under the headline "Needed: A Warren-Type Probe of Dr. King's Death." O'Leary, "Greatest Manhunt"; M. A. Jones to Mr. Bishop, MURKIN, 21 May 1968, Section 47, Louis E. Lomax, "King Killer Aided By Hoover's Hate!," Section 33, redacted to J. Edgar Hoover, 7 May 1968, Louis E. Lomax, "Needed: A Warren-Type Probe of Dr. King's Death," *St. Petersburg Times*, 4 May 1967, Section 37, King Assassination Documents.

11 Ray was at Joliet for just over a month, from 13 June to 19 July 1952. A. Rosen to Mr. DeLoach, 2 May 1968, Section 28, A. Rosen to Mr. DeLoach, 1 May 1968, Section 32, King Assassination Documents.

12 A. Rosen to Mr. DeLoach, 7 May 1968, Section 32, King Assassination Documents. See also Sides, *Hellhound*.

13 Louis Lomax, *To Kill a Black Man*, 49–50.

14 SAC, Mobile, to Director, FBI, 13 June 1968, Section 58, King Assassination Documents; *Palm Springs Desert Sun*, 2 June 1966, 1.

15 Historian Louis A. DeCaro has compared Lomax's sensationalistic *To Kill a Black Man* and its treatment of Malcolm X and Martin Luther King to James Crone's *Martin and Malcolm and America*, which he sees as a much more nuanced critical appraisal of the religious views of the two. DeCaro, *On the Side*, 298; Crone, *Martin*. Authors such as George Breitman were wholly dismissive of *To Kill a Black Man*: "Louis Lomax's book about Malcolm X (and Martin Luther King) is worthless as biography, history, or anything else." Breitman, Porter, and Smith, *Assassination*, 136.

16 Louis Lomax, *To Kill a Black Man*, 252–253.

17 To that end, Malcolm claimed that nonviolence was a rejection of self-defense, though he was intentionally representing King's vision. Malcolm "used his eloquence to pervert words." Louis Lomax, *To Kill a Black Man*, 9, 12–18, 60–64, 130, 249–255; Adams, review of *To Kill a Black Man*; Chappell, "Prophetic Religion," 1268.

18 The criminal suit against him was dropped on his death, but the civil suit remained, and the IRS reported that they were at least considering attempting to recover tax money from his estate. *Washington Evening Star*, 16 June 1970, A2; *LAS*, 21 May 1970, A1, 18 June 1970, A1; *BAA*, 30 May 1970, 21; *LAT*, 16 June 1970, A8; *NYT*, 16 June 1970, 43; *NYAN*, 23 May 1970, 3; "Author Louis Lomax Killed."

19 After Lomax's death, Binford contacted Hofstra president Clifford Lord to explain the visit in Los Angeles and to offer any further information if needed. Robinette Lomax, "It's All Around Me!," unpublished manuscript, box 1, series 1, subseries 3, folder 19, Lomax Papers; Sally R. Binford to Clifford Lord, 10 August 1970, box 12, series 7, folder 24, Lomax Papers; Wells, *Wild Man*, 367 (Russo); Clinger, *Our Elders* (Binford).

20 "Certificate of Death, State of New Mexico," box 17, series 8, folder 5, Lomax Papers; *BG*, 1 August 1970, 1, 21; *LAT*, 1 August 1970, 2; *NYT*, 1 August 1970, 23; *WP*, 1 August 1970, B6; *BAA*, 8 August 1970, 21; *CD*, 3 August 1970, 19; *ADW*, 4 August 1970, 1; *CD*, 1 August 1970, A10; "Louis Lomax, Author."

21 *LAS*, 6 August 1970, B3; *LAT*, 11 October 1992, E4; Wells, *Wild Man*, 367.

22 *LAS*, 29 October 1970, A1, A3, 5 November 1970, A1, A8. The police report for Lomax's crash no longer exists. Neither the Santa Rosa police department nor the New Mexico State Police hold a copy. The New Mexico State Police, in fact, retain records of fatal traffic crashes for only twenty-five years. Santa Rosa Police Department, correspondence with the author, New Mexico State Police, Inspection of Public Records Act request, 13 September 2018.

23 Despite her "surprise," Robinette had done her research on Hurkos, collecting newspaper articles and biographical material on the psychic before making the call. "Peter Hurkos materials," box 17, series 9, folder 13, Lomax Papers.

24 Peter Hurkos, interview, Syracuse, New York, 27 August 1970, box 17, series 9, folder 13, Lomax Papers.

25 Robinette Lomax, "It's All Around Me!," unpublished manuscript, box 1, series 1, subseries 3, folder 19, Lomax Papers; Hurkos, interview.

26 *LAT*, 3 August 1970, A2; *CD*, 4 August 1970, 6.

27 The pallbearers were William Walker, Bowman G. Wiley, Owen Knox, Celeste King, Hamilton S. Cloud, and Christopher S. Taylor. Lomax was buried at Rosedale Cemetery. He was survived by his aunt and uncle, James and Fannie Lomax; his wife, Robinette Kirk; two stepchildren, Robin and William; and his son, Hugh. James Edward Jones, "Introduction to Odyssey and Exodus of Louis Lomax," Westminster Presbyterian Church of Los Angeles, 5 August 1970, "Obsequies of Louis Emanuel Lomax, 1922–1970," box 17, series 8, folder 6, Lomax Papers; "Author Louis Lomax Dies in Auto Crash," box 17, series 8, folder 4, Lomax Papers; *LAS*, 6 August 1970, A1.

28 "Random House, Inc., Royalty Statement, 31 March 1970," "Random House, Inc., Statement, 30 June 1970," "Harper & Row, Publishers, Inc., Royalty Statement, 31 December 1970," "Random House, Inc., Royalty Statement, 30 September 1971," box 1, series 1, subseries 1, folder 5, Lomax Papers; "City of Los Angeles, in Tribute," Rex E. Layton to Mrs. Louis Lomax, 17 August 1970, box 17, series 8, folder 7, Lomax Papers; Robert E. Johnson to Mrs. Louis Lomax, 4 August 1970, Lerone Bennett Jr. to Mrs. Louie Lomax, 5 August 1970, Whitney M. Young Jr. to Mrs. Louis Lomax, 5 August 1970, William G. Nunn to Whom It May Concern, 1 August 1970, box 17, series 8, folder 12, Lomax Papers.

29 *NYAN*, 8 August 1970, 1, 15 August 1970, 25; "Lomax Fund Established," *Newsday*, 4 August 1970, box 17, series 8, folder 8, Lomax Papers; "Memorial Service Held for Lomax," box 17, series 8, folder 4, Lomax Papers; "Louis E. Lomax Memorial Service, 13 August 1970," "Louis Lomax Praised in Service at Hofstra," box 17, series 8, folder 8, Lomax Papers; *Hofstra University Evening Forum*, 21 September 1970, 3.

30 *LAS*, 6 August 1970, A7.

31 Leroy L. Ramsey, "Remembering Louis Lomax," *Newsday*, box 17, series 8, folder 4, Lomax Papers.

32 *LAS*, 29 October 1970, A1, A3, 5 November 1970, A1, A8.

33 *CD*, 5 November 1970, C16; *WP*, 6 November 1970, A4; *NYAN*, 21 November 1970, 52; *ADW*, 8 November 1970, 3; *PC*, 28 November 1970, 19; *LAS*, 5 November 1970, A1, A8.

34 *LAT*, 5 November 1970, E3.

35 *Robinette G. Lomax v. Ford Motor Company*, no. 995 090, Superior Court of the State of California for the County of Los Angeles, box 17, series 9, folder 14, Lomax Papers. Robinette also had trouble getting her insurance settlement from the Hartford, the delay hinging on whether Lomax was on official university business at the time of his death. The claim was eventually settled when Hofstra provided an official letter stating that Lomax was a full-time employee of the university and was engaged, however loosely, in official university business. F. Victor Palermo to Hubert M. Harvey Jr., 13 May 1971, G. Donald Guillet to Mrs. Herndon, 4 September 1970, box 17, series 9, folder 15, Lomax Papers.

36 The volumes Hobson saved were *The Reluctant African* (1960) and *When the Word Is Given* (1963). Subseries 5: Books, 1922–1976, series 20: Printed Materials, Papers of Julius Hobson, DC Community Archives; *PC*, 29 August 1970, 9.

37 Louis Lomax, *To Kill a Black Man*, 255–256.

Bibliography

ARCHIVAL MATERIALS

Amistad Research Center, Tulane University, New Orleans

Clifford Burdette, "Cullen on Those Who Have Made Good," WNYC, 22 June 1941
Eric Steele Wells Papers, 1855–1986

Assassination Archives and Research Center, Washington, DC

COINTELPRO—Black Extremism, FBI Central Headquarters File, 100-448006,
  FOIA, Federal Bureau of Investigation
John F. Kennedy Assassination File, Section 158, FBI 62-109060, Federal Bureau of
  Investigation
King Assassination Documents—FBI Central Headquarters File

Bentley Historical Library, University of Michigan, Ann Arbor

News and Information Services, University of Michigan, Faculty and Staff Files,
  1944–2005, 1960–1995, 2009097 Bimu C475 2, Y-1015-D
Mike Wallace Papers, 85472 Aa 2

**DC Community Archives, DC Public Library Special Collections,
Washington, DC**

Papers of Julius Hobson, 1960–1977

Dwight D. Eisenhower Library, Abilene, KS

Series II, Eisenhower Administration, 1953–1958, Maxwell M. Rabb Papers,
  1938–1958, 1989, A03-6, A03-6/1

Mary Ferrell Foundation, Ipswich, MA

US Department of State, "On the Record Unless Otherwise Indicated Transcript of
  Press and Radio News Briefing," 9 August 1963, Warren Commission Document
  1462

Asa H. Gordon Library, Special Collections, Savannah State University, Savannah, GA

Georgia Herald
Georgia State College Bulletin
The Hubertonian
The Tiger

Howard Gotlieb Archival Research Center, Boston University, Boston

Martin Luther King Jr. Papers, 1954–1968

Hargrett Rare Book and Manuscript Library, University of Georgia, Athens

Lillian Smith Letters to Rochelle Girson, MS1209

King Library and Archives, Martin Luther King Jr. Center for Nonviolent Social Change, Atlanta

Papers of Martin Luther King Jr.

Library of Congress, Prints and Photographs Division, Washington, DC

Radio Producer Clifford Burdette, LOT 13074, no. 85 (P&P)

National Archives and Records Administration, Washington, DC, and College Park, MD

Administration Folder K1, House Select Committee on Assassinations
    Administrative Folder, HSCA Tickler, vol. 2, NARA 124-10371-10103
Newspaper Clippings on the Assassination of President Kennedy
    (November 1963–February 1964), Central Intelligence Agency, 201 File, Lee
    Harvey Oswald, 201-289248, NARA 104-10300-10403
President John F. Kennedy Assassination Records Collection

Northeastern University, Archives and Special Collections, Boston

Phyllis M. Ryan Papers, M94

Office of the Clerk of Court, Chicago

Illinois v. Louis Lomax, case no. 49CR-2439, 49CR-2440, 49CR-2441, Files of the
    Criminal Court of Cook County

Office of Vital Records, Atlanta

Georgia Death Index, 1919–1998, Georgia Health Department

Paine College, Augusta, GA

COLLINS-CALLAWAY LIBRARY, P. RANDOLPH SHY SPECIAL COLLECTION
Paine College Bulletin, Register

REGISTRAR'S OFFICE
Louis Emanuel Lomax student file

Portland State University Library, Special Collections, Portland State University, Portland, OR

Oregon Public Speakers Collection

Rockefeller Archive Center, Sleepy Hollow, NY

Taconic Foundation Records, FA407

Schomburg Center for Research in Black Culture, Manuscripts, Archives and Rare Books Division, New York Public Library, New York

Lorraine Hansberry Papers, Sc MG 680
Wallace Terry Papers, 1938–2003, Sc MG 921

Social Security Administration, Washington, DC

US Social Security Applications and Claims Index, 1936–2007

Sudan Archive, Durham University Library, Archives and Special Collections, Durham, UK

Maurice Stanley Lush Papers, GB-0033-SAD

Syracuse University Libraries, Special Collections Research Center, Syracuse University, Syracuse, NY

Mike Wallace Papers

University of Minnesota Libraries, Special Collections and Rare Books, Minneapolis

McCarthy Historical Project, 1968 Presidential Campaign Records, SCRB
   Collection 14, Eugene J. McCarthy Papers

University of Nevada, Reno, Special Collections

Louis E. Lomax Papers, 82-30

Wisconsin Historical Society Archives, Madison

National Broadcasting Company Records, US Mss 17AF, Disc 45A, Micro 10, Micro 757, Micro 764, Micro 779, Micro 960

Robert W. Woodruff Library, Audio-Visual Recordings, Atlanta University Center, Atlanta

C. Eric Lincoln Collection

OTHER SOURCES

Abdullah, Zain. "Malcolm X, Islam, and the Black Self." In *Malcolm X's Michigan Worldview: An Exemplar for Contemporary Black Studies*, ed. Rita Kiki Edozie and Curtis Stokes, 205–226. East Lansing: Michigan State University Press, 2015.

Abernethy, Graeme. *The Iconography of Malcolm X*. Lawrence: University Press of Kansas, 2013.

Adams, Perry. Review of *To Kill a Black Man*, by Louis E. Lomax. *Probe*, January 1969. Harold Weisberg Archive, Digital Collection, Hood College. http://jfk.hood.edu/Collection/White%20Materials/Security-CIA/CIA%20 0212.pdf. Accessed 21 May 2018.

Adamson, June N. "Few Black Voices Heard: The Black Community and the Desegregation Crisis in Clinton, Tennessee, 1956." *Tennessee Historical Quarterly* 53 (Spring 1994): 30–41.

Aiello, Thomas. *The Grapevine of the Black South: The Scott Newspaper Syndicate in the Generation before Civil Rights*. Athens: University of Georgia Press, 2018.

Aiello, Thomas. "Jim Crow Ordained." In *Crossroads: A Southern Culture Annual*, ed. Ted Olson, 107–119. Atlanta: Mercer University Press, 2006.

Aiello, Thomas. "'Not Too Far Removed from Slavery': Police Brutality and Rights Activism in Valdosta, Georgia, 1945–1955." *Journal of Civil and Human Rights* 5 (Fall–Winter 2019): 34–67.

Ambar, Saladin. *Malcolm X at Oxford Union: Radical Politics in a Global Era*. New York: Oxford University Press, 2014.

Andrews, Kehinde. *Back to Black: Retelling Black Radicalism for the 21st Century*. New York: Zed, 2018.

"Announce Filming of Novel 'Burn, Killer, Burn!'" *Jet*, 31 January 1963, 58

Aptheker, Herbert. *A Documentary History of the Negro People in the United States*. Vol. 7, *1960–1968: From the Alabama Protests to the Death of Martin Luther King, Jr.* New York: Citadel, 1969.

Arnold, Eve. *In Retrospect*. London: Sinclair-Stevenson, 1996.

Arsenault, Raymond. *Freedom Riders: 1961 and the Struggle for Racial Justice*. New York: Oxford University Press, 2006.

Asserate, Asfa-Wossen. *King of Kings: The Triumph and Tragedy of Emperor Haile Selassie I of Ethiopia*. London: Haus, 2015.

"Author Louis Lomax Killed." *Jet*, 20 August 1970, 48–49.

Baldwin, James. *No Name in the Street*. New York: Dial Press, 1972.

Barnette, Aubrey, and Edward Linn. "The Black Muslims Are a Fraud." *Saturday Evening Post*, 27 February 1965, 23–29.

Bass, Amy. *Not the Triumph, but the Struggle: The 1968 Olympics and the Making of the Black Athlete*. Minneapolis: University of Minnesota Press, 2002.

Bass, Patrick Henry. *Like a Mighty Stream: The March on Washington, August 28, 1963*. Philadelphia: Running, 2002.

Beito, David T., and Linda Royster Beito. *Black Maverick: T. R. M. Howard's Fight for Civil Rights and Economic Power*. Urbana: University of Illinois Press, 2009.

"'Black Supremacy' Cult in US—How Much of a Threat?" *U.S. News & World Report*, 9 November 1959, 112–114.

Bodroghkozy, Aniko. *Equal Time: Television and the Civil Rights Movement*. Urbana: University of Illinois Press, 2012.

Boggs, Grace Lee, Danny Glover, and Scott Kurashige. *The Next American Revolution: Sustainable Activism for the Twenty-First Century*. Berkeley: University of California Press, 2012.

Boggs, James, and Stephen M. Ward. *Pages from a Black Radical's Notebook: A James Boggs Reader*. Detroit: Wayne State University Press, 2001.

Bogle, Donald. *Primetime Blues: African Americans on Network Television*. New York: Farrar, Straus and Giroux, 2001.

Bogus, Carl T. *Buckley: William F. Buckley Jr. and the Rise of American Conservatism*. New York: Bloomsbury, 2011.

Boskin, Joseph. *Sambo: The Rise and Demise of an American Jester*. New York: Oxford University Press, 1988.

Boyd, Bill. *Blind Obedience: A True Story of Family Loyalty and Murder in South Georgia*. Macon, GA: Mercer University Press, 2000.

Boyle, Sheila Tully, and Andrew Bunie. *Paul Robeson: The Years of Promise and Achievement*. Amherst: University of Massachusetts Press, 2005.

Branch, Taylor. *Parting the Waters: America in the King Years, 1954–63*. New York: Simon and Schuster, 1988.

Brath, Elombe. *Color Us Cullud! The American Negro Leadership Official Coloring Book*. Harlem, NY: Black Standard Publishing, 1963.

Brath, Elombe. *Selected Writings and Essays*. Ed. Herb Boyd. New York: Brath, 2018.

Breitman, George. *The Last Year of Malcolm X: The Evolution of a Revolutionary*. New York: Pathfinder, 1967.

Breitman, George, Herman Porter, and Baxter Smith. *The Assassination of Malcolm X*. Ed. Malik Miah. New York: Pathfinder, 1976.

Bronstein, Phoebe N. "Televising the South: Race, Gender, and Region in Primetime, 1955–1980." PhD diss., University of Oregon, 2013.

Broussard, Jinx Coleman. *African American Foreign Correspondents: A History*. Baton Rouge: Louisiana State University Press, 2013.

Brown, H. Rap. *Die, Nigger, Die! A Political Autobiography of Jamil Abdullah Al-Amin.* 1969. Chicago: Hill, 2002.

Brown, Scott. *Fighting for US: Maulana Karenga, the US Organization, and Black Cultural Nationalism.* New York: New York University Press, 2003.

Brown-Nagin, Tomiko. *Courage to Dissent: Atlanta and the Long History of the Civil Rights Movement.* New York: Oxford University Press, 2011.

Buckner, Julie Armstrong. *Mary Turner and the Memory of Lynching.* Athens: University of Georgia Press, 2011.

Burns, W. Haywood. *The Voices of Negro Protest in America.* New York: Oxford University Press, 1963.

Bush, Roderick D. *The End of White World Supremacy: Black Internationalism and the Problem of the Color Line.* Philadelphia: Temple University Press, 2009.

Cagin, Seth, and Philip Dray. *We Are Not Afraid: The Story of Goodman, Schwerner, and Chaney and the Civil Rights Campaign for Mississippi.* New York: Public Affairs, 2006.

Carmichael, Stokely, and Ekwueme Michael Thelwell. *Ready for Revolution: The Life and Struggles of Stokely Carmichael (Kwame Ture).* New York: Simon and Schuster, 2003.

Carpenter, Ronald H. "Father Charles E. Coughlin: Delivery, Style in Discourse, and Opinion Leadership." In *American Rhetoric in the New Deal Era, 1932–1945,* ed. Thomas W. Benson, 315–367. East Lansing: Michigan State University Press, 2006.

Carson, Clayborne. *In Struggle: SNCC and the Black Awakening of the 1960s.* Cambridge, MA: Harvard University Press, 1995.

Carson, Clayborne. "SNCC and the Albany Movement." *Journal of Southwest Georgia History* 2 (1984): 15–25.

Casey, Michael, and Aimee Rowe. "'Driving Out the Money Changers': Radio Priest Charles E. Coughlin's Rhetorical Vision." *Journal of Communication and Religion* 19 (March 1996): 37–47.

Catsam, Derek Charles. *Freedom's Main Line: The Journey of Reconciliation and the Freedom Rides.* Lexington: University Press of Kentucky, 2009.

Chafe, William H. *Civilities and Civil Rights: Greensboro, North Carolina, and the Black Struggle for Freedom.* Oxford: Oxford University Press, 1981.

Chappell, David L. "Prophetic Religion: A Transracial Challenge to Modern Democracy." *Social Research* 76 (Winter 2009): 1261–1276.

Clark, Kenneth. *Dark Ghetto: Dilemmas of Social Power.* Middletown, CT: Wesleyan University Press, 1965.

Clary, George E. *Paine College, Augusta, Georgia: An Account of Its Beginnings, 1882–1903.* Brunswick, GA: Lemmond Letter Shop, 1975.

Clegg, Claude Andrew, III. *The Life and Times of Elijah Muhammad.* Chapel Hill: University of North Carolina Press, 1997.

Clinger, Janet. *Our Elders: Six Bay Area Life Stories.* Bloomington, IN: Exlibris, 2005.

Cobb, Charles E., Jr. *This Nonviolent Stuff'll Get You Killed: How Guns Made the Civil Rights Movement Possible*. Durham, NC: Duke University Press, 2015.

Cole, Nat King. "Why I Quit My TV Show." *Ebony*, February 1958, 29–34.

Cromartie, J. Vern. "Harry Edwards and the Sociology of Sport: A Case Study of a Pioneer." *National Association of African American Studies and Affiliates Conference Monographs* (2013): 1420–1452.

Crone, James. *Martin and Malcolm and America*. Maryknoll, NY: Orbis, 1991.

Crump, Paul. *Burn, Killer, Burn*. Chicago: Johnson, 1962.

Cruse, Harold. *The Crisis of the Negro Intellectual*. New York: Morrow, 1967.

Curtin, Michael. *Redeeming the Wasteland: Television Documentary and Cold War Politics*. New Brunswick, NJ: Rutgers University Press, 1995.

Curtis, Edward E., IV. *Black Muslim Religion in the Nation of Islam, 1960–1975*. Chapel Hill: University of North Carolina Press, 2006.

Curtis, Edward E., IV. *Islam in Black America: Identity, Liberation, and Difference in African-American Islamic Thought*. Albany: State University of New York Press, 2002.

Curtis, Edward E., IV. "Islamism and Its African American Muslim Critics: Black Muslims in the Era of the Arab Cold War." *American Quarterly* 59 (September 2007): 683–709.

Darling, Frank C. Review of *Thailand: The War That Is, The War That Will Be*, by Louis Lomax. *Western Political Quarterly* 21 (December 1968): 754–755.

Dates, Jannette Lake, and William Barlow. *Split Image: African Americans in the Mass Media*. Washington, DC: Howard University Press, 1993.

Davidson, Osha Gray. *The Best of Enemies: Race and Redemption in the New South*. 1996. Chapel Hill: University of North Carolina Press, 2007.

Davis, Ossie, and Ruby Dee. *With Ossie and Ruby: In This Life Together*. New York: Morrow, 1998.

DeCaro, Louis A., Jr. *On the Side of My People: A Religious Life of Malcolm X*. New York: New York University Press, 1996.

Didion, Joan, and John Gregory Dunne. "The Hate Hour." *Saturday Evening Post*, 2 December 1967, 24–25.

Dunbar, Ernest. *The Black Expatriates: A Study of American Negroes in Exile*. New York: Dutton, 1968.

Edwards, Brent Hayes. *The Practice of Diaspora: Literature, Translation, and the Rise of Black Internationalism*. Cambridge, MA: Harvard University Press, 2003.

Edwards, Harry. *The Struggle That Must Be*. New York: Macmillan, 1982.

Eldridge, Lawrence Allen. *Chronicles of a Two-Front War: Civil Rights and Vietnam in the African American Press*. Columbia: University of Missouri Press, 2012.

Elmore, Charles J. *Athletic Saga of Savannah State College*. Savannah, GA: Savannah State College Archives and Faculty/Staff Development, School of Humanities and Social Sciences, 1992.

Essien-Udom, E. U. *Black Nationalism: A Search for Identity in America*. Chicago: University of Chicago Press, 1962.

Euchner, Charles. *Nobody Turn Me Around: A People's History of the March on Washington*. Boston: Beacon, 2010.

Evanzz, Karl. "Black Hollywood and the FBI." *Black Film Review* 64 (Winter 1987/88): 16–19.

Evanzz, Karl. *The Judas Factor: The Plot to Kill Malcolm X*. New York: Thunder's Mouth, 1992.

Fairclough, Adam. *Race and Democracy: The Civil Rights Struggle in Louisiana, 1915–1972*. Athens: University of Georgia Press, 1995.

Fanon, Frantz. *The Wretched of the Earth*. 1961. New York: Grove, 2005.

Farrar, Hayward. *The Baltimore Afro-American, 1892–1950*. Westport, CT: Greenwood, 1998.

Felber, Garrett. "'Harlem Is the Black World': The Organization of Afro-American Unity at the Grassroots." *Journal of African American History* 100 (Spring 2015): 199–225.

Felker-Kantor, Max. "Fighting the Segregation Amendment: Black and Mexican American Responses to Proposition 14 in Los Angeles." In *Black and Brown in Los Angeles: Beyond Conflict and Coalition*, ed. Josh Kue and Laura Pulido, 73–90. Berkeley: University of California Press, 2015.

Felzenberg, Alvin. *A Man and His Presidents: The Political Odyssey of William F. Buckley Jr*. New Haven, CT: Yale University Press, 2017.

Ferguson, Karen. *Black Politics in New Deal Atlanta*. Chapel Hill: University of North Carolina Press, 2002.

Fine, Sidney. *Violence in the Model City: The Cavanagh Administration, Race Relations, and the Detroit Riot of 1967*. East Lansing: Michigan State University Press, 2007.

Fischer, John. "What the Negro Needs Most: A First Class Citizens' Council." *Harper's*, 1 July 1962, 12, 14–15, 18–19.

Fleming, Cynthia Griggs. *Yes We Did? From King's Dream to Obama's Promise*. Lexington: University Press of Kentucky, 2009.

Forman, Seth. *Blacks in the Jewish Mind: A Crisis of Liberalism*. New York: New York University Press, 1998.

Frank, Gerold. *An American Death: The True Story of the Assassination of Dr. Martin Luther King, Jr. and the Greatest Manhunt of Our Time*. Garden City, NY: Doubleday, 1972.

Franklin, John Hope. *George Washington Williams: A Biography*. Chicago: University of Chicago Press, 1985.

Frederickson, Kari. *The Dixiecrat Revolt and the End of the Solid South, 1932–1968*. Chapel Hill: University of North Carolina Press, 2001.

Gabbard, Krin. *Better Git It in Your Soul: An Interpretive Biography of Charles Mingus*. Berkeley: University of California Press, 2016.

Gaillard, Frye. *Cradle of Freedom: Alabama and the Movement That Changed America*. Tuscaloosa: University of Alabama Press, 2015.

Gallen, David, ed. *Malcolm X: As They Knew Him*. New York: Carroll and Graf, 1992.

Galliccho, Marc. *The African American Encounter with Japan and China: Black Internationalism in Asia, 1895–1945*. Chapel Hill: University of North Carolina Press, 2000.

Garfinkel, Herbert. *When Negroes March: The March on Washington Movement in the Organizational Politics for FEPC*. New York: Atheneum, 1969.

George, Marsha Washington. *Black Radio . . . Winner Takes All: America's First Black DJs*. Bloomington, IN: Xlibris, 2001.

Gibson, Dawn-Marie. *A History of the Nation of Islam: Race, Islam, and the Quest for Freedom*. Santa Barbara, CA: ABC-Clio, 2012.

Gibson, Dawn-Marie. "Nation Women's Engagement and Resistance in the Muhammad Speaks Newspaper." *Journal of American Studies* 49 (2015): 1–15.

"'Go Shine Shoes,' Headmaster Tells Lomax's Son." *Jet*, 16 July 1964, 20.

Godshalk, David Fort. *Veiled Visions: The 1906 Atlanta Race Riot and the Reshaping of American Race Relations*. Chapel Hill: University of North Carolina Press, 2005.

Goldman, Peter. *The Death and Life of Malcolm X*. Urbana: University of Illinois Press, 2013.

Goodman, Jordan. *Paul Robeson: A Watched Man*. New York: Verso, 2013.

Goudsouzian, Aram. *Down to the Crossroads: Civil Rights, Black Power, and the Meredith March against Fear*. New York: Farrar, Straus and Giroux, 2015.

Gregory, James Noble. *The Southern Diaspora: How the Great Migrations of Black and White Southerners Transformed America*. Chapel Hill: University of North Carolina Press, 2005.

Grilli, Matteo. "Nkrumah's Ghana and the Armed Struggle in Southern Africa (1961–1966)." *South African Historical Journal* 70 (March 2018): 56–81.

Haley, Alex. *The Autobiography of Malcolm X*. New York: Ballantine, 1964.

Haley, Alex. "An Interview with Malcolm X: A Candid Conversation with the Militant Major-domo of the Black Muslims." *Playboy*, May 1963. Reprinted in *Voices in Our Blood: America's Best on the Civil Rights Movement*, ed. Jon Meacham, 218–234. New York: Random House, 2001.

Halper, Donna L. *Icons of Talk: The Media Mouths that Changed America*. Westport, CT: Greenwood, 2009.

Hamilton, Charles V. *Adam Clayton Powell, Jr.: The Political Biography of an American Dilemma*. New York: Cooper Square, 2001.

Hammon, Jupiter. *The Collected Works of Jupiter Hammon: Poems and Essays*. Ed. Cedrick May. Knoxville: University of Tennessee Press, 2017.

Handley, Paul M. *The King Never Smiles: A Biography of Thailand's Bhumibol Adulyadej*. New Haven, CT: Yale University Press, 2006.

Hano, Arnold. "The Black Rebel Who 'Whitelists' the Olympics." *New York Times Sunday Magazine*, 12 May 1968, 39.

Hartnell, Anna. "Between Exodus and Egypt: Malcolm X, Islam, and the 'Natural' Religion of the Oppressed." *European Journal of American Culture* 27 (2008): 207–225.

Heller, Celia Stopnicka, and Alphonso Pinkney. "The Attitudes of Negroes toward Jews." *Social Forces* 43 (March 1965): 364–369.

Higgins, Chester. "Talking About." *Jet*, 12 May 1966, 43.

Hill, Lance. *The Deacons for Defense: Armed Resistance and the Civil Rights Movement*. Chapel Hill: University of North Carolina Press, 2006.

Hooker, James R. *Black Revolutionary: George Padmore's Path from Communism to Pan-Africanism*. New York: Praeger, 1967.

Horne, Gerald. *Fire This Time: The Watts Uprising and the 1960s*. Charlottesville: University Press of Virginia, 1995.

Horne, Gerald. *Mau in Harlem? The US and the Liberation of Kenya*. New York: Palgrave Macmillan, 2009.

"Host with the Most." *Time*, 23 September 1957, 58.

Houston, Benjamin. *The Nashville Way: Racial Etiquette and the Struggle for Social Justice in a Southern City*. Athens: University of Georgia Press, 2012.

Huie, William Bradford. *Three Lives for Mississippi*. Jackson: University Press of Mississippi, 1965.

Hussein, Khuram. "Born of Our Necessities: 'Muhammad Speaks' Vision of School Reform." In *Critical Perspectives on Black Education: Spirituality, Religion, and Social Justice*, ed. Noelle Witherspoon Arnold, Melanie Brooks, and Bruce Makoto Arnold, 109–140. Charlotte, NC: Information Age, 2014.

"In the Matter of the Guardianship and Tutorship of Almaz Fufa, A Minor. Civil Case 132/56, High Court, Addis Ababa, Civil Division No. 1." *Journal of Ethiopian Law* 5 (1968): 79–82.

Jackson, Karl D., and Wiwat Mungkandi, eds. *United States–Thailand Relations*. Berkeley: Institute of East Asian Studies, University of California, 1986.

Jeffries, Judson L. *Huey P. Newton: The Radical Theorist*. Jackson: University Press of Mississippi, 2002.

Jones, William P. *The March on Washington: Jobs, Freedom, and the Forgotten History of Civil Rights*. New York: Norton, 2013.

Joseph, Peniel E. "The Black Power Movement, Democracy, and America in the King Years." *American Historical Review* 114 (October 2009): 1001–1016.

Joseph, Peniel E. *Waiting 'til the Midnight Hour: A Narrative History of Black Power in America*. New York: Holt, 2006.

Kay, Jack, George W. Ziegelmueller, and Kevin M. Minch. "From Coughlin to Contemporary Talk Radio: Fallacies and Propaganda in American Populist Radio." *Journal of Radio Studies* 5 (1998): 9–21.

Kempton, Murray. *The Briar Patch: The Trial of the Panther 21*. 1972. New York: Da Capo, 1997.

King, Martin Luther, Jr. *The Autobiography of Martin Luther King Jr.* Ed. Clayborne Carson. New York: Grand Central, 2001.

King, Richard H. *Civil Rights and the Idea of Freedom*. Athens: University of Georgia Press, 1996.

Kirby, John B. *Black Americans in the Roosevelt Era: Liberalism and Race*. Knoxville: University of Tennessee Press, 1980.

Kirschke, Amy. "Du Bois, *The Crisis*, and Images of Africa and the Diaspora." In *African Diasporas in the Old and New Worlds: Consciousness and Imagination*, ed. Genevieve Fabre and Klaus Benesch, 239–262. New York: Rodopi, 2004.

Knight, Frederick. "Justifiable Homicide, Police Brutality, or Governmental Repression? The 1962 Los Angeles Police Shooting of Seven Members of the Nation of Islam." *Journal of Negro History* 79 (Spring 1994): 182–196.

Kusch, Frank. *Battleground Chicago: The Police and the 1968 Democratic National Convention*. 2004. Chicago: University of Chicago Press, 2008.

Lawson, Richard A. "The Joliet Prison Photographs, 1890–1930." www.jolietprison .org. Accessed 18 January 2019.

Leclerc, Ryan. "Malcolm X and the Hajj: A Change in Tamed Power." Honors thesis, University of Michigan, 2010.

Lee, Martha F. *The Nation of Islam: An American Millenarian Movement*. Syracuse, NY: Syracuse University Press, 1996.

Lerner, Gerda, and Linda K. Kerber. *The Majority Finds Its Past: Placing Women in History*. Chapel Hill: University of North Carolina Press, 2005.

"'Let Whites Give Something' Lomax says in Bogalusa." *Jet*, 29 July 1965, 6–7.

Leuchtenburg, William Edward. *The White House Looks South: Franklin D. Roosevelt, Harry S. Truman, Lyndon B. Johnson*. Baton Rouge: Louisiana State University Press, 2005.

Levine, Robert S. *The Lives of Frederick Douglass*. Cambridge, MA: Harvard University Press, 2016.

Lewis, David Levering. *W. E. B. Du Bois: A Biography*. New York: Holt, 2009.

Liebenow, J. Gus. *Liberia: The Evolution of Privilege*. Ithaca, NY: Cornell University Press, 1969.

Lincoln, C. Eric. *The Black Muslims in America*. 1961. Trenton, NJ: Africa World, 1994.

Lomax, Betty Frank. "Afro-American Woman: Growth Deferred." *Liberator*, May 1966, 18.

Lomax, Louis E. "The Act and Art of Being a Negro." *Urbanite*, April 1961, 17, 30–33.

Lomax, Louis E. "The American Negro's New Comedy Act." *Harper's*, June 1961, 41–46.

Lomax, Louis E. "The Black Middle Class and the Fire This Time." *Boston Globe Magazine*, 21 April 1968, F48–F51.

Lomax, Louis E. "A Georgia Boy Goes Home." *Harper's*, April 1965, 152–159.

Lomax, Louis E. "Have Slums, Will Travel." February 1966. Boulder, CO: National Center for Audio Tapes, 1970.

Lomax, Louis E. "Integration with a Difference." *Nation*, 28 September 1957, 190.

Lomax, Louis E. "Inter-Racial Marriage—An American Dilemma." *Pageant*, November 1957, 6–13.

Lomax, Louis E. "The Kennedys Move In on Dixie." *Harper's*, May 1962, 27–33.

Lomax, Louis E. "Lord Help Me Not to Be Scared!" *Pageant*, October 1957, 112–117.

Lomax, Louis E. "Memo from Amman: The Death of Hussein's Peace Mission." *Look*, 14 May 1968, 95.

Lomax, Louis E. *The Negro Revolt*. New York: Harper and Row, 1962.

Lomax, Louis E. "The Negro Revolt against 'the Negro Leaders.'" *Harper's*, June 1960, 41–48. Reprinted in *Voices in Our Blood: America's Best on the Civil Rights Movement*, ed. Jon Meacham, 268–280. New York: Random House, 2001.

Lomax, Louis E. "A Negro View: Johnson Can Free the South." *Look*, 10 March 1964, 34–38.

Lomax, Louis E. "Prelude to a New Africa Policy." *New Republic*, 4 September 1961, 18–20.

Lomax, Louis E. *The Reluctant African*. New York: Harper, 1960.

Lomax, Louis E. "The Road to Mississippi." In "Mississippi Eyewitness: The Three Civil Rights Workers—How They Were Murdered." Special issue, *Ramparts Magazine*, January 1969, 6–23.

Lomax, Louis E. *Thailand: The War That Is, The War That Will Be*. New York: Vintage, 1967.

Lomax, Louis E. *To Kill a Black Man*. Los Angeles: Holloway House, 1968.

Lomax, Louis E. "Two Millionaires, Two Senators, and a Faubus." *Harper's*, March 1960, 73–86.

Lomax, Louis E. *When the Word Is Given*. 1963. New York: Penguin, 1969.

Lomax, Louis E. "The White Liberal." *Ebony*, August 1965, 60–68.

"Louis Lomax, Author, Killed in Auto Crash." *Negro History Bulletin* 33 (November 1970): 170–171.

"Louis Lomax Discusses the Book *Thailand: The War That Is, The War That Will Be*." WFMT Chicago, 1967. Chicago History Museum. https://studsterkel.wfmt .com/programs/louis-lomax-discusses-book-thailand-war-war-will-be.

Lovett, Bobby L. *The Civil Rights Movement in Tennessee: A Narrative History*. Knoxville: University of Tennessee Press, 2005.

Lucander, David. *Winning the War for Democracy: The March on Washington Movement, 1941–1946*. Urbana: University of Illinois Press, 2014.

Lynchings by States and Race, 1882–1959. Tuskegee, AL: Department of Records and Research, Tuskegee Institute, 1959.

Mailer, Norman. *Miami and the Siege of Chicago: An Informal History of the Republican and Democratic Conventions of 1968*. 1968. New York: Random House, 2016.

Makalani, Minkah. *In the Cause of Freedom: Radical Black Internationalism from Harlem to London, 1917–1939*. Chapel Hill: University of North Carolina Press, 2011.

Malcolm X. "The Ballot or the Bullet." In *Malcolm X Speaks: Selected Speeches and Statements*, ed. George Breitman, 23–44. New York: Grove, 1965.

Malcolm X. "The Race Problem." Lecture presented to the African Students Association and NAACP Campus Chapter, Michigan State University, East

Lansing, 23 January 1963. Transcript available at https://ccnmtl.columbia.edu
/projects/mmt/mxp/speeches/mxt17.html. Accessed 28 August 2020.

Manis, Andrew M. *Macon Black and White: An Unutterable Separation in the American Century*. Macon, GA: Mercer University Press, 2004.

Mantler, Gordon K. *Power to the Poor: Black-Brown Coalition and the Fight for Economic Justice, 1960–1974*. Chapel Hill: University of North Carolina Press, 2013.

Marable, Manning. *Black Leadership*. New York: Columbia University Press, 1998.

Marable, Manning. *Malcolm X: A Life of Reinvention*. New York: Viking, 2011.

McCartney, John T. *Black Power Ideologies: An Essay in African-American Political Thought*. Philadelphia: Temple University Press, 1992.

McKnight, Gerald. *The Last Crusade: Martin Luther King, Jr., the FBI, and the Poor People's Campaign*. Boulder, CO: Westview, 1998.

Meacham, Jon, ed. *Voices in Our Blood: America's Best on the Civil Rights Movement*. New York: Random House, 2001.

Meltsner, Michael. *The Making of a Civil Rights Lawyer*. Charlottesville: University of Virginia Press, 2006.

The Messenger from Violet Drive. Written, produced, and directed by Richard Moore. Bloomington, IN: National Education Television, 1965. https://youtu.be /NdMv-a4pSrQ. Accessed 15 May 2018.

Miller, Eben. *Born along the Color Line: The 1933 Amenia Conference and the Rise of a National Civil Rights Movement*. New York: Oxford University Press, 2012.

Mingus, Charles, and John F. Goodman. *Mingus Speaks*. Berkeley: University of California Press, 2013.

Modisane, William Bloke. *Blame Me on History*. Durban, South Africa: Ad Donker, 1963.

Moerman, Michael. "A Minority and Its Government: The Thai-Lue of Northern Thailand." In *Southeast Asian Tribes, Minorities, and Nations*, vol. 1, ed. Peter Kunstadter, 401–424. Princeton, NJ: Princeton University Press, 1967.

Moerman, Michael. *Western Culture and the Thai Way of Life*. Berkeley: Center for Southeast Asia Studies, University of California, 1964.

Moore, Tomas Franklin. *From Whence We Came: A Historical Overview of the Black Schools of Lowndes County and Valdosta, Georgia from the Period of Reconstruction to the Time of School Desegregation, 1867–1969*. Valdosta, GA: self-published, 2006.

Morgan, Iwan, and Philip Davies, eds. *From Sit-Ins to SNCC: The Student Civil Rights Movement in the 1960s*. Gainesville: University Press of Florida, 2013.

Morris, James McGrath. *Eye on the Struggle: Ethel Payne, First Lady of the Black Press*. New York: Amistad, 2015.

Morrison, James. "Success and Clifford Burdette: Negro Radio Impresario at 27." *Daily Worker*, 20 January 1942. Reprinted in *Encyclopedia of the Great Black Migration*, ed. Steven A. Reich, 3:31–33. Westport, CT: Greenwood, 2006.

Mulloy, D. J. *The World of the John Birch Society: Conspiracy, Conservatism, and the Cold War*. Nashville, TN: Vanderbilt University Press, 2014.

Murphree, Vanessa. *The Selling of Civil Rights: The Student Nonviolent Coordinating Committee and the Use of Public Relations*. New York: Routledge, 2006.

Murray, James Bradford. "A Study of the Editorial Policies of the Atlanta Daily World: 1952–1955." Master's thesis, Emory University, 1961.

Myers, Christopher. "Killing Them by the Wholesale: A Lynching Rampage in South Georgia." *Georgia Historical Quarterly* 90 (Summer 2006): 214–235.

Nemiroff, Robert. *To Be Young, Gifted and Black: Lorraine Hansberry in Her Own Words*. New York: Vintage, 1995.

Nicol, Mike. *A Good-Looking Corpse: World of Drum—Jazz and Gangsters, Hope, and Defiance in the Townships of South Africa*. London: Secker and Warburg, 1991.

1956 Democratic Party Platform. American Presidency Project, University of California, Santa Barbara. http://www.presidency.ucsb.edu/ws/index.php?pid =29601. Accessed 20 August 2018.

Norwood, Stephen H. "Bogalusa Burning: The War against Biracial Unionism in the Deep South, 1919." *Journal of Southern History* 63 (August 1997): 591–628.

Novotny, Patrick. *This Georgia Rising: Education, Civil Rights, and the Politics of Change in Georgia in the 1940s*. Macon, GA: Mercer University Press, 2007.

Ogbar, Jeffrey O. G. *Black Power: Radical Politics and African American Identity*. Baltimore: Johns Hopkins University Press, 2005.

O'Leary, Jeremiah. "The Greatest Manhunt in Law Enforcement History." *Reader's Digest*, August 1968, 62–69.

Parker, Maynard. "The Americans in Thailand." *The Atlantic*, December 1966, 51–58.

Pearson, Hugh. *When Harlem Nearly Killed King: The 1958 Stabbing of Dr. Martin Luther King, Jr*. New York: Seven Stories, 2004.

Pederson, Vernon L. *The Communist Party in Maryland*. Urbana: University of Illinois Press, 2001.

Pepper, William F. *An Act of State: The Execution of Martin Luther King*. Brooklyn, NY: Verso, 2003.

Perlstein, Rick. *Before the Storm: Barry Goldwater and the Unmaking of the American Consensus*. New York: Nation, 2009.

Perry, Bruce. *Malcolm: The Life of a Man Who Changed America*. New York: Station Hill, 1991.

Pfeffer, Paula. *A. Philip Randolph, Pioneer of the Civil Rights Movement*. Baton Rouge: Louisiana State University Press, 1990.

Poinsett, Alex. *Walking with Presidents: Louis Martin and the Rise of Black Political Power*. Lanham, MD: Rowman and Littlefield, 2000.

Porter, Eric. *What Is This Thing Called Jazz? African American Musicians as Artists, Critics, and Activists*. Berkeley: University of California Press, 2002.

Prattis, Percival L. "The Role of the Negro Press in Race Relations." *Phylon* 7 (1946): 273–283.

Prescott, Heather Munro. *The Morning After: A History of Emergency Contraception in the United States*. New Brunswick, NJ: Rutgers University Press, 2011.

Press, Bill. *Toxic Talk: How the Radical Right Has Poisoned America's Airwaves*. New York: Macmillan, 2010.

Priestley, Justine. *By Gertrude Wilson: Dispatches of the 1960s from a White Writer in a Black World*. Martha's Vineyard, MA: Vineyard Stories, 2005.

"Radio Reviews." *Variety*, 14 May 1941, 32.

Rashid, Samory. *Black Muslims in the US: History, Politics, and the Struggle of a Community*. New York: Palgrave Macmillan, 2013.

Rhodes, Jane. *Mary Ann Shadd Cary: The Black Press and Protest in the Nineteenth Century*. Bloomington: Indiana University Press, 1999.

Rickford, Russell J. *Betty Shabazz, Surviving Malcolm X: A Journey of Strength from Wife to Widow to Heroine*. Naperville, IL: Sourcebooks, 2003.

Ritchie, Donald A. *American Journalists: Getting the Story*. New York: Oxford University Press, 1997.

R. L. Polk & Co.'s Valdosta City Directory, 1923. Jacksonville, FL: Polk, 1923.

R. L. Polk & Co.'s Valdosta City Directory, 1925. Detroit: Polk, 1925.

Robinson, Jo Ann Gibson. *The Montgomery Bus Boycott and the Women Who Started It: The Memoir of Jo Ann Gibson Robinson*. Ed. David J. Garrow. Knoxville: University of Tennessee Press, 1987.

Sales, William W., Jr. *From Civil Rights to Black Liberation: Malcolm X and the Organization of Afro-American Unity*. Boston: South End, 1994.

Santoro, Gene. *Myself When I Am Real: The Life and Music of Charles Mingus*. New York: Oxford University Press, 2001.

Schmidt, Christopher W. "Conceptions of Law in the Civil Rights Movement." *UC Irvine Law Review* 1 (2011): 641–676.

Schmidt, Christopher W. "Divided by Law: The Sit-Ins and the Role of the Courts in the Civil Rights Movement." *Law and History Review* 33 (February 2015): 93–149.

Schmidt, Christopher W. *The Sit-Ins: Protest and Legal Change in the Civil Rights Era*. Chicago: University of Chicago Press, 2018.

Schmier, Louis. *Valdosta and Lowndes County: A Ray in the Sunbelt*. Northridge, CA: Windsor, 1988.

Schultz, John. *No One Was Killed: The Democratic National Convention, August 1968*. 1969. Chicago: University of Chicago Press, 2009.

Self, Robert O. *American Babylon: Race and the Struggle for Postwar Oakland*. Princeton, NJ: Princeton University Press, 2003.

Shaw, Tony. *Hollywood's Cold War*. Edinburgh: Edinburgh University Press, 2007.

Shelton, Jane Twitty. *Pines and Pioneers: A History of Lowndes County, Georgia, 1825–1900*. Atlanta: Cherokee, 1976.

Sides, Hampton. *Hellhound on His Trail: The Stalking of Martin Luther King Jr. and the International Hunt for His Assassin*. New York: Doubleday, 2010.

Sieving, Christopher. *Soul Searching: Black-Themed Cinema from the March on Washington to the Rise of Blaxploitation*. Middletown, CT: Wesleyan University Press, 2011.

Silberman, Charles E. *Crisis in Black and White*. New York: Vintage, 1964.

Simmons, Charles A. *The African American Press, 1827–1965*. Jefferson, NC: McFarland, 1998.

Sitkoff, Harvard. *A New Deal for Blacks: The Emergence of Civil Rights as a National Issue*. Vol. 1, *The Depression Decade*. New York: Oxford University Press, 1978.

Smallwood, Andrew P. "The Intellectual Creativity and Public Discourse of Malcolm X: A Precursor to the Modern Black Studies Movement." *Journal of Black Studies* 36 (November 2005): 248–263.

Strain, Christopher B. "'We Walked Like Men': The Deacons for Defense and Justice." *Louisiana History* 38 (Winter 1997): 43–62.

Streckfuss, David. "Kings in the Age of Nations: The Paradox of Lèse-Majesté as Political Crime in Thailand." *Comparative Studies in Society and History* 37 (July 1995): 445–475.

Swiderski, David M. "Approaches to Black Power: African American Grassroots Political Struggle in Cleveland, Ohio, 1960–1966." PhD diss., University of Massachusetts Amherst, 2013.

Swindall, Lindsey R. *Paul Robeson: A Life of Activism and Art*. Lanham, MD: Rowman and Littlefield, 2015.

Taylor, Bruce. "Black Radicalism in Southern California, 1950–1982." PhD diss., University of California, Los Angeles, 1983.

Theoharis, Jeanne. "'Alabama on Avalon': Rethinking the Watts Uprising and the Character of Black Protest in Los Angeles." In *The Black Power Movement: Rethinking the Civil Rights–Black Power Era*, ed. Peniel Joseph, 27–54. New York: Routledge, 2006.

Theoharis, Jeanne. "'I'd Rather Go to School in the South': How Boston's School Desegregation Complicates the Civil Rights Paradigm." In *Freedom North: Black Freedom Struggles Outside the South, 1940–1980*, ed. Jeanne Theoharis and Komozi Woodard, 125–152. New York: Palgrave Macmillan, 2003.

Thomas, Damion L. *Globetrotting: African American Athletes and Cold War Politics*. Urbana: University of Illinois Press, 2012.

Thomas, Norman. *Human Exploitation in the United States*. New York: Stokes, 1934.

Tinson, Christopher M. *Radical Intellect: Liberator Magazine and Black Activism in the 1960s*. Chapel Hill: University of North Carolina Press, 2017.

Tirella, Joseph. *Tomorrow-Land: The 1964–65 World's Fair and the Transformation of America*. Guilford, CT: Lyons, 2014.

Trowbridge, John M., and Jason LeMay. *Sturgis and Clay: Showdown for Desegregation in Kentucky Education*. Lexington: Commonwealth of Kentucky, 2006. https://kynghistory.ky.gov/Our-History/Major-Commands/Documents/sturgisandclayky1956.pdf.

particular, nineteen years old, were put in a clinical trial of low-estrogen birth control pills. Planned Parenthood affiliates director Naomi Gray, herself African American, met with the university's Black faculty in response. Carolyn Sofia, "OBC Says NOAH Sinking," *Hofstra Chronicle*, 23 October 1969, 2; Prescott, *Morning After*, 34.

44 "It's a Friend and Foe Day," n.d., "Hofstra Students Sit In to Seek Power, Peace, 15 April 1970," "Hofstra Protest Leads to Dissent, 16 April 1970," box 12, series 7, folder 26, Lomax Papers.

45 "Clifford Lord to the Hofstra Faculty and Student Body, 4 May 1970," "Clifford Lord to Members of the Hofstra Community, 5 May 1970," box 12, series 7, folder 25, Lomax Papers; "The National Strike," "Most LI Colleges Quiet at Bell; Hofstra Anti-War Group Active, 13 August 1970," "Organization of Black Collegians, National Strike Statement, Hofstra," "English 25—Dr. Wiley, Moratorium!, 28 October 1969," box 12, series 7, folder 26, Lomax Papers; *Hofstra Chronicle*, 11 May 1970, 1, 2, 4. For more on the Panther 21, see Kempton, *Briar Patch*.

46 In April 1970, Artie Seale, wife of Bobby Seale, and Afeni Shakur came to speak at Hofstra, providing an infusion of Black Panther radicalism to the campus. "The power structure's showing you that they're your enemy," said Seale. "And if you don't know what's happening then you're going to have to be dealt with too when the revolution comes." "National Strike," "Strike Newsletter," "Hofstra Test Verdict Given with a Smile," box 12, series 7, folder 26, Lomax Papers; Craig Dreilinger, "SMC Holds Black Panther Rally," *Hofstra Chronicle*, 9 April 1970, 1.

47 Carolyn Sofia, "Gov't Hearing: Change vs. Status Quo," *Hofstra Chronicle*, 12 February 1970, 1.

48 In October 1970, with the midterm elections approaching, President Lord sent guidelines to faculty concerning political activity on campus. Though they were couched in legal jargon, they basically concluded that everyone at Hofstra had a right to participate in the political process, but no member of the community "should speak or act in the name of the institution in a political campaign." Glen Taylor to Clifford Lord, 18 May 1970, "Clifford Lord to the Hofstra Community, 20 October 1970," "Guidelines on Questions Relating to Tax Exemption and Political Activities Statement of the American Council on Education," box 12, series 7, folder 26, Lomax Papers.

10. CONSPIRACIES

1 J. F. Bland to W. C. Sullivan, confidential memorandum, 22 August 1967, FBI File No. 62-102926; *Independent Star News*, 6 August 1967, 1, 4, 20 August 1967, 1, 3.

2 *New Orleans Times-Picayune*, 1 May 1969, 17; John F. Kennedy Assassination File, Section 158, FBI File No. 62-109060, Federal Bureau of Investigation, Assassination Archives and Research Center, Washington DC.

3 Percy Foreman, testimony, in US Congress, House, Select Committee on Assassinations, *Investigation of the Assassination of Martin Luther King, Jr.*, 235–236.

Tscheschlok, Eric. "Long Time Coming: Miami's Liberty City Riot of 1968." *Florida Historical Quarterly* 74 (Spring 1996): 440–460.

Turner, Richard Brent. *Islam in the African American Experience*. Bloomington: Indiana University Press, 2003.

Tyson, Timothy B. *The Blood of Emmett Till*. New York: Simon and Schuster, 2017.

US Congress. House. Select Committee on Assassinations. "An Analysis of James Earl Ray's Trip to New Orleans, December 15–21, 1967." *Appendix to Hearings before the Select Committee on Assassinations of the U.S. House of Representatives, Ninety-Fifth Congress, Second Session*, 13:265–282. Washington, DC: US Government Printing Office, 1979.

US Congress. House. Select Committee on Assassinations. "An Analysis of the Assassination Investigation of the Department of Justice and the Federal Bureau of Investigation." *Appendix to Hearings before the Select Committee on Assassinations of the U.S. House of Representatives, Ninety-Fifth Congress, Second Session*, 13:153–216. Washington, DC: US Government Printing Office, 1979.

US Congress. House. Select Committee on Assassinations. *Appendix to Hearings before the Select Committee on Assassinations of the U.S. House of Representatives, Ninety-Fifth Congress, Second Session*. Vol. 13. Washington, DC: US Government Printing Office, 1979.

US Congress. House. Select Committee on Assassinations. *Investigation of the Assassination of Martin Luther King, Jr.: Hearings before the Select Committee on Assassinations of the U.S. House of Representatives, Ninety-Fifth Congress, Second Session*. Vol. 5. Washington, DC: US Government Printing Office, 1979.

"U.S. Denies Hampering Writer's Visa from Cuba." *Jet*, 29 August 1963, 21.

US Warren Commission. *Investigation of the Assassination of President John F. Kennedy: Hearings before the President's Commission on the Assassination of President Kennedy*. Washington, DC: US Government Printing Office, 1964.

Valera, Alexandria Columbina. "The Politics and Aesthetics of American Art during the Cold War: Commissions for Philip Johnson's New York State Pavilion at the 1964–1965 World's Fair." Master's thesis, Hunter College, 2015.

Van Deburg, William. *New Day in Babylon: The Black Power Movement and American Culture, 1965–1975*. Chicago: University of Chicago Press, 1992.

Vandiver, Frank E. "Harper's Interprets 'The South Today.'" *Journal of Southern History* 31 (August 1965): 318–323.

Vieth, Benjamin L. "Kinderlou: Paradise for Vagabond Negroes." Unpublished manuscript in possession of the author.

Wagner, Christoph, and Udo J. Hebel. *Pictorial Cultures and Political Iconographies: Approaches, Perspectives, Case Studies from Europe and America*. Berlin: De Gruyter, 2011.

Walmsley, Mark Joseph. "Tell It Like It Isn't: SNCC and the Media, 1960–1965." *Journal of American Studies* 48 (2014): 291–308.

Warren, Harris Gaylord. *Herbert Hoover and the Great Depression*. New York: Norton, 1967.

Washburn, Patrick S. "George Padmore of the *Pittsburgh Courier* and the *Chicago Defender*: A Decidedly Different World War II Correspondent." In *War, Journalism and History: War Correspondents in the Two World Wars*, ed. Yvonne McEwen and Fiona A. Fisken, 95–119. New York: Lang, 2012.

Watson, Bruce. *Freedom Summer: The Savage Season of 1964 That Made Mississippi Burn and Made America a Democracy*. New York: Penguin, 2010.

Weems, Robert E. *Desegregating the Dollar: African American Consumerism in the Twentieth Century*. New York: New York University Press, 1998.

Wells, Tom. *Wild Man: The Life and Times of Daniel Ellsberg*. New York: Palgrave, 2001.

Wendt, Simon. "'Urge People Not to Carry Guns': Armed Self-Defense in the Louisiana Civil Rights Movement and the Radicalization of the Congress of Racial Equality." *Louisiana History* 45 (Summer 2004): 261–286.

West, Michael O., William G. Martin, and Fanon Che Wilkins, eds. *From Toussaint to Tupac: The Black International since the Age of Revolution*. Chapel Hill: University of North Carolina Press, 2009.

Wolters, Raymond. *Negroes and the Great Depression: The Problem of Economic Recovery*. Westport, CT: Greenwood, 1970.

Wright, Amy Nathan. "Civil Rights 'Unfinished Business': Poverty, Race, and the 1968 Poor People's Campaign." PhD diss, University of Texas at Austin, 2007.

Wyche, Billy H. "Paternalism, Patriotism, and Protest in 'The Already Best City in the Land': Bogalusa, Louisiana, 1906–1919." *Louisiana History* 40 (Winter 1999): 63–84.

Index

Heyman, Philip B., 135
Hicks, James L., 77, 94, 95
Hicks, Robert, 128
Hobson, Julius, 177, 220n36
Hofstra University: Lomax at, 161–166, 173–76, 214n30, 218n19, 220n35; unrest at, 164–166, 216n46, 216n48
Hollywood Unity Awards Committee, 208n50
Home Show, The, 60
Hoover, J. Edgar, 25–26, 27, 130, 213n4; Lomax and, 109, 151, 152, 170. *See also* Federal Bureau of Investigation (FBI)
Hope, John, 12
Hope, Lugenia Burns, 12
Horne, Lena, 60
Houphouët-Boigny, Félix, 67
Houston, Norman, 80
Howard, Charles, 83, 199–200n29
Howard, T. R. M., 24–26, 186n3, 186n7, 202n19
Howard University, 17, 19, 182n32
Hoyt, Stuart, 144
Hubert, Benjamin, 15
Huff, Curtis A., 185n52
Hughes, Langston, 79
Human Rights Political Association, 87
Humphrey, Hal, 125
Humphrey, Hubert, 120, 130
Hunter, William Joseph, 182n27
Huntley, Chet, 39
Hurkos, Peter, 174–175, 219n23

Imperial Courts housing project, 146
Independent Star News, 167
Invisible Man, The (Ellison), 102

Jackson, Mahalia, 201n37
Jackson State College, 173
Jaffee, Sam, 117
Jamaica Coordinating Committee for Urban Renewal and Neighborhood Conservation, 198n11
James, William, 196n36
Jet, 104, 129, 176

Jewish War Veterans of California, 138
Job-a-Thon, 147, 148
John Birch Society, 122, 125, 127–128, 137–139, 145–146, 155. *See also* Rousselot, John
Johnson, Frank J., 144
Johnson, James E., 145–146
Johnson, Lyndon Baines, 160: criticism of, 100, 101, 130, 140, 142; Lomax and, 97, 128, 154; Martin and, 134, 135; Sherwood and, 211n40
Johnson, Rafer, 214n22
Johnson, Reginald, 195
Johnson, Robert E., 176
Johnson Publishing Co., 78, 129
Joliet Correctional Center, 1, 21–22, 24, 170, 218n11
Jones, James, 175–176
Jones, LeRoi, 103, 116

Karenga, Ron, 214n22
Kazan, Elia, 114, 213n4
KCET, 147
KDAY, 127, 132, 207n40
Keating, Edward M., 108
Kelly, Anne, 82
Kennedy, Bob, 99
Kennedy, John F., 29, 86, 87–88, 91, 135, 172, 198n10
Kennedy, Robert F., 59, 157–158, 196n39, 214n22
Kent State University, 165, 173
Kentucky State University, 129
Kerner, Otto, 154
Khoman, Thanat, 143
Kilgore, Thomas, 205n9
Killens, John Oliver, 79, 83, 87, 88, 103, 104, 202n7
Kinderlou Plantation, 7
King, Martin Luther, Jr.: Albany movement and, 75–76; assassination attempts, 30, 155, 157, 168–171, 217n5, 217n7; criticism of, 38, 95, 123, 129, 138; Harper and, 50, 67; Lomax and, 1, 16, 30, 38, 61, 66, 70, 87, 101, 108,

Motion Picture Association of America, 151

Muhammad, Elijah, 31, 180n5; anti-Communism, 200n31; and Cuba, 83; and *The Hate That Hate Produced*, 31–33, 35, 36; and Malcolm X, 82, 84, 93, 104, 199nn23–24, 202n5; and *The Messenger from Violet Drive*, 109–110, 204n62; and *When the Word Is Given*, 90–93. *See also* Nation of Islam

Murphy, Carl, 24

Murphy, George, 130

Murray, James Buford, 49

Mutual Broadcasting System, 19

My Friend Tony, 155

My Lai massacre, 162

Nader, Ralph, 177

Nash, Diane, 60

Nasser, Gamal Abdel, 45

Nat King Cole Show, 113

Nation, The, 23

Nation of Islam, 199n24; Lomax and, 2, 35, 39, 157, 206n36; and *The Messenger from Violet Drive*, 109–110; and "Walk in My Shoes," 61, 62, 63. *See also* Muhammad, Elijah; Malcolm X; *The Hate That Hate Produced*; *Negro Revolt, The*; *When the Word Is Given: A Report on Elijah Muhammad, Malcolm X, and the Black Muslim World* (Lomax)

National Advisory Commission on Civil Disorders, 154

National Association for the Advancement of Colored People (NAACP): activism, 9, 30, 38, 58, 75, 88, 96, 97, 105, 108, 118; defenses of, 30, 38, 42; Freedom Fund Dinner, 148; *The Hate That Hate Produced*, 189n38; investigated by FBI, 186n3; Lawson and, 34; Legal Defense and Education Fund, 38–39, 66, 85, 104; Lomax and, 36, 37, 39, 42, 53, 60, 63–64, 66, 72, 78, 79, 80, 110, 146, 197n51; Malcolm X and, 33; and *The Negro Revolt*, 65–66, 68, 69, 70, 71

National Association of Negro Business and Professional Women's Clubs, 101

National Council of Negro Women, 88

National Educational Television, 109

National Guard, 27, 28, 121, 186n10

National Highway Safety Bureau, 177

National Memorial African Bookstore, 202n7

National Negro Publishers Association, 83, 135

National Review, 123, 124, 128, 144. *See also* Buckley, William F.

National Security Council, 134

National Urban League, 72, 88, 94, 107, 116, 176, 200n36; Lomax and, 37, 66, 68. *See also* Young, Whitney

NBC, 50; *Frontiers of Faith*, 55; *My Friend Tony*, 155; *Nat King Cole Show*, 113; *Today*, 79; *The Tonight Show*, 63

Negro History Week, 79

"Negro in American History and Culture, The" (Lomax), 161

"Negroes in Our Cities, The," 72

Negro Leadership Conference, 1, 2, 85, 122

Negro Political Association of California, 106, 121, 124

Negro Revolt, The (Lomax): later elaboration on, 76, 77, 95, 106, 110, 156; and NAACP, 65–66, 68, 69, 70, 71; and Nation of Islam, 68–70; overview, 67–70; publication, 64–66, 67, 194n30; reception, 70–71, 96, 194–195n33; sales, 4, 72, 73, 74, 75, 83, 98, 176; and Taconic Foundation, 200n36; and Urban League, 37, 66, 68; writing, 58–60, 61, 63

"Negro Revolt against 'the Negro Leaders,' The" (Lomax), 36–38, 42, 64, 78

Negro Speaks, The, 18, 19

Neighborhood Adult Participation Program, 123

New American Library, 74, 83

New Opportunities at Hofstra (NOAH), 215n43. *See also* Hofstra University